WHO NEEDS THE ABC?

Professor Matthew Ricketson is an academic and journalist. He heads the Communications group at Deakin University; before that, between 2009 and 2017, he was the University of Canberra's inaugural professor of journalism, and he ran RMIT's journalism program for 11 years. He has worked as a journalist for several newspapers and magazines, and is the author or editor of six books. Most recently, he co-edited *Upheaval: disrupted lives in journalism*. He has been a member of three Australian Research Council–funded projects on the media.

Patrick Mullins is a Canberra-based writer and adjunct academic at the University of Canberra's Centre for Creative and Cultural Research. His first book, *Tiberius with a Telephone: the life and stories of William McMahon* (2018), won the 2020 NSW Premier's Literary Award for Non-Fiction and the 2020 National Biography Award; his second book, *The Trials of Portnoy: how Penguin brought down Australia's censorship system* (2020), was short-listed for the 2021 NSW Premier's Literary Award for Non-Fiction.

Matthew Ricketson
& Patrick Mullins

WHO NEEDS THE ABC

why taking it
for granted is no
longer an option

SCRIBE
Melbourne • London

Scribe Publications

18–20 Edward St, Brunswick, Victoria 3056, Australia

Published by Scribe 2022

Typeset in Tiempos Text 9.75/14 pt by the publishers.

Printed and bound in Australia by Griffin Press, part of Ovato.

Scribe Publications is committed to the sustainable use of natural resources and the use of paper products made responsibly from those resources.

Scribe acknowledges Australia's First Nations peoples as the traditional owners and custodians of this country, and we pay our respects to their elders, past and present.

9781922310927 (paperback)
9781922586490 (ebook)

Catalogue records for this book are available from the National Library of Australia.

scribepublications.com.au

To the next generation of the ABC's audience

For Finlay, and for Claire.

CONTENTS

Chapter 1

WHO'S AFRAID OF THE ABC?

Try imagining life without the Australian Broadcasting Corporation (ABC). There would be no *7.30* or *Four Corners* or *Foreign Correspondent* or *Media Watch* or *Q&A* on television. No local radio across every capital city and close to 50 regional centres broadcasting news and interviews and taking talkback. No *Country Hour*, no *Landline*. No Radio National offering specialist programs covering many areas (religion, law, philosophy, cinema, health, and more), from novel directions (*Rear Vision*), in different ways (*All in the Mind*), focused on people (*Conversations*), and with national living treasures (Phillip Adams has hosted *Late Night Live* for more than three decades now).[1] No Triple J Hottest 100. No emergency broadcasting. No innovations like iview, which are now baked into everyday habits. No hidden pockets of the ABC's giant website offering valuable resources for schools, such as ABC Splash.

What have we missed? Lots, actually. Homemade dramas like *Mystery Road* or *Stateless* or *Rake*. Comedies like Shaun Micallef's *Mad as Hell* or Tom Gleeson's *Hard Quiz* or Kitty Flanagan's *Fisk* or Sarah Kendall's *Frayed*. Favourites imported from overseas — *Call the Midwife*, *QI*, and *Killing Eve*. Favourites among the 'massed five-year-olds', as John Clarke called them — *Bananas in Pyjamas*, *Play School*, and *Bluey*.

We could go on — two classical-music stations, gardening shows dating back to the 1960s with Kevin Heinze's *Sow What*, Boyer lectures annually since 1959 — but we won't. This is a short book and time is shorter because there is a very real possibility a world without the ABC might exist by the time of its centenary on 1 July 2032. Not because it is failing to meet its legislated charter. Not because its business model has been blown out of the water by the internet. No, the ABC is reaching more Australians every day than at any time in its history, through its online platform and social media, and is doing so with substantially less money. In nominal terms, the ABC's operational funding may have increased markedly since 1983–84, from $274 million to $881 million for 2021–22, but, adjusted for inflation, funding has actually dropped 4 per cent. So, too, staffing, from 6,800 in 1984 to 4,233 in 2021 — a 38 per cent fall.[2] The threat to the ABC is real precisely — and paradoxically — because it reaches more people now. That the ABC's footprint is large as well as deep has implications for the rest of the media industry and for an institution with which the ABC is inextricably entwined — its funder, the federal government. To paraphrase George Orwell's *Animal Farm*, published in the decade after the ABC began in 1932, all governments loathe the ABC equally, but some loathe it more equally than others. The coalition government, in power since 2013, really loathes the ABC and gives every indication that if it could get rid of the ABC it would.

Understanding the far-reaching changes in recent years to both the news-media and political contexts in which the ABC operates, then, is a key to solving the ABC's current predicament.

We'll outline these changing contexts and their impacts, but first we need to clear some space for what you're about to read. To write about the ABC today is a fraught exercise, such is the level of hostility swirling around the national broadcaster. When did you last hear a government minister say anything remotely positive about the ABC? The same question could be asked of the country's national daily newspaper *The Australian*. Nothing like the same animus is directed at other cultural institutions, such as the National Library of Australia or the National Museum or the Australian War Memorial. Yes, the ABC is part of the news media, an inherently noisy, contentious industry, but the noise surrounding the news media has only increased in recent years, and around the ABC in particular it is almost deafening. The relentlessness and loudness of the ABC's critics obscure from view the standing of the ABC as an important cultural institution. That seems to be part of the purpose: to carp and grind away at any and everything, large and small, real or not, to build a picture of the ABC as a hopelessly bloated, biased organisation that despite its name is somehow at root un-Australian.

Some sectors of the media, such as commercial radio and television or local and regional media, pretty much ignore the ABC as they have done in the past. Other sectors, like the Nine newspapers, have an eye on their own commercial interest but for the most part report the ABC straight, keeping in mind the need to cover a range of views on an issue. The problem is, that range of views now includes almost unremitting hostility from News Corp Australia, which publishes metropolitan daily newspapers in five states and a territory and one of the two national dailies in the country. The effect is to make scepticism bordering on suspicion a default setting for stories about the ABC.

Each week, though, more than two-thirds of all Australians watch ABC television or listen to ABC radio or read ABC Online. Since the beginning of 2020 — before the global pandemic — abc.net.au has been the most popular news website in Australia, ahead of news.com.au and nine.com.au, according to Nielsen Digital Content Ratings. The ABC delivers content on YouTube that reaches 22.6 million monthly unique viewers; on Facebook, which reaches 6.1 million monthly unique users; and on Instagram, which reaches 3.5 million users — the vast majority of them Australian, aged under 45, with a skew toward women. Podcasts produced from local ABC Radio content are downloaded 1.2 million times each month; from Triple J, they are downloaded 1.4 million times; from ABC News, it is 4.9 million times; and Radio National, which pioneered the popular new form in Australia, sees 7.8 million monthly unique downloads.[3]

These are remarkable figures. Doubtless most of these people are uninterested in the culture wars, in which, as journalist Benjamin Wallace-Wells puts it, 'every issue rings the same bell, and then everyone staggers bleary-eyed to their usual stations, like firemen at midnight'.[4] The ABC finds itself dragooned into these internecine outbreaks of hostilities whether it wants to be or not. For the public engaging with ABC content every week, it is likely they love some content, hate other content, and shrug about the rest. To the extent they think about the ABC at all, they might nod in thanks to their taxes being well spent, but they might not dwell on this connection — so much is free to download these days, after all. Older viewers and listeners probably appreciate the ABC's longevity in Australian life, quietly believing it should simply continue, like the National Library or the Museum or the War Memorial.

So, there is a gap in public discussion about the ABC.

Who can fill it? Who can provide an alternative, let alone supportive, perspective on the ABC?

The ABC can do this for itself, and sometimes it does, but campaigns spruiking yourself can look a tad unseemly, especially on a network that cherishes its ad-free status. Could the ABC Alumni provide this perspective? Perhaps yes. Set up in 2018, its members include former household names like Kerry O'Brien and Maxine McKew, who believe 'a strong public service broadcaster is essential in a healthy democracy' and advocate for it by giving speeches, making parliamentary submissions, and mentoring current ABC staff members. O'Brien also released a memoir in 2018 that provides detailed analysis of many of the important stories he worked on, as well as a robust defence of the ABC.[5] A knowledgeable, committed group, then — but, by definition, one drawn from the ABC. And the Friends of the ABC? Nobody doubts their commitment, but they are, well, friends. In the current media environment, regrettably, they are rarely called on for comment.

That is why we have written this book. We don't claim to speak for the millions of people who engage with ABC content. But we do hope to start a conversation among this audience. What we're worried about is the attack, in plain view, on a valued cultural institution. We know it is valued because that's what public opinion polls have been saying for decades. In recent years, however, there's been a drop in the proportion of people surveyed who think the ABC's news and current affairs is accurate and impartial. From a high point of 83 per cent in 2006 and 2009, the figure has dropped 10 percentage points to 73 per cent in 2021. The proportion of people who think the ABC offers a valuable service overall is still at 79 per cent, but it has dropped from 86 per cent in 2016. The highest rating is for ABC Online, at 92 per cent.[6] Do these figures mean the critics are right, or do they mean the unceasing attacks on the ABC are eroding public confidence in it? Or something else? Whichever, we don't think the ABC should suffer death by a thousand cuts, as one of its most respected alumni, Chris Masters, said he suffered, defending his landmark program about corruption in Queensland, 'The Moonlight State'.

We come to this topic from different backgrounds. One of us (Matthew) has worked as a journalist at both *The Age* and *The Australian*, has studied the news media as an academic, and assisted Ray Finkelstein QC in an inquiry into the media (set up in 2011 by the Gillard Labor government), which in recommending stronger regulation earned him few friends in the media. The other (Patrick) is an independent scholar and author, of a biography of Australia's least-loved prime minister, Billy McMahon, and an account of the censorship trials that engulfed the Australian publication of Philip Roth's *Portnoy's Complaint*. Neither of us has worked at the ABC, though like many we've been interviewed over the years on ABC programs.

We happily declare we believe in the value of the ABC as a national institution, which in the current environment means we probably will be dismissed as left-leaning, inner-city-dwelling, soy-latte-sipping self-abusers. Sigh. The ABC is far from a flawless institution. From our perspective as consumers, as well as in our professional assessment, a selected list of the ABC's shortcomings is still lengthy enough. It is too often monochromatically mainstream in its outlook on the world. It boasts that it does not run advertisements ... until it does, either in the form of endless cross-promotions for its own programs on its own network, or within programs themselves. It is Sydney-centric. It can be timid in the face of pressure from governments: the 'pre-emptive buckle', a term invented by the ABC's Michael Cosby nearly half a century ago, is still more common than it should be.[7] Like all large media organisations, the ABC is prey to office politics, but they take on a peculiarly dispiriting form at the national broadcaster that has curdled the creativity of many a program-maker. The ABC may no longer be part of the conventional public service, but it remains bound, some would say hidebound, by the strictures of bureaucracy. As Ken Myer said soon after becoming chair of the ABC in 1983, when the commander of an aircraft carrier orders 'Hard a-starboard', the ship ploughs on for another four kilometres before turning; while a member of his board, Robert Raymond, described the corridors of ABC headquarters being 'enfiladed by management intrigues' and 'union ambushes'.[8] The flip side of the ABC being the most accountable media organisation in the country is that its program-makers and executives spend an inordinate amount of their working day responding to complaints, whether from the public, from parliamentarians in Senate estimates, or from rival media outlets making use of the freedom-of-information laws to probe for stories.

We could go on, but as we've already said, time is short. Whatever faults the ABC has are far outweighed by its strengths, and, equally to the point, the ABC faces a more hostile government than at any time in its near 90-year history. As this book went to press, it was unclear when the next federal election would be held. Regardless of who wins, there is a lot that needs to be done to repair problems in the ABC's funding process and governance, as we will outline in later chapters. A barrage of funding cuts, internal turmoil, and a chorus of harping critics within government and outside of it have made the ABC's future a live issue. 'Many of my colleagues in the government see the ABC as the enemy and think it should be treated as such,' Nationals MP Darren Chester told us. 'A number of the more ideologically aligned MPs think we'd be better off if we didn't have the ABC anymore.'[9] Chester does not think the government would actually follow through on this threatened action: 'There's still National Party MPs and some of the sensible metro MPs who strongly support the ABC.' Perhaps. Nevertheless, talk of the 'enemy' by coalition members is telling. It suggests a fundamental hostility that may end in the kind of world we've just imagined — a world without the ABC. Is our imagination running away with us? We don't think so. In any case, forewarned is forearmed.

Chapter 2

HOW THE INTERNET BROKE THE MEDIA'S BUSINESS MODEL AND MADE THE ABC

When the internet arrived in Australia in the early 1990s, the commercial media was in its pomp and the ABC was in its box. By 2012, the nation's big newspaper companies were laying off more journalists than at any time in living memory and the ABC had become the darling of the digital age. It can be difficult to discern these changes from the perspective of today's media environment, which is superheated and seems to have been in upheaval for years. It is important to understand them, though, as they underlie much of the tension today.

Back then, the news media comprised print, radio, and television. It was a profitable industry for most companies and a highly profitable one for commercial television stations, which could charge many thousands of dollars for the airing of a single 30-second advertisement. The Nine Network was particularly successful and thus influential. Commercial radio was not quite as profitable, but AM radio networks drew large audiences, and star broadcasters such as John Laws and Alan Jones were paid lavishly, with the former earning $3 million annually.[1]

Metropolitan daily newspapers were profitable, too. Between the 1970s and the 1990s, they expanded their coverage, creating supplements about television, food, music, education, and personal finance — one for each day of the week — and on weekends began publishing magazines on glossy stock filled with ads. To give an idea of the scale of growth, by 1996 *The Age* published as many pages each weekday as it had on a Saturday four decades before, and its weekend edition was a whopping 250 pages.[2] Around this time, the Saturday editions of *The Sydney Morning Herald* and *The Age* were making a profit of $1 million each week.[3] The growth in advertising revenue for the metro daily newspapers enabled sizeable growth in the number of journalists. At their peak, *The Sydney Morning Herald* and *The Age*, then owned by Fairfax Media, each employed 450-plus journalists, while the number for *The Australian* was close to 350. As well as staffing the many supplements, there were ample resources for news breaking and investigative journalism.

Commercial television also invested resources in current affairs in the 1990s, ranging from sensation-seeking shows such as *A Current Affair* and *Today Tonight* — committed to pursuing dodgy dry cleaners with the righteous vengeance usually reserved for Nazi war criminals — to programs aimed at more serious discussion, such as *Sunday* and *Business Sunday* on the Nine Network, *Witness* on Seven, and *Meet the Press* on Ten.

Other parts of the news-media sector were vibrant. Around Australia, there were 37 regional daily newspapers, 250 suburban newspapers, and 66 multicultural newspapers. Magazine industry analysts used to boast that

Australians read more magazines per head than any other country.[4] More than 3,000 titles were available across 51 categories, taking in, among others, health, women's interests, food, wine, motoring, craft, fashion, science, entertainment, gardening, sport, and current affairs. *The Australian Women's Weekly* was selling more than one million copies per issue.[5]

Meanwhile, until the launch of ABC Online in 1995, the ABC was a radio and television broadcaster whose programs rated solidly but consistently well behind the commercial media powerhouses. Its news and current affairs programs were generally of high quality but did not break many stories. *Four Corners* had been extending the ambition of its investigative journalism since the 1980s, notably through the work of Chris Masters, Jonathan Holmes, and Peter Manning, but it was the exception rather than the rule at the ABC. Overall, ABC journalists relied for their news leads on what they read in the morning newspapers, something rarely commented on but well known within the industry. As Peter Jeppesen, a long-time ABC current-affairs reporter, used to wryly remark, the ABC's newsroom was one where the phone never rang. The point here is not to denigrate the ABC but to note the behaviour, because it changes over time, and the impact of the change is important. In the 1990s, ABC journalists looked for news leads primarily in the Fairfax Media newspapers, which were then highly regarded and influential in setting the daily news agenda. There was also a broad confluence between the editorial outlook of Fairfax Media outlets and the ABC, as well as between the audiences they reached. As a media outlet, the ABC was still known among its commercial rivals as 'Aunty', a nickname that at its core saw the ABC as unthreatening.

Alongside news and current affairs, the ABC had sizeable divisions for music, drama, and the performing

arts. Since its early days as the Australian Broadcasting
Commission, the ABC had been integrally involved in
broadcasting music, especially classical music, on radio.
Included in its operations for many years were symphony
orchestras around the country. The increasing costs of
running the orchestras prompted the ABC to corporatise
them in 1996. They remained wholly owned subsidiary
companies of the ABC but were supported by a combination
of federal and state government funding, philanthropy, and
sponsorship.[6] For those with more modern musical tastes,
its youth station, 2JJJ, had been brought into the Triple J
network in 1989 and by the following year was available in
all state and territory capital cities as well as Newcastle.
The ABC had extensive in-house production facilities for
radio and television, enabling it to create programs across
a range of genres, including drama, comedy, chat shows,
documentaries, and miniseries. Spending on Australian-
made drama had trebled between 1986 and 1991.[7] That is
to say, the ABC was not simply a news and current-affairs
network. A good deal of its activities, and its staffing, were
in other areas — music, and the production of programs for
radio and television.

Disruption in the commercial media sector

It was more than a decade before the internet laid waste to
the business model that had long sustained print media
companies in Australia, mainly because in 2000 the dotcom
bubble burst, fuelling scepticism about the internet's
commercial potential. Meantime, news-media companies
doubled down on their strategy of making content freely
available, in the belief that substantially expanding their
audience online would draw more advertisers. From today's
perspective, this seems an inexplicably foolish move, but

that glib judgement overlooks the extent to which print media had always been a hybrid business where the paper was provided for less than the cost of a coffee. As readers, we think newspapers (and magazines) are about the journalism. They are, and they aren't. What newspapers really have been about is selling space to advertisers to reach prospective customers. Newspaper proprietors understood that those prospective customers were more likely to read the ads if they were surrounded by interesting, entertaining information. That is where news and journalism come in. News is perennially interesting to people; the journalist's job is to find it and tell it in a clear and compelling way.

Producing a newspaper has always carried costs in paying for journalists, paper, printing presses, and delivery by truck. Media companies earned part of their income from the cover price, but the great bulk of their revenue came from advertising. Over many years, the public became accustomed to getting their daily paper for next to nothing, which worked for them. It worked for the newspaper companies, too, earning them plump profits. Handsome rates for advertisements could be charged because the hefty costs of production and distribution ensured there were few, if any, competitors to the main newspaper companies. Since the 19th century, classified advertisements had given the Fairfax family, owners of *The Sydney Morning Herald*, a level of profitability envied by other media proprietors, such as the Packer family and Rupert Murdoch, the latter of whom dubbed classifieds the 'rivers of gold'. Fairfax protected these rivers against all comers so successfully that by the 1980s competitors had all but given up on diverting them away.[8]

Illustrating the maxim that sometimes your greatest strength can be your greatest weakness, however, Fairfax failed to protect its classified advertising revenue when the internet arrived. The internet enabled the creation of standalone advertising websites to meet customers' individual needs. By the mid-2000s, if you wanted to hunt for a house or a car or a job, you could do that for free. Instead of purchasing a newspaper and wading through pages of newsprint, you could narrow your search and quickly turn up precise information. If you were selling, meanwhile, you posted an ad to these sites for next to nothing. The new online classified-advertising sites could undercut Fairfax's rates because they were in that business only and had none of the costs associated with gathering and distributing news.

It is easy to heap scorn, but no mainstream print media company in the English-speaking world has yet found a successful replacement for that old business model. Even acknowledged industry giants like Rupert Murdoch for many years misread the internet's potential. Remember Myspace? No? Nor does anyone else now, but Murdoch acknowledged mistakes and mismanagement after he sold it in 2011 for a tiny fraction of what he had paid six years before.[9] It took time for the changes made possible by the internet to unfold, but they were irreversible. In less than a decade, around $8 billion of market capitalisation in Fairfax Media was sucked away to REA (realestate.com.au), Carsales, and Seek, according to Colleen Ryan's *Fairfax: the rise and fall*.

The print media companies' struggle to compete with the standalone online advertising sites was aggravated by Google and Facebook. According to the Australian Competition and Consumer Commission's (ACCC) Digital Platforms report of 2019, online advertising grew as a share of all advertising from 25 per cent to 53 per cent between 2012 and 2018. As of 2019, these two companies were receiving two-thirds of all online advertising revenue in Australia, and that proportion is rising.[10] Google and Facebook garnered such a large chunk of the available advertising market because they offered consumers an enticing range of services. We don't need to rehearse the list of things you can do online or through a mobile device; suffice to say they extend way beyond what any daily newspaper can offer. This has enabled Google and Facebook to become immensely profitable and powerful. By 2020, their market capitalisation was US$919 billion and US$583 billion respectively; by 2022, Google's market capitalisation was US$1.816 trillion and Facebook's was US$934 billion, making them the fourth- and seventh-largest companies in the world. Rupert Murdoch's News Corp, historically the 800-pound gorilla in the media sector internationally, did not even make the top 1,000 companies.[11]

In addition to being popular online destinations, the global tech companies provide precision advertising. About a century ago, American businessman John Wanamaker summed up the shortcomings of advertising in newspapers and, later, radio and television: 'Half the money I spend on advertising is wasted; the trouble is I don't know which half.' Google and Facebook's algorithms — the 21st-century equivalent of Colonel Sanders's 11 secret herbs and spices — enable them to maximise the likelihood that ads will be put in front of consumers when they are thinking about a particular purchase. As Amanda Lotz wrote in *Nieman Lab*, 'Social media and search give advertisers better tools to target messages to more precise groups of potential consumers. It is a phenomenally better mousetrap.'[12]

There's been a further twist of the knife for mainstream media companies. Google and Facebook became so deeply embedded in people's lives, especially younger people's, that they drew attention away from conventional news media. This forced the outlets to chase audiences. One way of doing this was to join news-aggregating services, such as Google News or Apple News or Flipboard, which bundled content from a range of outlets and sold a smorgasbord-style service to subscribers. Alternatively, news-media outlets could make their content available to the 'feeds' of social-media platforms. News and journalism continued to be a way of drawing people's attention, but the difference now was they were only one among many drawcards. All of this meant the news-media companies needed Google and Facebook a lot more than the latter needed them. In the ACCC's dry phrase, Google and Facebook became 'unavoidable trading partners' for news-media companies.[13] Media researcher Emily Bell put it more vividly: 'Facebook is eating the world.'[14]

Searching for a new business model

From its high-water mark in the 1990s, the commercial media has struggled to find a new business model to replace the one that served it so well for so long. As income dropped, media companies looked for ways to save money. They made their content available online, which appealed to many, but retained the expensive printing plants to assuage the substantial minority who still wanted to read a physical copy of a newspaper. They experimented with all sorts of ways of holding open the door, hoping the horse might re-enter the stable, including paywalls (please pay us for what we've been giving you freely for the past decade), micropayments (please pay us such a small amount you'll hardly notice it), and crowdfunding (please pay us just for the stuff you really want), with some but nowhere near enough success to offset the drop in advertising revenue. In the past few years, media companies have had more success in building digital subscriptions, or digital and print subscriptions for those still wedded to hard copy, which has led to a net increase in overall subscriptions for the major publishers.[15] If this strategy is about gradually persuading people to pay for news, others went a different way: *Guardian Australia* (and its parent company in the United Kingdom) continued to offer its journalism for free while asking readers to donate so the company could continue doing the kind of journalism they valued. Again, there are signs of success, with 150,000 people donating financially to *Guardian Australia* only seven years after it launched in Australia.[16]

One way the commercial media dealt with its business-model problem was to slash the numbers of journalists. In 2012, Fairfax Media and News Limited (as News Corp Australia was then known) laid off more journalists than at any time in their history, and continued cutting over the next several years. There was a brief respite in the second half of the decade as it dawned on media companies that they were endangering a key element of what they offered readers, and so they began hiring again, albeit in modest numbers. Then COVID-19 arrived, prompting another wave of redundancies. By the end of 2020, the journalists' union, the Media, Entertainment, and Arts Alliance (MEAA), estimated that between 4,000 and 5,000 journalism jobs had been lost in the past decade.[17] Where there had been several hundred journalists in the big-city newspaper newsrooms, there were now fewer than 200. In regional and local media, the pressures led to the closing of mastheads. Between 2008 and 2018, more than 100 — or 15 per cent — of all regional and local newspapers were shut down.[18] The arrival of COVID-19 led to the further shuttering of more than 100 local newspapers.[19]

Another way to reduce costs has been to cut entire programs. Most of the current-affairs programs mentioned earlier no longer exist: *Business Sunday* closed in 2006, and *Sunday* closed two years later; *Witness* lasted only a couple of years, while *Meet the Press* continued until 2013; *Today Tonight* began closing state editions in 2014 and finished altogether in 2019. Most programs begun more recently, such as *Inside Story* (Nine), lasted only a few seasons. *The Project*, which began on Ten in 2009, is a rare example of a commercial network trying, and succeeding in, a new approach to news and current affairs.

The impact of sustained job losses and the closing of news outlets took their toll. News deserts, as they were called, began to appear. Courts were covered less frequently, as was local government. In 2019, researchers from the Public Interest Journalism Initiative (PIJI) interviewed 12 editors and newsroom managers working across various media platforms around the country. They found that many outlets felt their reporting lacked 'desirable depth', that breadth had suffered, that investigative reporting was untenable for small and local publications, and that the news agenda of local outlets was more likely to be driven by advertising considerations. One finding was particularly dire: 'Where local news outlets are unable to serve their communities, it tends to undermine their position, and thus their ability to gather news in the future.'[20]

What this makes clear is that the commercial media is no longer the dominant force in providing information and shaping public debate. The internet's near-universal availability offers infinitely more sources of information, and the widespread take-up of social media means people conduct many of their conversations beyond the reach of mainstream news media. What's good about this is an increase in the range of voices and perspectives feeding the national conversation. What's bad is the turbocharged spread of deliberate distortion and misinformation.

The splintering of established media structures combined with winnowed newsrooms also prompted an unwelcome shift in the news media's approach to its work. As Sean Kelly, a former Labor media adviser turned political commentator, told *Guardian Australia*'s Katharine Murphy:

> News has always been a business, no point pretending otherwise. And what do you do if you need to create more content with less money? You create cheap content. What are the cheapest types of content to produce? Opinions and breaking news. The beauty of opinions is everyone's got one. The beauty of breaking news is that it doesn't have to be important, or even difficult to get: it just has to have happened in the recent past. So suddenly you've got opinions and breaking news everywhere.[21]

What this means, Murphy concludes, is that, courtesy of the internet, the news cycle 'got a whole lot more breathless, and a lot more shouty'.

Within the commercial media, there have been changes in what American journalist Tom Wolfe used to call the status totem pole. The Nine Network's influence gradually waned. When Kerry Packer, owner of that network, switched his allegiance from Labor to the Liberals in 1995, then prime minister Paul Keating was livid, mainly because he feared that Nine's coverage would carry weight with voters. Within a year of Packer's death in 2005, however, his son, James, had begun selling off the media interests that had been in the family's hands for four generations. Since the mid-1990s, the influence of Fairfax Media's big city newspapers has diminished, while the influence of News Corp Australia's newspapers, especially *The Australian*, has expanded thanks to the unified messaging they achieve by syndicating content and the columns of star writers like Andrew Bolt to their daily papers in Sydney, Melbourne, Brisbane, Adelaide, Hobart, and Darwin.

Aunty slips off her cardigan

If the scale and influence of the commercial mainstream media have been diminished in this period, what about the ABC? As a broadcaster not reliant on advertising, it was in tune with the information-wants-to-be-free ethos of the early internet. It caught up and, in some areas, overtook commercial media as the latter began to struggle. From the mid-1990s, it began making programs available online, sometimes including full transcripts, and then began reporting news online. A few years later, it extended online coverage to include news analysis and made good use of its experience in audio and video to create multimedia packages about newsworthy events, such as the 2009 Black Saturday bushfires. The following year, it extended into round-the-clock news coverage with ABC News 24. Program-makers on Radio National were probably the first in the Australian media to embrace podcasting, which has become one of the most successful new media forms of the 21st century. Canadian-born engineer Dan Fill worked in-house at the ABC to create a catch-up recording service, which was launched in 2008 as iview and became wildly popular, prompting commercial networks to follow suit. Within a decade of its creation, iview was attracting around 50 million plays monthly and accounting for around half of the total time streamed by Australian TV video services.[22]

On television in particular, the ABC provides far more current affairs than the commercial networks, and far more variety of current affairs. There is nothing on commercial free-to-air television that resembles *Q&A*, an hour-long weekly discussion program driven by questions from a studio and online audience, and little apart from *The Project* that resembles *The Drum*, an hour-long panel discussion program that runs five nights a week. *Four Corners* is the longest-running long-form current-affairs program in Australia, celebrating its 60th anniversary in 2021. It has produced more investigative journalism than perhaps any other television program in the country.

Apart from *Four Corners*, which was already well established when the internet arrived, the ABC now generates many more of its own news leads, especially since 2010, when a unit devoted to investigative journalism was established.[23] The unit is not tied to particular programs, like *Four Corners*, though its work may well end up there. Rather, the investigations unit works up individual stories while at the same time looking at how best to tell them and where. The effect is to invest a sharper journalistic focus into more programs and platforms on the ABC. Among numerous examples, investigations led by Anne Connolly on aged care and Mark Willacy on war crimes allegedly committed by Australian troops in Afghanistan originated in the investigations unit and had significant impact.[24] Investigative journalism by definition goes beyond reporting to scrutinise and criticise individuals and organisations, and so attracts controversy, resistance, and sometimes counterattack from the subjects of stories. The greater volume of investigative journalism, and the spread of that work across ABC outlets and platforms, is another important shift in the ABC's operations and affects its presence in the public eye.

Outside of this, though, it remains true that ABC local and regional news still rely on the morning's newspapers for stories. The difference is that for at least the past decade News Corp Australia has been the dominant media company in the country, overshadowing Fairfax Media, which merged with Nine in 2018. To the extent that the daily news agenda of the ABC is influenced by the surrounding dominant news media, it is News Corp rather than Nine that provides the influence.

The shape of the ABC as an organisation has shifted, too, since the mid-1990s. News and current affairs has always been a substantial division in the corporation, but over time other divisions have diminished in size. The ABC no longer owns symphony orchestras, though it continues to broadcast a lot of music. It no longer has an in-house radio and television production division, preferring instead to contract independent producers to create programs. It remains a cultural organisation, but, relatively speaking, news and current affairs looms larger than it did, sharpening the ABC's image in the public eye. Much less often is it referred to as Aunty these days.

The ABC was founded on the idea of broadcasting right around the country, and as commercial media outlets began abandoning costly or less profitable services in regional Australia, the ABC's importance grew. To the commercial media, the ABC was no longer the easy target for jokes about cardigan-wearing timeservers but another threat to their viability. The ABC not only gave away its content for free but was doing so in a new medium — online — that commercial media was desperately trying to tap as a new revenue stream. That their efforts were failing in the face of Google and Facebook's 'better mousetrap' did not stop commercial media outlets from loudly criticising the ABC's expansion into online and social media. Two issues were in play here: first, since the ABC's earliest years, commercial media companies have lobbied governments to prevent it encroaching on their territory, whether in the granting of licences or in limiting how much news could be taken from the daily newspapers.[25] Second, the arrival of the internet posed a far greater threat. Because the spectrum for broadcasting radio and television was a scarce resource, the federal government stepped in to control access to it. But government was not able to control access to the internet. Commercial media outlets that in the past tolerated or even supported the ABC now felt antagonistic toward it. Murdoch's newspapers, never friendly to the national broadcaster, became increasingly antagonistic, driven equally by commercial self-interest and ideology.

Happy as they were to tap-dance on the ABC's windpipe, News Corp Australia realised Google and Facebook posed a bigger problem than the national broadcaster. In 2019, it led a sustained and successful lobbying effort to persuade the Liberal–National federal government to set up an inquiry into the threat posed by Google and Facebook to the local media sector's survival. The self-interest was stark and eventually made plain in public hearings of a Senate inquiry into media diversity when Robert Thomson, CEO of News Corp globally, was asked his view of media regulation of Facebook and Google: 'I would like for it to be relaxed for us and intensified for them.'[26] The ACCC, a well-resourced federal agency that reports to Treasury and is influential in budget deliberations, conducted its Digital Platforms inquiry. Its research amply demonstrated the scale of the problem and recommended the creation of a News Media Bargaining Code by legislation that would use a final-offer arbitration process to force the global tech giants to make deals with media companies and compensate them for the use of their journalism.

Two things were happening simultaneously: first, the federal government, to its credit, was engaging with the real problem of Google and Facebook's dominant market power.

But, second, the government was enabling a shakedown. As former Ninemsn executive Hal Crawford said on *Q&A*, Google and Facebook would be paying 'protection money'.[27] What Crawford identified was that the government was applying the wrong solution to the right problem. The problem is not that Google and Facebook have 'stolen' the journalism; it is that they have taken the advertising revenue. Communications minister Paul Fletcher, appearing on the same episode of *Q&A*, perpetuated the misunderstanding when he said of the media companies, 'These are businesses that make their money out of journalism. That's their strategy. That's their competitive advantage.' The solution is couched in terms of funding journalism, but Google and Facebook have rightly argued they do not earn a great deal from anyone's journalism.

Google and Facebook and the government then engaged in a game of high-stakes poker. The tech companies were prepared to do deals to compensate media outfits ahead of the News Media Bargaining Code being actually legislated, according to Crawford, for two reasons: to head off the possibility that governments overseas would introduce similar legislation that would pose a much larger threat to their revenue, and, by acting ahead of the code being implemented, they would control the terms of any agreements made. The companies did a few deals but not enough to satisfy the government or the ACCC. They also intensively lobbied the government to protect details of how exactly their algorithms work. The government gave ground on that point while keeping pressure on the two companies by pushing through the legislation in February 2021. As media academic Andrea Carson noted: 'An important concession was that the federal treasurer would exercise discretion over whether the platforms would be formally "designated" under the code, a necessary step before the arbitration process would apply. At time of writing in July 2021, neither Facebook nor Google had been "designated". Rather, both Facebook and Google have avoided arbitration by sealing several multi-million dollar deals with major media companies.'[28]

Since then, the two tech behemoths have continued to do deals, but the terms of the code, not to mention Google and Facebook's perch outside it, mean that a critical piece of public policy contains serious flaws even as it paves the way for a new revenue stream to commercial media. It is certainly good that, according to one informed estimate, around $200 million per year will flow to media companies in Australia from Google and Facebook.[29] However, the benefits may be outweighed by the problems. First, it is not clear if the News Media Bargaining Code will apply to other new or emerging media technology companies. Second, the code does not specify the money has to be spent on public-interest journalism, or indeed journalism at all, even though some media companies have since begun hiring more journalists. Third, the terms of the deal are protected by commercial-in-confidence provisions. Fourth, overwhelmingly it is the biggest media companies, like News Corp Australia, Nine, and Seven West Media, that have secured deals. Small or alternative media outlets have been snubbed or ignored. Finally, most of the companies and individuals whose job it is to disclose to the public important information have a vested interest in keeping secret information about how and to what extent two immensely powerful companies are helping keep their businesses alive. As Hal Crawford wrote in an industry journal, 'This is a game without rules being played out of sight.' He adds that, when most of the current deals expire in 2024, 'Australian news companies will find the platforms playing the hardest hardball they can muster. Unless News has managed to ramp up the political pressure, the deals will be a lot less lucrative.'

The ABC and SBS watched intently as these negotiations unfolded. The ACCC recommended they be included in the code, but the government demurred before agreeing they should be included, even though, by definition, Google and Facebook's ability to attract advertisers does not impinge on the viability of broadcasters funded almost entirely (or mainly, in the case of SBS) by taxpayers. Exactly how much money Google and Facebook will hand over to the ABC had not been disclosed at time of writing, but the ABC has committed to spending it on public-interest journalism. In September 2021, meanwhile, Facebook decided to discontinue negotiations with SBS.[30] There is only one certainty about the News Media Bargaining Code and the public broadcasters. Unlike the commercial media companies, the ABC will be required to disclose the amount, either in its annual report or under questioning in Senate estimates.

The disparity in the way public broadcasters and privately owned media companies are treated by government is an issue we will discuss in a later chapter. Before that, we need to look at the political context in which the ABC operates. New communication technologies have been a factor in its changing fortunes, but far more important has been a rise in hyper-partisanship. Yes, like Nine and News Corp Australia in the past decade, the ABC has had to let go of many experienced journalists, and has cried loudly about the pain of doing so. Lost in the noise, however, has been a crucial distinction: the job losses at the ABC were driven not by a broken business model or technological change but by deliberate and repeated cuts, orchestrated by government, to its budget.

Chapter 3

ALL GOVERNMENTS LOATHE THE ABC EQUALLY, BUT SOME LOATHE IT MORE EQUALLY THAN OTHERS

When the ABC announced job losses for 250 people in 2020 because of cuts to its budget, the prime minister, Scott Morrison, responded bluntly: 'I've got to say, if you're working in the media industry today, if you're a journalist today, the safest place for you to be is actually at the ABC because your revenue is guaranteed in that industry by the government.'[1] It was a vintage Morrison answer: a dash of truth, lots of mixer, topped with a wedge of lemon and a smirk of ice. Yes, the government of the day funds the ABC and to that extent jobs are guaranteed. Yes, the media industry has been forced to shed thousands of jobs. But this particular government has delivered harsher cuts to the ABC than any of the past four decades, and its decision to do so has been driven by hyper-partisanship.

To understand how poisonous relations are between the coalition government and the ABC, we need to delve into relations between the ABC and successive governments. Just as the media environment has changed since the internet's arrival three decades ago, so, too, the political environment the ABC operates in has changed. There is a key difference, though: almost everyone agrees the media landscape has changed. Not so the political landscape. Or not in the way that we want to discuss in this chapter. We're not thinking here about the broad political environment, but the circumstances of the ABC within the political environment. That the ABC depends on government for its funding is a statement of the bleeding obvious. Equally obvious is that the ABC is always in a state of tension with government, of whichever political stripe. This is because the ABC is a statutory authority bound by its charter to provide an independent broadcasting service.[2] Its 34-page editorial policies document requires that the ABC follow 'fundamental journalistic principles of accuracy and impartiality', and that it report on Australia, and the world, 'without fear or favour, even when that might be uncomfortable or unpopular'.[3] This includes the government of the day, whose activities are routinely covered by ABC news and current affairs.

You might think this does not need to be spelled out, but think of it this way: how often do you see commercial media outlets report critically on their own company? How often do News Corp Australia outlets criticise their proprietor, Rupert Murdoch? Look through back issues of *The Australian* if you like, but we can save you the time: rarely is the answer. Nor is Murdoch an exception. The same applies to Seven West Media, *The West Australian*, and their proprietor, Kerry Stokes. Ken Inglis, surveying in 2006 the ABC's then half-century-plus history, wrote:

> Just as the most precious singularity of the public broadcaster as statutory authority is that it is endowed to make a product which may contain severe

judgements of its patrons, so the most exacting test of the governing body [the ABC board] may well be its will to stand firm in the face of overt or implied threats or inducements of a fiscal nature from those patrons.[4]

The inherent tension between the government and the ABC surfaces on the government's side in various overt and covert methods of controlling the public broadcaster, and on the ABC's side in routine proclamations of independence from government, whether Labor or Liberal. ABC managers and journalists are at pains to say they report without fear or favour and that if government is annoyed by their reporting they must be doing something right.

This is an important half-truth. The legislated tension built into the ABC's operations means that every government has been irritated, upset, or outraged by the national broadcaster's journalism, and that every government has sought to use the levers at its disposal to persuade at best and punish at worst the ABC. What this half-truth skates over is that one side — the Liberal–National Party coalition — has been substantially more hostile toward the ABC, both in outlook and in action, than the other. This has important implications, but they are rarely discussed publicly, because it is not really in the major political parties' interests to do so. Nor is it in the ABC's. Everyone stays quiet, and the public is not encouraged to see what is actually going on.

The act of parliament changing the ABC from a commission to a corporation came into effect in July 1983. In the 39 years since, the two major parties have been in power for almost the same period of time: just under 19 years for Labor (1983–96 and 2007–13), and just over 20 years for the coalition (1996–2007 and 2013 to now). This provides, fortuitously, a good basis for comparing how different governments have treated the ABC. The first 50 years of the broadcaster's existence is not irrelevant to this debate, but it took years for the ABC to be allowed, let alone be able, to establish a news service with its own journalists reporting the news rather than presenters reading excerpts from the newspapers.

In the original *Australian Broadcasting Commission Act*, passed in 1932, the commission was charged with broadcasting 'adequate and comprehensive programs'. Independence was not mentioned. The ABC initially came under the control of the postmaster-general's department, which had the power to interfere with programs and on occasion did just that. An early postmaster-general, Archie Cameron, gruffly proclaimed in 1938 that he knew nothing about broadcasting, did not like it, and if given a choice would have stopped it. 'No time for these mechanical things. Don't know anything about music. As for people who give talks and commentaries over the air, if I had my way I would poison the blanks blanks — would bring them under the Vermin Act.'[5]

Nothing like a bit of plain speakin', as *Mad as Hell* host Shaun Micallef would say. It took most of a half-century for the ABC simply to assert a level of independence as a statutory authority. Between 1946 and 1955, prime ministers Ben Chifley (Labor) and Robert Menzies (Liberal) allowed staff numbers to almost double, while also being seen to stand apart from the organisation.[6]

In 1979, during his prime ministership of the coalition government, Malcolm Fraser set up what was a landmark inquiry into the ABC. The public took a keen interest in the inquiry, headed by businessman Alex Dix, sending in 2,200 written submissions — three times as many as had been sent to a comparable inquiry about broadcasting in the United Kingdom.[7] Dix's recommendation that the ABC be allowed to accept 'corporate underwriting' — that is, advertising — was widely opposed (including by newspapers worried about a new competitor for the ad-revenue pie) and not taken up by government, but Dix had other ideas that have shaped the ABC since. The most notable was his argument that the ABC should be a comprehensive broadcaster aiming to meet the information needs of all Australians — not just a niche broadcaster aimed either at the relatively small number of classical-music lovers or at counterbalancing what was then a generally conservative political outlook from the commercial print and broadcast media.[8] There was an inconsistency here, or at least confusion, in Dix's proscription for a broadcaster that catered for all, and it continues to bedevil public perceptions and debates about the ABC's role. This is because Dix also recommended the ABC worry less about bidding big sums to broadcast popular sports and concentrate more on those neglected by commercial media, such as basketball, netball, and hockey. That is, on sport, the ABC should become a niche broadcaster. The ABC did this, broadcasting women's sport and other (then) less popular sports, but oscillating between providing a comprehensive and a niche service has led to confusion about the ABC's purpose that some of its critics have exploited.

Our focus here, then, is to ask: since the passing of the *Australian Broadcasting Corporation Act*, which closely followed the election of the Hawke Labor government in March 1983, how has the ABC fared with successive governments? Tension between government and the ABC is to be expected, but apart from that, which governments have increased funding, which have cut it, and by how much? Which have sought to improve the independence of the organisation's governance and which have sought to interfere? Which have been hostile and which supportive?

'Have you read the fuckin' Act?':
the ABC and the Hawke/Keating Labor
governments, 1983–96

The Hawke Labor government inherited the bill flowing from Dix's report. It had not been passed before the 1983 election, because Labor, with the Australian Democrats, had blocked Fraser-government plans to step beyond Dix and introduce an external commissioner of complaints for the ABC. This commissioner was necessary, according to the broadcasting minister, to quash 'the ABC's now well-established bias toward Labor and the socialist side of politics'.[9] Over the 13 years of Labor governments, led during five terms by Bob Hawke (1983–91) and Paul Keating (1991–96), the overall relationship between government and the ABC was one of healthy tension. The prime ministers and most of their cabinet colleagues were supporters of public broadcasting in general and the ABC in particular. They wanted to see the ABC succeed and were keen to see it modernise.

In 1986, foreign minister Bill Hayden sent a congratulatory telegram saying the ABC's coverage of the Marcos regime's fall in the Philippines was quicker and more reliable than official sources. Hawke wrote a foreword for a book by ABC broadcaster Mark Aarons about alleged Nazi war criminals entering Australia; the book grew out of Aarons' *Background Briefing* series on Radio National, which had prompted Hawke to set up an inquiry and then a Special Investigations Unit. There were, however, plenty of tense moments between the government and the ABC. The first arrived only weeks after Labor won office, when a revitalised *Four Corners* program broadcast allegations of corruption in New South Wales that ensnared Labor premier Neville Wran. Soon after, there was tension over an interview with a Free Papua Movement representative in another *Four Corners* program that imperilled international relations. Later, tension ensued over government proposals to introduce advertising on the ABC and over managing director David Hill's famous 'eight cents a day' campaign to prod government into providing more money (which led Keating as treasurer to threaten punishment in the next budget — a threat unfulfilled, as it turned out).

The ABC enjoyed the highest level of real funding in its history in 1985–86, and it was under Hawke that the ABC's many years of lobbying for budgetary certainty were answered with the introduction of triennial funding rounds. But it also suffered budget cuts on more than one occasion under Labor. The Hawke/Keating governments, unlike the previous Labor government, under Gough Whitlam, believed in the virtues of privatising government services and economic rationalism, or neoliberalism, as it is now known. On this, they were closer to Liberal Party ideology, though they still hewed to social-democratic policies. Hawke, keen to contrast himself with the profligacy, real and perceived, of Whitlam, was 'ostentatiously frugal' with public money.[10]

On governance, Labor broke with the previous coalition government's practice by consulting with the Liberal Party opposition about its choice of chair for the new ABC board in 1983, and by reinstating a staff-elected board member. Like previous governments of all persuasions, Labor appointed board members sympathetic or aligned to it, though, importantly, these appointees favoured stewardship over political loyalty. As one anonymous board member told Ken Inglis, 'We leave our guns outside'.[11] However, Labor did not, or chose not to, understand that, while the *ABC Act* enabled it to select a chair and board members, it did not provide for the government to select the managing director.

It chose Hill as chair in 1986, and, when the inaugural managing director, Geoffrey Whitehead, resigned a few months later, Labor moved to persuade the board to choose Hill as managing director without advertising the position and without consulting the opposition. Nearly a decade later, when Hill's combustible energy finally blew himself up, he blamed the government, probably wrongly, for leaning on the board.

The Labor government was acutely aware of the power of the news media. It hated the investigative journalism done about its activities by *Four Corners* and other ABC news programs: 'We have had enough of you cunts, and now it's the full frontal assault,' Keating told Hill in 1988.[12] When *Four Corners* scrutinised the business activities of his close friend Peter Abeles, Hawke was blunt: 'We don't fund the ABC to do stories on Peter Abeles.'[13] Labor government ministers, especially those of the right faction, grumbled about the ABC, arguing in one caucus meeting in 1984 that the ABC's independence should be changed. 'Have you read the fuckin' Act?' demanded the communications minister, Michael Duffy, who stands out among this portfolio's ministers over the past four decades as a strong advocate for public broadcasting.[14] The idea was dropped.

Overall, the ABC figured less in Labor's thinking than either those newspaper companies perceived as enemies — such as the historically conservative Herald and Weekly Times Ltd and John Fairfax and Sons Ltd, which published investigative journalism about the government, primarily in *The National Times* — or those the government thought would be friends, including Rupert Murdoch's newspapers and especially Kerry Packer's Nine television network. The cross-media ownership laws passed in 1987 were primarily aimed at punishing perceived enemies and rewarding 'media mates', as Paul Chadwick documented.[15] And they did so with disturbing success, opening the door to Murdoch becoming the dominant print media owner in Australia, which he remains today, and fuelling a massive increase in the value of the commercial television stations, from which Packer benefited to the tune of hundreds of millions of dollars.[16]

The nadir of relations between the ABC and Labor came late in Hawke's prime ministership. It centred on his anger at the ABC's coverage of the Gulf War, in particular commentary in ABC television's current-affairs programs by Robert Springborg, a Middle East expert from Macquarie University. After Iraq invaded Kuwait in August 1990, Springborg wrote an opinion piece for *The Herald* in Melbourne arguing that Hawke's decision to dispatch naval vessels to help enforce an American blockade of the Persian Gulf had been 'made precipitously and with little consultation, suggesting that we are every bit as much of a one-man show as is the country we may be fighting'. Springborg had then been retained on the ABC as a commentator on the war after the United States–led alliance of nations that included Australia began bombing Iraq and Iraqi-held areas in January 1991. At that point, Gerard Henderson, a former chief of staff in opposition leader John Howard's office and head of the Sydney Institute, wrote a *Sydney Morning Herald* opinion piece criticising the lack of balance in the ABC's choice of commentators and singling out Springborg, who he argued was not 'an uncommitted, impartial observer'.[17]

Hawke was furious about the use of Springborg, whose past views, he thought, should have been made clear to viewers and whose presence should have been balanced by another analyst. He vented to ABC chair Bob Somervaille and managing director David Hill. The latter set up an internal inquiry into the ABC's Gulf War coverage, conducted by a senior ABC executive, Derek White. He concluded that the national broadcaster 'provided comprehensive and balanced coverage of the Gulf crisis' while acknowledging that there would have been fewer complaints about Springborg if his earlier stated opposition to the war had been made clear to viewers. The inquiry did not dwell on the primary complainant being the prime minister. Separately, Rodney Tiffen, a political scientist, analysed the controversy and concluded that the ABC's sin, if there was one, was one of tone. Did the standard 'adversarial-cum-sceptical' manner of current-affairs interviewing need to be calibrated during a war in which Australia had committed troops? Tiffen also concluded, like White, that the ABC's coverage of the war was comprehensive and balanced, and added that it shone when compared with the 'parade of false alarms' that characterised much newspaper coverage, especially in the Sydney tabloids.[18]

The controversy surrounding Springborg overshadowed another controversy, sparked by special programs aired by the ABC's international service, Radio Australia, for sailors deployed to the Persian Gulf and some citizens who had been captured and held as hostages in Kuwait. The government wanted the service to continue; Radio Australia worried about losing independence in programming decisions. The ABC was warned by communications minister Kim Beazley that he might invoke a rarely used clause in the *ABC Act* empowering the minister to require or prevent broadcasting of certain items. Somervaille and Hill assured the minister that this would not be necessary and put in place a plan that appeared to give the government what it wanted without jeopardising the ABC's independence. The arrangement protecting the ABC's independence was a 'fiction' according to Radio Australia's acting general manager, Geoff Heriot.[19] It was an example of the ABC's proclivity for a 'pre-emptive buckle'.

Four points emerge from the confrontations between the ABC and the Hawke government over the Gulf War. First, the prime minister's pressure appears to have led to the ABC using Springborg less and ensuring a greater diversity of views. Second, the Springborg controversy obscured from view the conclusion of both an internal inquiry and academic analysis that, overall, the ABC's coverage was strong. Third, the ABC jeopardised its editorial independence under pressure from Beazley. And fourth, the ABC's budget was substantially cut later in 1991 — though it is not clear whether or to what extent the cut was retribution for the war coverage. Michael Duffy, for one, told Ken Inglis that governments should neither applaud the ABC nor punish it, and that Hawke's antagonism 'always stopped short of punishment'.[20]

The prime ministership of Paul Keating contained no event as confrontational as the Springborg controversy, though Keating was notorious in media circles for phoning both newspaper editors and ABC editorial executives and delivering lengthy sprays, flecked with the bluest language. Keating was more supportive of the arts than almost any PM before or since. His Creative Nation policy in 1994 recognised both that the nation's cultural diversity extended well beyond traditional high-art forms like opera and ballet and that the value of the arts to the economy should be recognised and encouraged.[21] A lover of classical music, Keating wanted Australia to have a world-class symphony orchestra and decided that Sydney's should be uncoupled from the ABC. Creative Nation would see $252 million in additional funding allocated to the arts over four years. The ABC had expected to be included in this largesse and so had not pressed hard for more in its triennial budget submission to government. To its disappointment, though, the ABC was excluded.[22]

Over their time in office, the Hawke/Keating Labor governments maintained a productive relationship with the ABC, supporting it on important initiatives and interfering on only a limited number of occasions. Labor generally adhered to good governance. It perpetuated the practice of appointing politically sympathetic or aligned people to the board, though it did appoint two former Liberal MPs, Neville Bonner in 1983 and Ian Macphee in 1994.[23] It increased ABC funding early on and introduced triennial funding but later wavered between budget cuts and modest funding increases. Over the period 1983–96, the Labor government increased funding for the ABC by 7 per cent in real terms, according to a detailed analysis of ABC budgets prepared for this book by Michael Ward (see Appendix B).

'Fair game': the ABC and the Howard coalition governments, 1996–2007

John Howard led the Liberal–National Party coalition to office in 1996 and remained prime minister until 2007. At a personal level, Howard had an odd relationship with the ABC. There were many things about its broadcasting that he had long loved, especially its cricket coverage, and, at the opening of the ABC's new headquarters at Ultimo in Sydney in 2002, he put aside his prepared speech and delivered a paean to the ABC, praising it for contributing to media diversity, for challenging as well as shaping public attitudes, and for its role 'in nurturing and understanding of different facets of the way of life of our fascinating and lovely country'.[24] He also made a pact with the long-time friend he chose to chair the ABC, Donald McDonald: 'I will never speak to you about the ABC, I will never raise the ABC as an issue with you, [and] if you want to talk to me about the ABC, contact my office, make an appointment, and come and we'll formally meet and discuss it.' As McDonald recalled, Howard kept his word: while they met three or four times over funding issues, 'never did he speak to me about a program, either happily or unhappily'.[25]

But Howard had also always liked his senior adviser Grahame Morris's description of the ABC as 'our enemy talking to our friends', and, within two months of being elected in 1996, he launched a direct attack on the ABC's programs, describing them as 'politically correct' ('woke' in today's parlance). Throughout his prime ministership, Howard made himself available to be interviewed on the ABC, especially on radio, but he was frequently critical of the national broadcaster, especially about what he thought was its tendency to focus too much on issues such as the treatment of asylum seekers.

Richard Alston, communications minister under Howard, had a hostile relationship with the ABC. He had held the portfolio in opposition for three years before Howard won office and would continue to hold it until 2003. (Labor's Stephen Conroy, serving from 2007 to 2013, is the next-longest-serving minister in a portfolio normally marked by brief tenures; the Hawke/Keating governments actually had seven communications ministers in total.) Alston made clear that the ABC could not expect funding increases, and he opened the door to changes in ABC funding by tying funds to particular purposes, such as digitisation and rural and regional programming.[26]

The relationship between the government and the ABC was often tense. At times, that tension, as during the Hawke/Keating governments, could be described as healthy, but mostly it was unhealthy. The hostility began early. Having promised during the election campaign that brought them to power not to cut the ABC's funding, Alston announced exactly that four months later — a 10 per cent cut to the ABC's budget in the triennial beginning 1997–98.[27] This was a cut bigger than the 8 per cent cut imposed by Hawke in 1986 and the 7 per cent cut by Malcolm Fraser in 1976.[28] The coalition government claimed the cuts were forced on them by a budgetary 'black hole' they inherited, but the Liberals had been planning to cut the ABC's budget for some time.

Laura Tingle, writing for *The Age*, revealed a cabinet submission from Alston outlining two options for the ABC while acknowledging they were 'inconsistent with government election commitments'. The first option included budget cuts and the setting up of an independent review of the ABC's charter 'by an eminent person, which would make recommendations to government on a future, narrower role for the ABC'.[29] If setting up an independent review with a preconceived result in mind was not bad enough, the second option proposed an immediate, savage budget cut of 20 per cent, followed by further cuts in the next four years. In his memoirs, Alston denies ever seeing this draft of the cabinet submission and what he terms its 'totally unauthorised and false assertion' about the coalition's broken promise, but he did not dispute journalist Pamela Williams's claim, in her inside account of how the Liberals won office, that the coalition always intended to cut the ABC's budget and concealed this during the election campaign. 'It was too dangerous to provoke the broadcaster during an election campaign when every minute of good news counted,' wrote Williams, drawing on views from Liberal headquarters. 'The ABC would be quarantined until its current funding ran out. But after that it would be fair game for the chop'.[30]

Apart from promising, before the 1996 election, not to cut the ABC's funding, Alston declared there would be no stacking of the ABC's board.[31] Reminded of this in 2000 by Ken Inglis, Alston replied that it was the sort of policy that appealed to politicians in opposition.[32] If a candid answer, it was also breathtakingly cynical; Alston and Howard went on to stack the ABC board with political appointments. This began in 1998, when they chose to break with a 40-year convention, extending back to Robert Menzies's prime ministership, of appointing a board member with a trade-union background. Instead, they chose barrister Ian Callinan QC, only to replace him almost immediately, after appointing him to the High Court. They then broke another convention, that of keeping a national balance on the board, by replacing Callinan, a Queenslander, with Michael Kroger, a Victorian. A former national president of the Liberal Party, Kroger was also openly partisan. 'Hopefully, having a board representative who is clearly seen to be an ally of the federal government can dent criticisms of bias from which the ABC has suffered for decades,' he said.[33] On this, he was as good as his word, reportedly telling the board a planned *Four Corners* program about Sydney shock jock Alan Jones should not be made and, if it was, it should be positive, because that was how the people of New South Wales viewed Jones.[34] That Kroger was a friend of Jones and a member of his 'pick and stick' club did not for a moment, apparently, cloud his judgement.[35]

The stacking continued with ideological appointments such as Ron Brunton (2003–08), a member of the right-wing think tank the Institute of Public Affairs, ABC critics such as Janet Albrechtsen (2005–10), and culture warriors such as Keith Windschuttle (2006–11). Brunton said he was a supporter of public broadcasting, and Kroger admired how Radio National devoted an entire day's programming to commemorating the millennium's end, but Albrechtsen, Windschuttle, and Kroger all trenchantly criticised the ABC before, during, and after their board terms, accusing it, among other things, of being a workers' collective with an ingrained bias against those on the right of politics. In 2003, Kroger declined the opportunity of a second term on the board, telling Inglis that 'time and again the government had appointed people who they hoped would reform the ABC but who had been seduced by its patronage'.[36] Kroger's remark suggested, no doubt unintentionally, that the ABC possessed some kind of weird superpower for which no kryptonite could be found.

This period also saw the disastrous managing directorship of Jonathan Shier, who in the eyes of many appeared to be acting as the government's agent in smashing the ABC's culture, though chair Donald McDonald claims it was less a case of malice and more a case of 'miscasting' the role. Whatever the intent of the board in signing off on his appointment, Shier's chaotic tenure generated fear and loathing inside the ABC, lots of headlines (including plans to get rid of Kerry O'Brien as host of *The 7.30 Report*), and eventually a revolt led by news and current affairs head Max Uechtritz, who persuaded McDonald and eventually the board that Shier's disruptive, demoralising management style could not continue. Supported by Kroger to the end, Shier stepped down after less than two years in charge.[37]

Richard Alston's hostility continued to be cold and intense. He first complained formally about bias in the ABC's coverage of the bitter dispute prompted by the government's campaign to break the waterfront union in 1998; during the Iraq War, in 2003, he took exception to supposedly anti-American language in the ABC's coverage and launched a volley of complaints — 68 in all — using his ministerial office.[38] The ABC's complaints-review executive, Murray Green, issued a 130-page report, concluding that two of the 68 complaints had merit. Alston was unhappy ('a sneeringly dismissive response') and appealed to the ABC's Independent Complaints Review Panel, which included senior commercial and SBS television executives, print journalists, and a law professor.[39] The panel found merit in 17 of Alston's 68 criticisms and, like Green, no evidence of systemic bias. Instead, it praised the ABC's coverage of the war for enabling listeners 'to grasp what was happening on the battlefields and in the war rooms of a controversial conflict'. Still not satisfied, Alston took his complaints early in 2004 to an external body, the Australian Broadcasting Authority (ABA), which increased the number of complaints upheld to 21. It was still less than a third of the total, and the ABA also found no evidence of systemic bias, concluding that the coverage overall was of a high standard and included a good range of viewpoints on the war. In his memoirs, Alston termed this a 'substantial vindication' and, understandably, given his feelings of vindication, was perplexed when the ABC failed to acknowledge guilt, apologise, or change its editorial policy and/or practices.[40]

What came out of this extraordinarily focused attack on the ABC's journalism? First and foremost, it showed that its work stood up under intense scrutiny. Second, the controversy distracted people from a key point — that the ABC had been right to resist becoming a cheerleader, as others in the media had been, for the government's support of the Bush administration's invasion of Iraq. By mid-2003, when Alston was launching his first volley of complaints, it was already becoming clear that the grounds on which the 'shock and awe' bombing campaign had been initiated were spurious. Given the certitude with which Alston prosecuted his case, it is important to underscore the damning verdict on the war: it was unjustified, it cost hundreds of thousands of Iraqi lives, and by 2006 it had cost more American lives than were lost in the terrorist

attacks of 11 September 2001, which had been the initial —
wrong — impetus for invading. Third, though it is hard to
say with any certainty, the complaints campaign may have
had an effect on internal morale at the ABC. Did it cause
journalists to begin self-censoring? Did it perhaps give rise
to a reflexive defensiveness among ABC journalists around
coalition governments? If so, did that do anyone any good?

Over 11 years marked by unhealthy tension and hostility
toward the ABC, the government sought to bend the
broadcaster to its will. In real terms, funding for the ABC
dropped 5 per cent between 1996 and 2007 (see Appendix
B). The government extended and worsened previous
governments' tendency to stack the ABC with political
appointees. It engaged in campaigns to prosecute the idea
that the ABC's journalism was systemically biased against
the right side of politics. Positive moments were piecemeal,
grudging, and not actually all that positive, as when
McDonald was forced to make a formal appointment with
the prime minister in 2000 to plead his case to stave off the
closing down of Radio Australia.[41]

Tender processes: the ABC and the Rudd/ Gillard/Rudd Labor governments, 2007–13

The relationship between the national broadcaster and the
Labor governments led by Kevin Rudd and Julia Gillard
between 2007 and 2013 was the most harmonious and least
eventful in the nearly four decades of the modern ABC.
And the most unremarked on. This might have something
to do with all the tumult created by Rudd's shock ouster,
which dogged Gillard's government and obscured from
view what the government and the ABC did accomplish
during these years.

The fact is that of the four periods of Labor or coalition

government between 1983 and 2021, the Rudd and Gillard Labor governments increased the ABC's funding in real terms by the most — 10 per cent, according to Michael Ward's analysis (see Appendix B). The government supported the ABC in switching from analog to digital transmission, with $33 million in tied funding, and supported the commercial broadcasting networks to do the same by reducing their licence fees. Such support was similar to that provided by the Howard government, but the Labor government went further in driving progress toward digital multi-channels, which the commercial free-to-air networks had successfully persuaded previous governments to delay. In 2009, the government provided an additional $136 million for the creation of a separate, dedicated children's television channel, ABC Kids, and for new Australian drama, resourcing for which had been slowly starved.[42] In the 2013 budget, the government also provided more than $60 million over four years for 'enhanced news gathering', specifically to set up a National Reporting Team, new regional bureaus, state-based digital teams, and a fact-checking unit.[43]

Wearying of the toxic influence of political appointments to the ABC board, Labor resolved in 2002, while in opposition, to reform the process for board appointments. In 2010, Labor brought to parliament amendments to the ABC's governing legislation to introduce an arms-length process for appointments to the boards of the ABC and SBS, by which an expert nomination panel assessed applicants and provided a list of recommended appointees to the minister. The process drew on the work of a former United Kingdom judge, Michael Nolan, who outlined seven principles for good governance in public life, including openness and transparency, independent scrutiny, and merit. The amendment was not supported by the Liberal

Party.[44] The new system began late in the government's life, in 2012, but, before then, communications minister Stephen Conroy had in any case avoided making political appointments to the board. He also reinstated the position of staff-elected board member, which had been abolished by the Howard government in 2006.

During the government's two terms of office, the shift from analog to digital media became pervasive. In the 2007 election that saw Rudd become prime minister, the two main political parties were only just beginning to experiment with using online videos and social media to bypass political journalists and communicate directly with people. The ABC, led by a forward-thinking managing director, Mark Scott, wanted to extend the national broadcaster's digital services as far as possible, as we have seen, but its success was met with opposition from commercial media outlets. The ABC could make digital media available for free; commercial media outlets needed to make money, of course, and were increasingly worried the ABC was closing off revenue streams for them. The establishment in 2009 of the online analysis and commentary site *The Drum* was a particular cause of ire. Behaving in the digital age as if the ABC should be confined to broadcasting made no sense, but it did signal the commercial media's desperation as it struggled to adapt its business model.[45] In March 2013, the government introduced to parliament a package of six bills to reform media regulation. One of the bills would amend the *ABC Act*, enabling the ABC to provide digital services. Commercial media providers were still opposed but were so busy lobbying against the other bills, which they saw as a draconian incursion on freedom of the press, that they either ignored or paid less attention to the ABC amendment, which duly passed.

Perhaps the murkiest episode in Labor–ABC relations

in this period concerned the television service the ABC had been offering to expatriates and others in the Asia-Pacific region since 1993. That service, the Australia Network, became embroiled in a bitter power struggle within the government and between the government and Sky News Australia, which was then part-owned but largely managed by News Limited. In 2011, Rudd was no longer prime minister, but as foreign minister he was keen for his department to have as much say as possible in the running of the network, whose role was to exercise 'soft power' in the region. Julia Gillard and Stephen Conroy wanted to put the service out to tender for ten years and favoured the ABC continuing to provide it. Sky News had produced some programs for the service and wanted to become the primary provider. The process broke down amid leaking of confidential tender bid information. The contract was eventually awarded to the ABC for ten years even though the assessment board had favoured Sky News's bid. Auditor-general Ian McPhee said the government was entitled to make the decision but was scathing about the process, which had 'presented the Australian government in a poor light' and cost the two tenderers time and money.[46]

Overall, however, the governments led by Rudd and Gillard enjoyed good relations with the ABC. Funding was increased in real terms and substantial steps were taken to depoliticise appointments to the ABC board. There were no repercussions for the ABC when a Triple J presenter tweeted that Gillard was a 'whore', nor when Germaine Greer went on *Q&A* and criticised Gillard's clothing and body.[47] The only time Emma Dawson, the communication minister's media-policy adviser, remembers Conroy calling Mark Scott to complain was when the ABC announced plans to shut down local production, cutting some jobs in Tasmania and Western Australia, and that was mainly because he was angry that the first he'd heard about it was through the media.[48] Scott, meanwhile, said that the only instance of pressure he experienced from Conroy was benign: 'It would be on the availability of *Doctor Who* merchandising in his local ABC Shop, it would be whether in fact we were fast-tracking the new series when it arrives ...'[49] Gillard, moreover, waited until she had left parliament before criticising the ABC's four-part sitcom *At Home with Julia*, which focused on her relationship with partner Tim Mathieson.[50]

'Whose side are you on?': the ABC and the Abbott/Turnbull/Morrison coalition governments, 2013 to the present

In an interview with SBS on the night before an election that few doubted he would win, Liberal Party leader Tony Abbott promised there would be 'no cuts to education, no cuts to health, no change to pensions, no change to the GST, and no cuts to the ABC or SBS'.[51] The promise was broken in his government's first budget, in 2014. It was dismally reminiscent of the Howard government's broken election promise in its first year.

The relationship between the coalition government and the ABC has been almost unremittingly hostile ever since. The notion that the ABC should be privatised was floated during the Howard years but not seriously considered, partly because the National Party valued the ABC in regional and rural Australia and partly because Howard could see how well regarded the ABC was among the general public. This was not the case by 2013. The rise in hyper-partisanship in the media that saw News Corp Australia outlets become constant critics of the ABC resulted in politicised public perceptions of the national broadcaster, including in rural Australia, where Sky News has become a significant presence thanks to content-sharing deals with regional TV networks.[52] And where the National Party once praised the ABC's presence in rural and regional Australia, its increasing focus on the mining and coal industries has made it resentful of the ABC's coverage of climate change. These factors have combined to make privatisation a live issue.

The first blows arrived in the 2014 budget, with the cancellation of the $196 million contract the ABC had signed with the Rudd government to provide the Australia Network, and a 1 per cent cut to overall funding to the ABC. This was nowhere near as steep as when the last coalition government broke an election promise about ABC funding, but, later in the same year, new communications minister Malcolm Turnbull announced further cuts. These led to the loss of 400 jobs and the axing of the ABC's state-based Friday evening *7.30* programs. Funding was cut further in the 2015 and 2016 budgets. The 'enhanced news gathering' program was renewed but cut by a third. In the 2019–20 budget, an 'indexation pause' froze ABC funding at 2018–19 levels for the next four years. This prompted another 250 job losses and cuts to services, such as the dropping of the longstanding 7.45 am radio news bulletin, and halving of the length of the *World Today* and *PM* radio programs. In media interviews, communications minister Paul Fletcher refused to concede funding was being cut, and, when RMIT's Fact Check unit spent 3,500 words demolishing the minister's claims, labelling them 'misleading', he responded with desiccated hairsplitting. The minister said the fact-checking unit had drawn on budget papers that did not take into account intergovernmental transfers of funds, such as workers' compensation payments made by the government's self-managed insurance fund, Comcover, even though these are not included in calculating the ABC's operational budget.[53]

The analysis of the ABC's funding by Michael Ward in Appendix B is clear: the current coalition government's record is the worst since 1983 — an 11 per cent decline in real terms since it came to power in 2013. And *The Australian* reported that the forward estimates in the 2021 budget papers forecast a 6 per cent decline in the next triennial agreement. To the best of our knowledge, the minister has not taken *The Australian* to task for misreporting the budget papers. At the time of writing, the next triennial agreement has not been finalised, but internal hopes at the ABC are, at most, that indexation will be restored and funding for local and outer-suburban news will be made permanent.[54] The current triennial funding agreement expires on 30 June 2022.[55]

There has been as much turmoil in the coalition government's leadership as in the previous Labor government's, but each of the three coalition prime ministers has been hostile toward the ABC in their own particular way. Tony Abbott was fond of quoting the aphorism that it is easier to beg forgiveness than to seek permission, and his record as opposition leader between 2009 and 2013 revealed that his reflex was indeed to hit first and ask about his opponent's health later. Within two months of becoming prime minister, Abbott responded angrily to a story jointly published by the ABC and *Guardian Australia* about Australian intelligence agencies looking to tap the mobile phone of the Indonesian president and his inner circle in 2009. He told Ray Hadley's morning radio program: 'I think it dismays Australians when the national broadcaster appears to take everyone's side but our own'. Abbott wanted the ABC to have 'at least some affection for the home team'.[56] Not only did this ignore the genuine public interest in what was an alarming breach of international diplomacy, and that the ABC was a joint partner rather than the sole creator of the story, it assumed the national broadcaster's role was to be a cheerleader for government.

Abbott made similar noises after the ABC broadcast allegations that Australian naval personnel had wilfully burned the hands of asylum seekers. He told Hadley that the ABC should not have leapt to be critical of Australia and 'certainly ought to be prepared to give the Australian Navy and its hardworking personnel the benefit of the doubt'. Amid a pile-on from other politicians and commercial media outlets over its patriotism and the veracity of the story, the ABC eventually acknowledged imprecisions in its reportage. But the damage was done. 'Let the culture war begin,' declared conservative radio presenter Steve Price.[57]

In 2015, Abbott dialled up the jingoistic rhetoric by asking the broadcaster, 'Whose side are you on?' after the ABC invited a convicted criminal, Zaky Mallah, onto *Q&A*. Mallah was certainly a controversial choice, having pleaded guilty to threatening to kill ASIO officials and having been narrowly acquitted of charges over planning a terrorist attack. Abbott imposed a blanket ban on his ministers appearing on the program, and interfered with the ABC's statutory independence by lobbying its chair, James Spigelman, to have the program moved into the news and current affairs division.[58]

When Turnbull ousted Abbott as prime minister in 2015, the ABC might have hoped for a change of course from a politician known as a darling of *Q&A* audiences as well as a technologically innovative communications minister. He was a strong supporter of the ABC, but Turnbull believed it needed to improve its journalism to the point that it was beyond reproach. 'This was harder than ever of course,' he wrote later, 'not because of left-wing bias but because the rest of the media had, by and large, become debased to the level of social media: light on facts, dripping with bias, full of fake news and outrage'.[59] We will discuss in a later chapter to what extent it is appropriate to judge the ABC by a different standard to other sectors of the news media, but Turnbull is not remembered fondly inside the ABC. Matt Peacock, who left the ABC after a long career there, including a stint as the staff-elected member of the board, recalled for a parliamentary committee Turnbull's first visit as minister. 'It was a bit like him touring Channel Nine or something as Kerry Packer. He behaved as though he owned the place and was requesting briefings from all the executive directors — director of TV, director of radio, et cetera. I certainly do recall Mark Scott being quite shaken by the visit.'[60] Under Turnbull's prime ministership, the previous government's attempt to depoliticise the board appointments process was almost wholly flouted: two avowed ABC critics were appointed to the independent nomination panel, and of the five board members appointed between 2015 to 2018, only one was interviewed and recommended by the nomination panel. Two were interviewed but not recommended, and two had not even been considered.[61]

For his part, Turnbull became increasingly irritated by the ABC's journalism, in particular by chief economic correspondent Emma Alberici and political reporter Andrew Probyn, who were the subject of calculated, angry phone calls and texts from the PM's office and a series of official complaints from communications minister Mitch Fifield.[62] Jonathan Holmes, who spent five years scrutinising the nation's journalism as host of *Media Watch*, concluded that there were minor errors in Alberici's work and that Probyn's choice of words was occasionally 'sloppy', but he emphasised that the government had massively overreacted to stories critical of its policies or actions.[63] The animosity between the government and the ABC during this period was every bit as bad as during Richard Alston's complaints crusade of 2003–04, and became central to the unprecedented events of September 2018.

In that month, the ABC board sacked managing director Michelle Guthrie, and within three days forced chair Justin Milne to stand down following publication of emails that showed him willing to sacrifice the careers of Alberici and Probyn to keep alive a $500 million proposal for an elaborate content management system called Project Jetstream. A parliamentary committee set up to investigate was unable to disentangle all the claims and counterclaims between Guthrie and Milne, but, at the very least, Milne had a view of his role that was fundamentally at odds with the ABC's governing legislation and pointed to how pivotal the government's animosity was in the whole affair. In a *Four Corners* program about the forced departures of the managing director and the chair that aired on ABC television on 12 November 2018, Milne described the federal government as the ABC's shareholder, its banker, and its regulator, and questioned whether annoying the government, in this context, was wise.[64] The government may be the ABC's banker, but it is not the ABC's shareholder, a role that belongs to the public. Even the term 'shareholder' defines people narrowly as financial stakeholders rather than as citizens. Nor is the government the ABC's regulator; that role belongs to ACMA, a statutory authority that acts independently of the executive, and of the ABC.

A month before Guthrie's and Milne's departures, Turnbull lost his prime ministership in the culmination of a long campaign against him by the party's right wing. His successor, Scott Morrison, did not substantially worsen relations with the ABC, but they could scarcely have been worse in any case. Funding continued to decline (though the government refused to concede this), and the formal appointments process was flouted again when Morrison named as the new chair someone who had not even applied for the job. Ita Buttrose was a choice that looked carefully calibrated to both be unarguable — Buttrose had an impeccable media pedigree — and to irritate the 'luvvies', as she had primarily worked in commercial media and, though a pioneering female editor, did not trumpet herself as a feminist. Buttrose, however, soon showed herself to be a firm believer in public broadcasting and a robust advocate for the ABC, both in public and with government. Communications minister Paul Fletcher continued the government's everyday iciness toward the ABC when he ignored Buttrose's plea for standard board practice to be followed in consultation about appointments. Even if the appointments themselves were less controversial and less political than those made earlier in the government's term, the very fact that ABC insiders were quoted saying 'It's not as bad as we expected' showed what a low ebb things were at.[65]

In summary, antipathy toward the ABC has been entrenched in the eight-plus years so far of the coalition government. Government ministers barely bother hiding their hostility, while the Liberal and National party rooms view almost any ABC program critical of the government as confirmation of ingrained bias. The government has cut ABC funding in real terms more sharply than any government since 1983, trashed reforms to the ABC's governance, and interfered in internal ABC work by, for example, compelling it to produce confidential reports on its coverage.[66] Moreover, two months before Morrison became prime minister in 2018, the Liberal Party's national council voted by a two-thirds majority to sell off the ABC. The prime minister has since said nothing to dissuade anyone from thinking that should the opportunity arise he would enact the council's wishes.

Chapter 4

A CALM VOICE IN THE CACOPHONY
public broadcasting in modern times

Public-sector broadcasting was born in a time of media scarcity and now operates in an era of media abundance. Never before have people had so much choice about the news and entertainment they want to hear or watch or read online, or, for that matter, create for themselves. Portability and intimacy are core characteristics of radio and have been modernised and magnified by podcasting. The daily television program guide was supplanted first by video recorders, then by live streaming. 'Appointment viewing' is a term glowing with a sense of network exclusivity and mass viewer enthusiasm. It is also one falling into disuse as free-to-air television offerings are crowded out by an ever-expanding range of standalone program providers — Stan, Apple TV+, Disney+, Amazon Prime. Long-time ABC journalist Jonathan Holmes noted wryly in 2019 that at 70 he was only fractionally older than the average age of those who watch the ABC's main TV channel.[1] Some of the programs aired on the ABC's main channel — *Hard Quiz* and *Mad as Hell* — joke about this point so often you'd be forgiven for concluding the program-makers think the viewers aren't just older but have dementia as well.

Has public-sector broadcasting reached its natural use-by date? Do the ideas that propelled it early in the 20th century still apply? If they don't, have different issues arisen in the media that make public-sector broadcasting relevant in a different way? In the transition from an age of media abundance to one of media cacophony, is there still a role for public broadcasting?

The Beeb

When public-sector broadcasting began early in the 20th century, the primary popular medium was the newspaper. In Australia and in other English-speaking democracies, newspapers were the main provider of news. They were overwhelmingly held in private hands. Some proprietors and editors — but not all — asserted that newspapers provided a public service, but all knew they needed to make a profit to survive. In theory, anyone could start a newspaper, but the costs of printing presses and staff made the barriers to entry high. This led to the building of big newspaper houses whose proprietors wielded a lot of power and influence in society.

The arrival of new communication technologies — first radio, then television — required a role for government to find a way of allocating and regulating the broadcasting spectrum, a scarce commodity. A parliamentary committee set up in Great Britain to consider radio broadcasting concluded that the airwaves were 'public property' and should be a 'public utility'. The person who translated these unlovely bureaucratic terms into practice was John Reith, the first director-general of what became the British Broadcasting Corporation (BBC). Reith believed the BBC should inform and educate as well as entertain, and that it should lead rather than follow public taste. In this, Reith was reacting against American commercial broadcasting, which was market driven and saw entertainment as the surest way to maximise profits. Instead, he invoked the late-19th-century English reformer Matthew Arnold, for whom culture should be harnessed as a means of reducing social divisions and class warfare.[2]

Newspapers had begun spreading literacy among uneducated people from the late 19th century on. In Reith's mind, broadcasting could continue that process and ensure citizens were informed and able to exercise their democratic rights. This sounds noble enough, but it should be remembered that Reith, along with others in the upper classes and intellectual elite, was deeply anxious about the 'unready state of ordinary people for the responsibilities of citizenship', as Georgina Born writes in her 2004 history of the BBC. Reith comes down to us in history as a paternalistic, authoritarian, humourless Scottish Presbyterian, as well as a key figure in the development of public-sector broadcasting, but, according to Born, what is overlooked in many accounts of the BBC's development is that it was nowhere near as monolithic as it is painted. Reith tempered his early commitment to broadcasting's educative role by supporting more entertainment programs, even those that playfully sent up the BBC, and by allowing, encouraging even, a degree of internal debate and self-criticism, which bolstered the organisation's democratic health.[3]

Moreover, Reith introduced three main measures, which were all grounded in the BBC being a universal service. It should be available to everyone in the United Kingdom, cater for the country's social and cultural diversity in cities and regions, and encompass a wide range of genres, including news, talks, sport, drama, religion, light

entertainment, and both classical and popular music.[4] The
BBC was both a part of the state and apart from it. It was
set up by a royal charter, overseen by a board of governors,
and funded by licence fees, levied first on radio sets, then
on televisions; but the charter was also reviewed every ten
years, the governors appointed on the recommendation of
government, and government, too, could alter or abolish
the licence fee. In other words, the BBC may have enjoyed
advantages in funding and in reach that would be the envy
of generations of ABC managers, but it remained subject to
similar tensions inherent in state-funded broadcasting.

The BBC was the first and remains, with an annual
budget of just under £5 billion (equivalent to A$9.34 billion),
the biggest public broadcaster in the world.[5] Its example and
the ideals that have motivated its work have encouraged
similar initiatives, to the point that public broadcasting is a
staple in many countries. UNESCO describes it as a public
service that is neither commercial nor state-controlled,
that speaks to all citizens, and that encourages access to
and participation in public life, developing knowledge,
broadening horizons, and enabling people to understand
the world and each other, and thus enabling them to better
understand themselves as well.[6]

This brings with it, of course, considerable tensions.
The BBC, now in its centenary year, occupies a larger part of
the overall media in the United Kingdom than most if not
all other public broadcasters do in their countries. It did not
face competition from a commercial television broadcaster
until 1955, whereas when television began in Australia in
1956 there were two commercial outlets, Seven and Nine,
alongside the ABC. Public broadcasting is funded primarily
by the state but has always needed to ensure it does not
become a creature of the state, as, for instance, China
Central Television (CCTV) is. Public broadcasting needs

to appeal to the bulk of the population and also cater for the country's social, cultural, and linguistic diversity — not an easy balance to strike. Commercial media companies patrol their territory vigilantly, while other commentators are forever mindful that taxpayers' money should be spread further than highbrow programs about the arts. The tensions inherent in balancing these competing goals have been magnified in recent decades with the development of online, digital, and social media. As we have seen, public broadcasters were well placed to take advantage of new media technologies because they could use them to distribute their content further for free — but that antagonised commercial broadcasters struggling to adapt their business model to the digital world.

Moving fast, breaking things

It was common in the early years of the 21st century for techno-evangelists to laud the democratising possibilities of new media technologies, and to dismiss public broadcasters as yesterday's media, hamstrung by fusty ideas. Who wanted to be lectured anymore by middle-aged white male broadcasters when you could create your own media at the click of a mouse or a tap of your smartphone? And who wasn't inspired by the social-media-fired people power of the Arab Spring, which promised to upend a range of repressive regimes? A decade later, it is clear that some progress has been made on the fustiness problem, through the BBC's 50:50 equality project in 2017, with the ABC following suit the next year. These projects, which have quotas to drive diversity of both presenters and people interviewed for programs, are welcome recognition of the media's longstanding sidelining of, among others, women, First Nations people, and those from diverse ethnic backgrounds, though progress remains slower than many might like. On new media's power to create major change, it is painfully clear that democracy has not come to the Middle East, a point shockingly underscored in Syria, one of more than a dozen jurisdictions that saw Arab Spring uprisings, which has since descended into a civil war that continues a decade later and has cost the lives of more than 500,000 Syrians.[7]

Instead, in a few short years, the agile new tech companies offering a cornucopia of wonderfully quick, tailored, convenient services — Google and Facebook — morphed into predatory global behemoths whose market capitalisations are bigger than the gross domestic product (GDP) of all but the ten largest economies in the world, along the way scooping into their maw innovative startups like Instagram, WhatsApp, and Fitbit, among many others.[8] Google's early motto 'Don't be evil' gave way in 2015 to 'Do the right thing', by which time most could see that, if the company hadn't actually been evil, its motto might be more aptly rendered as 'Do the right thing — by Google'. Facebook founder Mark Zuckerberg's famous line 'Move fast and break things' encapsulated the company's cheerfully ruthless early years as it grew exponentially and outshone Friendster, Second Life, and Myspace. A succession of scandals ensued over the past decade, exemplified by the exposé of Cambridge Analytica in *The Guardian*, which showed that the personal data of millions of Facebook users had been collected without their consent by the British consulting firm for the purpose of political advertising, especially in the 2016 United States presidential election.[9] Thanks to a steady stream of disclosures by investigative journalists, former Silicon Valley executives, and whistleblowers such as Frances Haugen, it has become increasingly clear that the central nervous system of search engines, news feeds, and social-media networks — their use of algorithms — is designed not for the seemingly beneficent purpose of connecting everyone together but to connect users with advertisers, thereby making gobsmackingly large sums of money for the big tech companies.

Allied to the more precise use of advertising is the configuring of those search engines, news feeds, and social-media networks so that users are not provided with a wide range of information but are fed more and more material that appeals to and manipulates their emotions and reinforces their beliefs, hardening these into prejudices. As media critic Margaret Sullivan wrote, 'Outrage, hate, and lies are what drive digital engagement, and therefore revenue.'[10] Conflict has long been one of the core news values, illustrated in the cynical line about the evening television news: 'If it bleeds, it leads.' Google and Facebook, through their algorithms — the precise make-up of which remains closely guarded — have built a better mechanism for connecting audiences with conflict, as well as connecting audiences with advertisers. So successful have they been that they have whipped many around the world into a state of hyper-arousal or hyper-partisanship. The space for rational debate about issues large and small has shrunk, replaced by red-faced, sometimes-violent disagreement, anonymous trolling in the vilest of terms, especially toward women, people of colour, and those who identify as other than heterosexual, and slews of misinformation about urgent global issues like climate change and COVID-19. The damage caused by the misuse of social media reached its apotheosis in the depressingly familiar occurrence in 2021 of people, most often in the United States, pleading on their deathbed for the vaccine to combat COVID-19 after repeatedly, sometimes mockingly, denying the virus even existed.

A framework for understanding the impact of misinformation on the public sphere is provided in a landmark study of the American media system by Yochai Benkler, Robert Faris, and Hal Roberts. Published in 2018, *Network Propaganda* charts how distrust of the news media is decidedly more concentrated among voters identifying as right wing than among those identifying as left wing. The authors attribute this to the then US president Donald Trump's relentless denigration of critical or embarrassing news as 'fake news'. There is a connection, the authors argue, between this distrust and the nature of the right-wing news-media system. As legacy news organisations have been winnowed, there has been a proliferation of right-wing news sites that mimic those organisations in name but not in style or character.[11] There has been a near-unchecked movement of stories sourced from far-right 'news' sites such as Breitbart, Truthfeed, Infowars, and the Gateway Pundit — which, the authors note, do *not* claim to follow the norms or processes of professional journalistic standards — to more mainstream outlets, such as Fox News, which *do* claim to follow those norms and processes. Fox News unhesitatingly broadcast outrageous, unverified claims Hillary Clinton was involved in a child sex ring run out of a pizza shop in Washington and in the death of Democrats staffer Seth Rich. By comparison, the authors note that a claim that Donald Trump had raped a 13-year-old in the early 1990s had been raised on the left and scotched shortly afterward by prominent mainstream media organisations that examined its veracity.[12]

From these and other case studies, Benkler, Faris, and Roberts make three observations: first, the prominence of far-left news sites pales in comparison to the prominence of those on the right; second, the most visible left-wing news sources correlate at most to *moderate*-right news sources, not *far*-right news sources; and third, the traditional news media is tightly integrated with those left-wing news sources, exerting constraints of fact-checking, objectivity, and evidence-based reportage. They argue that the conception of a news spectrum with two extremes that mirror one another is false: there is an endemic strain of false stories on the right end of the news spectrum that is *not* mirrored on the left. As they conclude: 'Conspiracy theories, falsehoods, and rumours that fit the tribal narrative diffuse more broadly and are sustained for longer on the right than in the rest of the media ecosystem. Echo chambers ringing with false news make democracies ungovernable'.[13]

Exactly how misinformation spreads through society, in what ways it affects people's understanding of the world, and their response to it continues to be studied with growing urgency. Researchers at New York University and Université Grenoble Alpes in France found that during the 2020 US presidential election, news publishers known for spreading misinformation received six times as many likes, shares, and interactions on Facebook as did conventional trustworthy sources of news, including CNN and the World Health Organization.[14] Misinformation is false information spread by people who think it is true, while disinformation is false information spread by people who know it is false. Anti-vaccine misinformation, especially about COVID-19, is widespread across social media, but a 2021 study by British-American non-government agency the Center for Countering Digital Hate found that two-thirds of anti-vaccine disinformation was spread on social media by just 12 people, whom they dubbed 'the Disinformation Dozen'.[15] Australia is not America, of course, but there are similarities — in the trend toward the use of social media to spread misinformation and disinformation, in hyper-partisanship among political parties and media outlets, in the willingness of politicians to deploy the term 'fake news', and in the diminished influence of the conventional news media on public debate.

Sizing up the public square

One important difference between Australia and the US in this context is the role of public broadcasting. In the US, public broadcasting has always been a marginal player, far outweighed by the big three commercial television networks, and by the rise of partisan talk radio from the 1980s, and underfunded by government throughout. Undoubtedly there is good material broadcast on public radio and television in the US — that's where *This American Life* originates, after all — but its low government funding and reliance on audience donations mean it struggles for scale in the overall US media market. On lists comparing per capita funding for public broadcasting, the US ranks near the bottom. In an analysis of 23 countries, most of them members of the Organisation for Economic Cooperation and Development (OECD), the United States ranked last, spending A$13 per head on public broadcasting. Switzerland spent more per head — A$274 — than any of the other countries, while Australia ranked equal 13th with Japan, spending A$66. (For details, see Appendix D.) Australia's standing is unlikely to have improved since 2016, the year in which the analysis was performed, given the federal government's cuts to the ABC's funding.

Misinformation spread by social media is a phenomenon affecting most countries around the world. There is at least some evidence, though, that the existence of a public broadcaster acts to counter this misuse of social media. A 2016 study comparing public broadcasting and private media found:

> Public service media tend to broadcast more news and current affairs programs at peak times, and proportionally more hard news. In many cases, this creates media environments where citizens have better opportunities to become informed. As a direct result, both individual exposure to public service media news — or living in a public service–oriented media environment — is associated with increased knowledge of a variety of hard news topics, including politics, current affairs, and international events.[16]

Accordingly, the authors — from Oxford University's Reuters Institute for the Study of Journalism — found that public broadcasters help increase political knowledge and political participation and have a positive impact on trust, knowledge, diversity, and social cohesion. Another study, by Toril Aalberg and James Curran, examined individual news consumption and public-affairs knowledge in six countries — the United States, the United Kingdom, Sweden, Finland, Belgium, and the Netherlands — and concluded, 'Public service television sustains a higher level of public affairs knowledge than market-based television' and that 'this is borne out, not merely by the difference in the level of knowledge in the US and northern Europe, but also by differences within nations'. Even those uninterested in news are still better informed than they might otherwise be, as the reach of public broadcasting means they are more likely to *incidentally* encounter news and current affairs.[17]

These studies all have limitations. Some found results could be substantially affected by a person's education level, suggesting that this variable is at least as important, while others found broadsheet newspapers generally provided as much news as public broadcasters, if not more. Most studies paid less attention to online and social media, which of course is how and where many, perhaps most, people now consume news and current affairs.

Nor are the principles of impartiality underpinning public broadcasting without problems. They're good for information but struggle with emotion, not to mention nuance. The laudable principle of balance can curdle into false balance, epitomised in talk shows where a Holocaust denier is given equal airtime with a Holocaust historian. Not surprisingly, politicians have long since learned to game the rules of impartiality. Any president or prime minister knows that they will be quoted in a news story almost irrespective of what they say, simply because they head the government. And if the government is criticised, it is automatically given the right of reply — a courtesy not always extended to less powerful or dissenting voices.

These qualifications noted, the Reuters Institute authors' analysis indicates the healthy contribution made by public broadcasters to citizens' awareness and knowledge of current events. Implicitly, it is an argument for them being more, not less, relevant in the third decade of the 21st century. Impartiality may not be flawless, but the journalistic method for finding and verifying information provides at least a bulwark against hyper-partisanship, misinformation, and disinformation. 'The forces threatening broadcasting impartiality make its practice all the more necessary. The more society atomises, the more important a common thread of meaning becomes,' as one commentator in England noted.[18] Certainly, in the United States, scholars such as Victor Pickard have argued that the comparative weakness of public broadcasting there, and the primacy of commercially driven media, are key elements in the problems that have been besetting journalism, and more broadly democratic society, for well over a decade.[19]

Importantly, public-sector broadcasters continue to attract high levels of trust, according to the annual Reuters Institute Digital News Report, which in 2021 included 46 countries in Europe, the Americas, Africa, and the Asia-Pacific region. The comprehensive nature of public broadcasters' websites, which have provided detailed local breakdowns of COVID-19 as well as fact-checking and other explanatory journalism, has extended their reach, too. These gains in audience were generally not reflected in countries where public broadcasters are less well trusted. The report's authors say this boost for the sector has been welcome as its 'legitimacy and funding have been threatened by a combination of changing consumer behaviour and attacks by populist and right-wing politicians. Before the [COVID-19] crisis, for example, Boris Johnson's Conservative government in the UK was considering turning the BBC into a subscription operation. Now MPs are recommending any change to funding arrangements should be shelved until at least 2038.'[20] That may look like a vote of confidence in the BBC from the government, but it is more likely a tactical retreat in a long-running war between conservative governments in the UK and the BBC.[21]

As we will see in the next chapter, a similar push has been occurring for many years in Australia.

Chapter 5

A BILLION REASONS
the push to privatise the ABC

In June 2018, nearly 100 delegates of the Liberal Party's federal council gathered at Sydney's Hilton Hotel to listen to speeches, to debate ideas, and to vote on a series of resolutions. Some of the latter were humdrum. Others were contentious. A few, such as the call to transfer Australia's embassy in Tel Aviv to Jerusalem, were even controversial. But all played second fiddle in the next day's press coverage to the resolution that the government should privatise the ABC.

While the overwhelming margin by which it was adopted was notable — roughly two-thirds of the delegates voted in its favour — so too was the immediate scorn that Liberal government ministers and elders heaped on the resolution and, by extension, the council. 'It [the ABC] is a public broadcaster. It always has been, and it always will be,' said then prime minister Malcolm Turnbull.[1] There was no way the resolution would become government policy, said then treasurer Scott Morrison. It was a 'vent' of frustration only, said then energy and environment minister Josh

Frydenberg. 'An act of madness,' sneered one anonymous Liberal MP.[2]

Overlooked in all of this was the shoddy reasoning offered by the resolution's proposer, federal Young Liberals vice-president Mitchell Collier. Declaiming that sentimentality and his love for *Bananas in Pyjamas* should not stand in the way, Collier argued there was no justifiable economic case for keeping the broadcaster in public hands — with one exception. The ABC should be privatised, his resolution ran, 'except for [those] services into regional areas that are not commercially viable'.[3]

As ever, seeded within a call for the ABC's abolition was a justification for its existence: an acknowledgement that the ABC performs functions no commercial organisation would willingly perform; that those functions are sufficiently important to override a strict economic argument; and that in the absence of a commercial provider, government must fund those functions.

The resolution marked a new phase in debate about the ABC's future. Calls for the ABC's abolition or privatisation have been made since it was established, but they have peaked at times when neoliberal and libertarian policies have been in the ascendancy around the globe. This was particularly evident in the 1980s. In the UK, Margaret Thatcher's Conservative government (1979–90) actively considered proposals to abolish the licence fee that funded the BBC; in Canada, appropriations for public broadcaster CBC were reduced by Brian Mulroney's Progressive Conservative government (1984–93); in the USA, the Reagan administration (1981–89) placed public broadcaster PBS on what Ken Inglis later called 'a still leaner diet of public money'; and in New Zealand, the Labour government led by David Lange (1984–89) and influenced by the economic-rationalist ideals of finance minister Roger Douglas halted funding of the two public radio and television broadcasters, requiring them to raise money from advertising instead.[4]

Opponents of public broadcasting in Australia became most vociferous at this time. In 1984, *Australian Financial Review* columnist Padraic McGuinness argued that 'large sums of public money are being wasted' on an ABC he derided as 'moribund'.[5] By 1985, the argument had been absorbed sufficiently for that newspaper to editorialise that the ABC should be sold off.[6] Two years after that, while setting out the austere neoliberal policies he believed should anchor a future Liberal–National Party government, Australian Institute for Public Policy fellow John Nurick argued that it was 'stupid and immoral' to make taxpayers support the ABC when it was so 'hostile to the liberal-democratic consensus'. Nurick called for the ABC to be wholly funded by advertising within seven years and suggested a good start would be achieved via an immediate 30 per cent cut to the ABC's budget.[7]

A similar tune was seemingly heard the following year in the title of public-policy scholar Glyn Davis's book, *Breaking Up the ABC*. As the title indicates, Davis argued the ABC should be broken up into discrete units that would target specific objectives. But while there were some who believed this a prelude to privatisation, Davis's was a song in a completely different key to the basso profundo of the likes of McGuinness and Nurick. Davis's argument was posited as a solution to a predicament he identified, in which the ABC was confused and struggling, catering to too many priorities and audiences, and dividing its resources too widely. It was against this context that Davis's proposal was made — alongside an articulation of the 'overwhelming need' for some form of public broadcasting in Australia, and a reiteration that the ABC's abolition was 'unacceptable' without some kind of replacement.[8]

Davis's proposal to break up the ABC has never found much public favour, even if it has been mulled over by advocates for the ABC's privatisation.[9] But his insistence on the necessity of the ABC did represent the consensus in Australia. Even though John Howard believed it was preoccupied with a 'left-wing social agenda', he knew there was little public appetite for the ABC's privatisation, to the point that, in 2001, he professed to have no memory of Nurick's recommendation. Much though he disliked the ABC, Tony Abbott was similarly aware. Both men's governments would cut the ABC's budget, but their reviews — the Mansfield review in 1996, and the Commission of Audit in 2014 — proved not to be immediate fundamental threats: both confirmed the ABC was a necessary fixture of the Australian media landscape. This has given some a false sense of security, or at least reason to dismiss privatisation as a non-starter, as former communications minister Richard Alston did in January 2021: there was no one in the federal parliament, he declared in *The Australian Financial Review*, who favoured privatising the ABC.[10]

In coming to this conclusion Alston must for the past decade have been distracted by a passing butterfly. For there are certainly many in the parliament whose stated views contradict him and whose ascendancy in the last decade reflects the resurgence of neoliberal and libertarian thought. The recently retired senator and communications minister member Mitch Fifield told the Adam Smith Club in 2008 that there was merit in privatising the ABC.[11] During a Liberal–National party-room meeting in 2014, at least one MP suggested that the whole of the ABC should be 'put out to tender'.[12] Before becoming a Liberal senator for Victoria, James Paterson applauded the axing of the Australia Network contract and called for the axe to be wielded again: 'The Abbott government should go a step further, and privatise the ABC.'[13] Tasmanian senator Eric Abetz voted in favour of privatising the ABC at that 2018 Liberal Party federal-council conference, NSW senator Jim Molan declared in 2020 that he would advocate until he died for the ABC and SBS to be 'smash[ed]' together and the ABC to be defunded, and in 2021 Queensland LNP senator James McGrath reiterated his 2014 threat that privatisation would follow if the ABC did not change its ways.[14]

Some are confident there are sufficient supporters of the ABC among government MPs to rule out privatisation, but the growing popularity of the calls for privatisation and the continuing enmity between the government and the ABC make clear that the broadcaster's future is not assured. As we have seen, parliamentarians are increasingly willing to defund, penalise, intimidate, and destabilise the ABC in the hopes of setting it on a path toward obsolescence and eventually privatisation. Confidence in the ABC's future is surely misplaced when a resolution such as Collier's can gain approval by such a dramatic margin within the policy-making body of the Liberal Party: it is abundantly clear that there are many on the political right who believe the ABC's future should be severely limited.

Against public broadcasting

Two men who share that view are Chris Berg and Sinclair Davidson. Co-founders of the Blockchain Innovation Hub at RMIT, where Berg is a principal research fellow and Davidson a professor of institutional economics, both are academics with strong links to libertarian think tank the Institute of Public Affairs (IPA), which has long advocated the ABC's privatisation or abolition and been a reliable purveyor of anti-ABC 'research', much of which is as substantive as gossamer and equally full of holes.[15] Davidson has been an adjunct fellow of the IPA since 2008, and Berg was a senior fellow until 2017. Publication of their 176-page book *Against Public Broadcasting* preceded Collier's resolution by one month and to date is the most sustained argument made in Australia for the privatisation of the ABC. Theirs is a book first and foremost defined by what it is against, not what it is *for*. Moreover, it is not a disinterested, academic work but rather a manifesto, stemming from an ideological view that is hostile to public broadcasting and framed almost entirely by neoliberal economic thinking.

Berg and Davidson are scornful in their discussion of the traditional arguments for public broadcasting more broadly, which they present as half-baked, aspirational, and woolly, and declare to be nothing but a post-hoc justification for the establishment of the UK's BBC. As for the ABC, they argue that its proponents in the early 1930s — in particular, in the Scullin Labor government — were motivated by the anti-Labor bias of major press outlets and were ideologically disposed toward 'nationalisation as a mode of economic control'. The creation of the ABC, however, actually began with the conservative Bruce government late in the 1920s, continued with the Scullin Labor government, and was enacted by the (non-Labor) United Australia Party government led by Joseph Lyons. Berg and Davidson nevertheless argue that elements of paternalism and the cultural cringe informed the decision to press ahead with the legislation that established the ABC. They discount arguments the ABC should not be a niche or specialist broadcaster, and dismiss the manifold reviews of the ABC and its functions, declaring that all 'skirt' the real question that should be answered: why should Australia have a public broadcaster?

Berg and Davidson give short shrift to all of the customary answers to this question. Claims that the ABC is necessary to resolve 'market failure' in the broadcast market are, in their telling, fatally undermined by the existence of online media. 'It is important to recognise that the accessibility of "quality" media content has never been higher,' they write. 'The globalisation of media content has opened up vast new avenues through which the highest quality content can be delivered.'[16] Online media is also Berg and Davidson's answer to the argument that the ABC contributes to diversity and pluralism: 'With online media, the number of firms and the variety of content they can offer is functionally infinite ... Virtually limitless niche content online should satisfy this policy requirement [of diversity].'[17] Berg and Davidson offer the same answer yet again to the argument that the ABC provides an independent counterbalance to commercial media organisations. Critics of those organisations, write Berg and Davidson, 'have more outlets for their critiques than ever before in history, and social media provides a historically unparalleled mechanism for distributing those critiques'.[18] Digital media is also their solution to the problem of providing content in rural and regional areas: 'There has been no better time for people in regional and remote areas to access and produce content.'[19]

The repeated resort to online media is rather like seeing a student going into an exam hoping that having one answer alone will be enough to secure a pass. It won't, and nor should it. Nor should Berg and Davidson be able to do so. The idea that online media can be a substitute for what the ABC does — in diversity and pluralism, as a counterbalance to commercial media organisations, to the lack of media in and for rural and remote areas — is a nice idea in theory but has hardly been borne out by reality. Furthermore, it relies on an ellipsis between the accessibility and opportunity of online media — that anyone could publish online, for anyone to access — with the reality of mass media concentration in Australia. The ACCC agreed in 2019 that the advent of the internet had 'increased the plurality of journalism available online' but added, pointedly, that the commercial media organisations remain the highest providers of content and that two such organisations, in Nine and News Corp Australia, enjoy an overwhelmingly large audience share.[20]

To be fair to Berg and Davidson, however, they do not merely point to digital media as the reason that the ABC need not exist. Any 'need' for an alternative to commercial media organisations, they argue, has been obviated by the legacy media's declining power: 'Media moguls have never had less power — both direct political power and diffuse, cultural power — than they do today.'[21] They disagree that the ABC offers content of a superior 'quality' to that offered by commercial media providers, scoffing that such content cannot be superior or more valuable if it does not attract audiences of a size greater than the commercial media providers. They deride claims of the ABC's value in rural and remote areas by pointing to the shrinking percentage of people who live in those areas, and question whether the ABC's presence in these areas — via a 'subsidy', they call it — is even desirable. Berg and Davidson point to a range of organisations, from Screen Australia to the Flying Fruit Fly Circus, who fund or produce content that contributes to a 'sense of national identity', as the ABC claims to do, and suggest that there is something deplorable in the ABC's doing so as a government organisation: 'It is not at all clear why we should welcome a democratic government that seeks to manipulate its citizens in this way.' They also dismiss arguments that a national broadcaster scrutinising and criticising government is necessary in a democracy, suggesting instead that public broadcasting is empirically associated with 'less liberal, less democratic' governments in other countries.

All of these are contentious arguments and many are risible. The suggestion that media moguls have less power than they once did, arguable at any rate, does not mean that the power of those moguls today is small; any suggestion that this power is small enough to be ignored would doubtless produce a guffaw of laughter from any observer of or participant in Australian political and cultural life. It also begs the question whether, if the media moguls' power happened to grow, Berg and Davidson would advocate for its reduction. The suggestion that the ABC's audience share undermines its claims to produce quality content is a complete non sequitur. The suggestion other providers can contribute to a sense of national identity is nothing more than an attempt to begin winnowing, on grounds of duplication and efficiency, any organisation with this mission. Their implication that the ABC is a vehicle for government manipulation is preposterous, given not only the ABC's statutory independence from government, but also the regularity with which it irritates government — and their attempt to link the ABC with public broadcasting in non-democratic countries is so comically distorting as to be hallucinatory.

But all of the above are ultimately secondary issues to Berg and Davidson's chief bugbear — principally, that the ABC is a 'burden' on Australia that manifests in three ways: as a cost to the taxpayer, as a competitor to commercial media organisations, and as a biased organisation acting in its own self-interest.

What do we really pay for the ABC?

Berg and Davidson concede it would be churlish to quibble with the ABC's daily cost to individual Australians — a figure of around 14 cents per day — before quibbling anyway. If the ABC's funding were divided by the number of taxpayers, they point out, its cost would be closer to 30 cents per day, and if the cost of the ABC were divided among those taxpayers 'who pay more tax than they receive in social welfare payments', and who thus are *really* the ones who 'pay for the ABC', the figure would be higher still: maybe a few dollars, at best.[22] This is bizarre logic, not to mention cruel. Are roads funded on the basis that only wage earners can use them? And is social welfare funded on the basis that it is available only to those who earn enough not to need it?

What is ostensibly more conducive to Berg and Davidson's argument that the ABC is a 'burden' to Australia is the magic number: the roughly $1 billion the ABC receives each financial year. This is the figure repeatedly invoked, and not merely by Berg and Davidson: 'The ABC should be privatised to save the taxpayer more than $1 billion it costs each year to run,' *Australian* columnist Peter van Onselen argued in 2013.[23] 'The ABC will spend $1.1 billion this financial year,' wrote *The Spectator*'s William Hill in 2017, in the course of arguing for the ABC's privatisation.[24] 'Their annual budget funding now exceeds $1 billion,' exclaimed Richard Alston in 2019, 'but the ABC still complains that it needs more!'[25] Indeed, van Onselen, with frequent collaborator Wayne Errington, reiterated the weight of that burden in 2021 while simultaneously conceding that the ABC and SBS had been underfunded for decades. Perhaps we should not take too much notice of this schizoid thinking. In what might very well explain why they dub it one of the 'pariah policies' examined in their short book *Who Dares Loses,* van Onselen and Errington call for the ABC to carry advertising so that government may use the resulting savings in ABC funding to pay commercial networks and news providers to do better journalism.[26]

We will set aside the simple fact that the ABC does not actually cost $1 billion a year: as any survey of the budget papers shows, just under a fifth of the total government appropriation to the ABC (or around $185 million) is spent on transmission and distribution — i.e. getting the ABC's broadcast signals and digital content into homes and businesses — and is all but an unavoidable, fixed cost that, until 1999, was not part of the ABC's funding.[27]

The ABC's critics like to use the larger figure because it sounds like — and is — a considerable sum of money. But it is hard not to hear confected outrage and exaggerated scaremongering when this figure is repeatedly invoked. Is the billion-dollar cost a 'burden', as Berg and Davidson suggest? After all, policymaking should not be determined solely by how expensive or cheap a policy might be. Plenty of policies are expensive but funded anyway; plenty of policies are cheap but go unfunded. There are other factors at play.

That billion-dollar price tag is also better understood as a proportion of government spending. Out of the $677 billion of budgeted government spending in 2020–21, the federal government devoted $227 billion to social security, $94 billion to health, $35 billion to defence, and $41 billion to education.[28] The money that went to the ABC in 2020–21 constituted 0.15 per cent of that budget's spending. *Is that really so much?* Berg and Davidson might mull over their answer, but it would be churlish to say anything but no.

Another consideration should be the efficiency of that spending. Taxpayer money should not be wasted. There is

a long record, however, of the ABC squeezing every dollar
to its last drop — an ability necessitated by the parsimony
of successive governments and the broadcaster's awareness
of the need to make do with what funding it had. There is
abundant proof of this ability. At the behest of the Howard
government, auditing firm KPMG reviewed the ABC's
funding in 2006 and found it was a 'broadly efficient
organisation' providing a 'high volume of outputs and
quality relative to the level of funding it receives'.[29] In 2014,
Malcolm Turnbull commissioned his department to conduct
an efficiency study of the ABC and SBS, which suggested
joint savings opportunities but stressed both organisations
were already attentive to such opportunities.[30] Turnbull
commissioned another efficiency study in 2018 that made
suggestions for further efficiencies, but which stressed that
these efficiencies could not eventuate without a significant
short-term investment of funds, in order to modernise the
outdated systems that were causing inefficiencies. A further
perverse unintended consequence of cuts to funding in the
name of efficiency is that it can lead to the ABC becoming
more centralised, and the Sydney-centric character of the
ABC has been a common criticism. This is what happened
after the state-based editions of *The 7.30 Report* were cut
in the early 1990s, according to ABC Alumni's submission
to the Senate inquiry into media diversity.[31] The 'ongoing
funding constraints' the authors noted were imposed
in the first place by the federal government and were
preventing anything more than incremental improvements
in the ABC's efficiency. As they concluded, 'More profound
changes are required.'[32]

Another consideration should be the effectiveness of
the spending, whatever its level. Is that money being spent
wisely? Berg and Davidson would say not, making much
of the ABC's comparatively low audience share to argue

that its services are a failure. But this is to ignore entirely the ABC's historically consistent low audience share — though this share has improved alongside investment in online services over the last decade.[33] Moreover, a rejoinder to the argument about audience share might be provided by Macquarie Bank, which in 2002 found that the ABC's funding was 'significantly lower' than that of its international peers and domestic competitors, and that the ABC was 'quite distinctive' in its appeal to diverse communities and demographics. The Macquarie consultants concluded that one consequence of the ABC's low funding and its commitment to distinctiveness was a relatively small market share.[34]

Is the ABC a burden on the taxpayer, then, as Berg and Davidson suggest? Between the overall cost compared to other government initiatives, the efficiency of the ABC, and the effectiveness of the money spent by the ABC, it would appear not — or, if it is, then any efficiency gains would be marginal, and in any case the ABC remains a burden that taxpayers are overwhelmingly willing to shoulder. The $1 billion price tag may be repeatedly invoked with a Dr Evil–like flourish, but even Berg and Davidson concede that the public has been almost entirely unmoved by the supposed monetary benefits of privatising the ABC.[35]

A tank on the lawn?

The second manifestation of the 'burden' of the ABC is its footprint in the media market. Berg and Davidson argue that the ABC is a constantly expanding competitor to commercial media organisations, crowding out and distorting what is already a small market. This is an argument mounted many a time by commercial media organisations bewailing the current media environment

— indeed, Berg and Davidson even cite former Fairfax Media CEO Greg Hywood on the 'additional pressure' that the ABC, via its provision of free content, supposedly puts on local commercial media. They give the establishment of the ABC's dedicated children's channel, in 2009, and the establishment of its Fact Check group, in 2013, as examples of this phenomenon: the first was followed by a reduction in commercial media investment in children's television, the second by the closure of fact-checking outfits at Fairfax and *PolitiFact Australia*.[36] But this is a complex issue that relies on much more than a simple after-the-fact rationalisation. Berg and Davidson go some way to conceding this, noting that 'the evidence does not strongly favour Hywood's position' and that the supposed distortion created by ABC Kids would need to be considered against a context of content rules, audience preferences, the role of advertising, and provisions of the ABC charter.[37] Moreover, commercial media organisations themselves lobbied to be allowed to reduce or cease their investment in children's broadcasting on grounds that *other* sources of such broadcasting — notably, YouTube and Netflix — were available.[38] Barring the closure of the Fairfax and *PolitiFact* fact-checking outfits, these decisions had less to do with the ABC than with other factors.

To be fair, there are other instances where commercial media providers have been critical of ABC media decisions. Eric Beecher — chair of Private Media, the owner of news site *Crikey* — loudly criticised the establishment of ABC online opinion site *The Drum* (2010–16), echoing *Guardian* editor Alan Rusbridger in likening the initiative to seeing 'tanks roll up' on the lawn of commercial media providers.[39] A similar view was held by Fairfax CEO Brian McCarthy, predecessor to Greg Hywood, who argued the ABC's Open project — where online producers went into regional areas

to help produce locally generated, community content —
threatened the viability of commercial media organisations
in regional and rural Australia: 'I do not believe that it is the
role of the ABC to disrupt the commercial media landscape
by building empires with public funds'.[40] *Australian* media
writer Geoff Elliott was sympathetic to both, noting that
the ABC was 'soak[ing] up bandwidth, attract[ing] eyeballs
away from niche operators, and poach[ing] writers on the
government dime to the detriment of those trying to earn a
buck setting up a new media business'.[41]

But the reality was not as clear as these advocates
were making out. Were audiences *only* accessing the
ABC's content? The answer was no. Barely a week after
making those comments, Beecher conceded he had seen
no impact on *Crikey*'s traffic or advertising revenue since
the launch of *The Drum*. Was the ABC really duplicating
what those commercial media providers were offering,
and thereby muscling in on a space which commercial
enterprises should have to themselves? The answer was no.
The obligations of the ABC's charter ensured a diversity of
voices would be published on *The Drum* — as Chris Berg's
six years' worth of columns and ABC TV appearances show.
And, as journalism scholar Jason Wilson pointed out,
Fairfax had no similar initiatives to that proposed in the
ABC's Open project.[42]

The question that should be asked of Berg and
Davidson, and indeed of commercial media providers
critical of the ABC, is whether or not the ABC's content
and expansions are so significantly similar to commercial
media providers as to constitute unfair competition — and
if so, whether the potential damage to commercial media
providers is sufficiently justified by the public interest in
having an ABC presence. This question was at the heart
of an inquiry set up by the government after a request by

Pauline Hanson. In 2018, it found the two national public broadcasters, taking into account their market shares, were 'not causing significant competitive distortions beyond the public interest'.[43] It is also a question better understood on a case-by-case basis, with an awareness of the lack of media diversity in Australia and of the public interest in having more outlets, more perspectives, and more participants in the Australian media market.

A great leap left?

The third manifestation of the burden of the ABC, Berg and Davidson argue, is its irredeemable bias and tendency to act in its own self-interest, typically by asserting the quality of its content and its independence, and by a relentless quest for funding increases.

The claim the ABC is biased toward the left is often made to buttress arguments that the ABC should be privatised. In 1987, John Nurick cited six articles from the Institute of Public Affairs's *IPA Review* and conservative magazine *Quadrant* to argue that the ABC conformed to a 'radical left' agenda. The argument was undermined by Nurick's admission that, even with such reliably critical sources, the 'anti-western, anti-capitalist, anti-liberal-democratic slant' he sensed in ABC programming was 'harder to demonstrate', but he did not allow this to stand too much in the way: the ABC had to be privatised.[44] Berg and Davidson work similarly — to the point that they also admit that 'direct and uncontested evidence for bias in the ABC is hard to come by'.[45] One piece of evidence that Berg and Davidson muster, and proceed to retail in a tone both scandalised and approving, is an academic study published in 2013 that, they say, shows ABC journalists are nearly five times more likely to vote for the Greens than is the general population, and twice as likely to vote Green than journalists in other organisations.[46] Repeated during publicity events for their book, the claim has since become a stock-standard part of the argument that the ABC is biased — or, as Davidson would have it, 'infested by extremist left-wing progressives who use small-l liberalism to destroy our way of life and civilisation'.[47]

The conclusion that Berg and Davidson draw and have repeatedly invoked is flimsy. The study they cite was a survey of 600 journalists, drawn from a variety of media organisations, of whom 59 were from the ABC. Twenty-five of those journalists elected not to answer the question about their voting intentions. Of the 34 who did answer, 14 said they would vote for the Greens.[48] Given that the news division of the ABC at this time employed 1,178 people, the sample of ABC journalists was small and unrepresentative, a point the author of the study, Folker Hanusch, made when he disputed any extrapolation of the results, à la Davidson. 'I would caution against comparisons to the results of this study with much larger and far more robust studies of the voting intentions of the general Australian public,' he told the ABC's fact-checking operation, 'in the way that appears to have been done here.'[49] No matter. In the two years since it was first adopted as a talking point, proponents of the claim have doubled down on it, with the IPA's Daniel Wild even stating it had been 'confirmed' by fact-checking.[50]

More important than this claim about the personal political beliefs of ABC journalists and staff is the argument that the predominance of left-wing ideological views influences the reportage and work of ABC journalists and staff. Berg and Davidson argue that the ABC's coverage of the coal industry betrays a bias against fossil fuels so pronounced it is 'effectively campaigning for renewable energy'. They argue the ABC's editorial standards are selectively enforced: the ABC dropped *Australian* journalist Glenn Milne and *Daily Telegraph* columnist Piers Akerman from panels of its *Insiders* program but was all too willing to publish claims that Australian Defence Force personnel had mistreated asylum seekers, to publish an erroneous piece by Emma Alberici on corporate tax cuts, and to broadcast a faked photo of *Australian* commentator Chris Kenny having sex with a dog. 'With this record,' write Berg and Davidson, apropos these claims, 'it is hard to see how the ABC might function as an institution where "we try to work out the future together".'[51]

There are many other critics who have made similar claims about bias in the ABC. The aforementioned Kenny claimed that the ABC's news operations are firmly anchored by a left-of-centre sensibility and are 'relentlessly anti-conservative'. Fellow *Australian* columnist and former *Insiders* panellist Gerard Henderson repeatedly argues the ABC 'is a conservative-free zone', bereft of a 'conservative presenter, producer, or editor for any of its prominent television, radio, or online outlets' — a grouping from which he excludes Radio National programs *Counterpoint* (hosted by former Howard-government minister Amanda Vanstone) and *Between the Lines* (hosted by Tom Switzer, executive director of libertarian think tank the Centre for Independent Studies).[52] Switzer identifies a similar point: the producers' rooms of most ABC programs are filled with people who are ideologically and politically uniform, with the result that they think alike and dissenting views — such as his — go missing.[53] The effect, in this view, is that the ABC produces content that is not representative of Australia. A 1,016-person poll commissioned by the IPA in 2019, for example, prompted IPA fellow Gideon Rozner to declare the broadcaster completely unrepresentative: 'Only thirty-two per cent of Australians believe the ABC represents the view of ordinary Australians.'[54] That almost a third declined to express an opinion one way or the other did not trouble Rozner. It was another example of the ABC being *theirs*, not *yours*, as the ABC's slogan would otherwise have had it.

To its critics, it is unacceptable that an organisation funded by taxpayers should be so biased and unrepresentative. The ABC had failed to 'fulfil its most basic duty', declared Rozner: therefore it should be privatised.[55] 'When the ABC is sold off and capital is returned to the federal budgets,' Tom Switzer concluded, 'the journalists could put on all the ideologically-tainted content they like. Some programs may not sell, and others will continue to aggravate many Australians. But at least we will not be forced to pay for it.'[56]

The problem with this argument is that the step from suggestions of bias — which are the subject of considerable, continuing scrutiny and are contested by the ABC, and for which critics have long been unable to muster real proof beyond an unswerving belief in their own perceptions — to the necessity of privatisation is less a step than a jump, twist, and flip.[57] It posits that this bias is conscious and irredeemable and so overwhelming that the whole endeavour of the ABC should be tossed aside. In this argument, what Switzer calls a 'great and important institution', with 'highly professional and intelligent members of the "fourth estate"', should be privatised.[58] What Berg and Davidson call an 'icon' of Australia, with a 90-year history, should be brought down, they say, flogged for parts like an old car. The problem is that the car is still working, and, while it may be in need of a service, wrecking it is an overreaction. The conclusion is a non sequitur.

Public opinion about the meeting place

A final point should be made about Berg and Davidson's book. In search of a purpose that is 'grounded and utilitarian', they forgo consideration of one of the most widely cited arguments for the importance and necessity of public broadcasting: public service. As we have seen, public broadcasting is widely regarded as important to the functioning of democratic societies, as outlined by UNESCO:

> Public broadcasting is defined as a meeting place where all citizens are welcome and considered equals. It is an information and education tool, accessible to all and meant for all, whatever their social or economic status. Its mandate is not restricted to information and cultural development — public broadcasting must also appeal to the imagination and entertain. But it does so with a concern for quality that distinguishes it from commercial broadcasting.[59]

We might quibble that commercial broadcasting certainly has produced high quality programming, but there is considerable evidence most Australians understand UNESCO's position. As Berg and Davidson grumble at the end of their glib little tract, the single largest impediment to privatising the ABC is public opinion.[60]

Chapter 6

IDENTIFYING BIAS EVERYWHERE BUT YOURSELF
the ABC and the media watchdoggers

'I can understand your frustration, Ray, because at times there does appear to be a double standard in large swathes of our national life.'

— Tony Abbott, sympathising with 2GB's Ray Hadley and his erroneous claim that the ABC is exempt from ACMA oversight while Hadley is not.[1]

The ABC is funded by taxpayers, so its news and current affairs must be held to a higher standard than the rest of the media. This statement, or something like it, is made so often that it has taken on the aphoristic tone of the opening lines of a Jane Austen novel: 'It is a truth universally acknowledged ...' Yet, is the same idea applied to the rest of the ABC's services? Does it have to broadcast world-class dramas? Must its equipment be cutting edge? If its comedies draw fewer laughs than those shown on commercial stations, should a special session of Senate estimates be convened to ensure taxpayers' funny bones are not being short-changed? The answer is no.

Every now and again, there will be a controversy about a particular ABC show, such as *The Chaser's War on Everything* or, more recently, *Tonightly with Tom Ballard*, when a particular joke or stunt is seen to have gone too far. But the debate tends to centre on questions of taste rather than whether the Chaser team or Ballard's offerings should be superior to comedies on other networks *because* they are funded by taxpayers. Nor is the notion of a higher standard applied to other services whose provision is split between public and private, like health care or transport. There is an expectation of a baseline level of service whether it is publicly or privately funded. If anything, the assumption underpinning services like health or transport is that if you want a higher standard, be prepared to pay for it.

There is certainly a general perception, though, that the ABC's news and current affairs should be of a higher standard than the rest. There is both a good reason and a bad reason for this. The former is because the ABC is required by its governing legislation 'to ensure that the gathering and presentation of news and information is accurate according to the recognised standards of objective journalism'. Fair enough. The bad reason is it suits anyone with a vested interest or an axe to grind to claim the ABC's journalism should be held to a higher standard. How? By giving critics a platform afforded by legislation to attack the ABC and, in doing so, avoid or at least deflect scrutiny of whatever was reported about them by the ABC in the first place.

Paradoxically, the 'recognised standards of objective journalism' are similar, if not the same, across the news media. You might find this hard to believe given how wide the spectrum is between the exemplary and the execrable. There is journalism that wins the highest award in Australia, the Gold Walkley, which may be produced by the ABC (Mark Willacy won in 2020 for his exposé of alleged war crimes committed by Australian troops in Afghanistan) but equally could be produced elsewhere. The *Herald Sun*'s Anthony Dowsley and Patrick Carlyon won in 2019 for their reporting on the Lawyer X scandal, and in 2013 Joanne McCarthy of *The Newcastle Herald* won for her revelations about clerical child sexual abuse. At the same time, listeners over many years of Alan Jones's morning radio program or eponymous Sky News TV program could be forgiven for thinking he is barely on nodding terms with the 'recognised standards of objective journalism'. The same could be said of his former confrères on what is called Sky News 'after dark' or, for that matter, much of what is published in *The Australian* or *The Daily Telegraph* or the *Herald Sun*, where Andrew Bolt has worked for around three decades. These outlets, to a greater or lesser extent, have been regularly accused of publishing tendentious opinion within news reports, of failing to give people a right of reply, of subjecting critics to relentless, often personal attacks, and of coverage that goes well beyond campaigning into distortion by declining to publish anything like a range of views on an issue.[2]

Codes and clauses

In Australia, journalism is supposed to abide by a range of codes and self-regulatory or co-regulatory regimes. The Australian Journalists' Association (AJA), the journalists' union, led the way by introducing a code of ethics in 1944. The first of its eight clauses reads thus: 'Report and interpret news with a scrupulous honesty'.[3] The union revised its code in 1984 and again in 1999, by which time it had become the Media, Entertainment, and Arts Alliance (MEAA), expanding the number of clauses to 12, providing an overarching statement of principles, and including a guidance clause. The union's code is well regarded but covers only union members. The large-scale redundancy rounds across the media over the past decade have seen membership fall from a high point in the 1980s of around 12,000 to 5,020 in 2021. Also, the code is written for employees who have limited autonomy, as is evident in clause 11 — 'Journalists have the right to resist compulsion to intrude' — and clause 12 — 'Do your utmost to achieve fair correction of errors'.

The AJA/MEAA code was the first of its kind in Australia and, while limited in application, provided a template for later codes. The ABC introduced a code of editorial policies in 1949 and has reviewed it several times since, most recently in 2019.[4] At 34 pages, it is more detailed than any other code operating in Australian journalism, though that stems partly from its inclusion of a range of other ABC content, not just news and current affairs. A preamble says the code upholds the core journalistic principles of accuracy and impartiality, in order to protect the ABC's independence and integrity. It also explicitly endorses the need to be 'brave in reporting without fear or favour, even when that might be uncomfortable or unpopular'.

The Australian Press Council (APC), meanwhile, is a self-regulatory body established by newspaper publishers in 1976. It hears complaints about journalism in newspapers, magazines, and more recently some online outlets as well as the online versions of members' print publications. Its statement of principles is also updated from time to time and contains eight clauses covering four areas similar to the union's code: accuracy and clarity, fairness and balance, privacy and avoidance of harm, and integrity and transparency.[5] Commercial radio and television broadcasters are required under the *Broadcasting Services Act 1992* to register codes of practice with the Australian Communications and Media Authority (ACMA), which covers news and current affairs. A similar code for pay-TV broadcasters was developed by its peak body, the Australian Subscription Television and Radio Association (ASTRA), in consultation with ACMA.[6] Section 3 of Commercial Radio Australia's code of practice has ten clauses, requiring that news and current affairs be presented accurately, substantial errors be corrected as soon as possible, reporting be distinguished from commentary, reasonable efforts be made to present a range of views on issues, material not be presented in a misleading way, and people be protected from 'invasions of privacy' unless there is a clear public interest to do so.[7] Section 4.3 of Free TV's code of practice covers the same principles, with additional emphasis on the power of visual images to 'seriously distress or seriously offend a substantial number of viewers'.[8] The nation's second public broadcaster, SBS, has a code of practice that is updated regularly and covers similar issues of accuracy, balance, impartiality and timely correction of significant errors.[9]

In 1993, editor-in-chief of the Herald and Weekly Times Ltd (HWT) Steve Harris introduced a professional practice policy that was considerably more detailed than the MEAA's code of ethics and was influential in shaping later codes created for other newspapers within the HWT group and across its parent company, News Limited, and for its historically linked rival West Australian Newspapers.[10] *The Age* created its own code of ethics in 1998, and *The Sydney Morning Herald* followed suit a few years later.[11] The HWT policy contained a valuable preamble setting out principles, including: 'The freedom of the press to bring an independent scrutiny to bear on the forces that shape society is a freedom exercised on behalf of the public', and 'Good faith with the reader is the foundation of good journalism'. The *Age* code said its overriding principles are 'fairness, integrity, openness, responsibility and a commitment to accuracy and truth'. The current News Corp Australia code was updated more than five years ago and has done away with the preamble espousing principles, but contains 25 clauses dealing with, among other matters, the importance of accuracy, correcting mistakes, avoiding misrepresentation and harassment in gathering news, and respecting privacy except where exposure is in the public interest. Clause 1.1 says 'Publications should take reasonable steps to ensure reports are accurate and not misleading', while clause 1.5 says 'Try always to tell all sides of the story when reporting on disputes and with such stories, reasonable steps should be taken to contact adversely named parties'.

In summary, according to the various codes and policies, there is agreement among news organisations, including the ABC, that they aim to produce accurate, honest journalism, and there is similarly broad agreement about what constitutes good journalism and what constitutes poor journalism. This does not mean all the codes are identical; there are differing emphases. Some are 'green-light codes', which treat journalists as professionals capable of ethical decision-making in context; others are 'red-light codes', laying down prescriptions about what journalists should not do. The MEAA code is an example of the former, while the current News Corp Australia code exemplifies the latter. The key point here is that the basic principles of journalism apply across the board.

Chasing cars

Once we understand this, the important questions to be asked about the ABC's news and current affairs coverage are simple. Do ABC news and current affairs programs abide by the corporation's own code of editorial policies? Do other news outlets adhere to their own codes? If they don't, what happens?

Let's begin with the ABC, which has always had its critics, some of whom have legitimate complaints of the kind that all news outlets receive. Mistakes are a hazard for any product or service created afresh every day, from unverified or contested information, or 'facts' confected by public-relations operatives. There are those who complain about particular programs on particular nights and then there is the small army of ABC watchers, the most prominent of whom work for other media outlets, especially those owned by News Corp Australia: Piers Akerman, a columnist with *The Daily Telegraph*; Tim Blair, a blogger with the same newspaper; Gerard Henderson, founder of *Media Watch Dog* and a columnist with *The Australian*; Chris Mitchell, a long-time editor-in-chief turned media columnist with the national daily newspaper; and the aforementioned Bolt, whose reach across News Corp Australia's tabloid mastheads and his weeknightly eponymous program on Sky News is matched by his energy — Bolt was an early adopter of blogging and has kept at it ever since. Rarely will you find these members of the 'commentocracy' writing anything positive about the ABC. Their resting face is by turns scabrous (Akerman), sneering (Blair), sour (Henderson), scathing (Mitchell), and sanctimonious (Bolt).

We doubt many would challenge the assertion that these journalists are habitually critical of the ABC, but, in the interests of accuracy, we examined the output of one of them over an extended period. Gerard Henderson's *Media Watch Dog* began in 1988 but was published less frequently until 2009, when it became a weekly online newsletter. We surveyed one in four issues between November 2010 and December 2020 with the following two questions in mind: How often does Henderson mention the ABC? And how often are the mentions positive overall, negative overall, or neutral? Here's what we found, remembering that the number of mentions is about one-quarter of Henderson's total output on *Media Watch Dog*, each of whose issues runs on average to 6,900 words, and does not include his appearances on ABC television's *Insiders* or on Sky News programs. In the decade to the end of 2020, Henderson mentioned the ABC 987 times, of which 926 — or a tick under 94 per cent — were negative mentions. Given one-quarter of *Media Watch Dog* was surveyed, these figures can be confidently multiplied by four; that is, Henderson mentioned the ABC 4,000 times in his newsletter in a decade, denoting a level of attention bordering on the obsessive. There were 44 positive mentions (just over 4 per cent) and 17 neutral mentions. By comparison, *Media Watch Dog* rarely mentions news and current affairs programs on commercial radio and television. If the ABC was mentioned 987 times in a decade in our sample, the comparable figure for the rest of the commercial broadcast media was 38 mentions. For someone whose mantra is the need for balance on the ABC, these figures reveal a decidedly imbalanced focus of attention. To say he is a (*Media Watch*) *Dog* with a bone is simply accurate. (In the interests of balance, we note that Henderson judged Kerry O'Brien to have been fair and professional in his moderating of the political leaders' debate on ABC television ten elections ago, in 1993.)[12]

A couple of points flow from this. Negative or hostile coverage of the ABC has become louder and more insistent in recent years, and this, as we have said, stems from a combination of media outlets becoming more partisan to keep hold of their audience and the stories broken by the ABC's investigative-journalism unit. In the interests of keeping an open mind, though, it is worth asking whether the negative coverage is simply a reflection of partisan media competitors or whether there is evidence of declining standards at the ABC — or indeed systemic bias. It is easy to find individual articles criticising individual pieces of ABC journalism — and you can find them every now and then in the Nine newspapers — but it is much harder to locate properly conducted academic studies that find serious or systemic faults with the ABC's journalism. For a start, there is little evidence that ordinary members of the audience are particularly exercised about the 'left-leaning groupthink' that Gerard Henderson et al. believe infests the ABC.[13] When the Howard coalition government set up a review of the ABC soon after being elected in 1996, it attracted a large number of submissions — more than 10,000 — from the public and various interested bodies. Most did not mention bias at all, and the minority who did said the ABC was 'unbiased in presentation of issues'.[14] Later in the coalition's four terms of office, when communications minister Richard Alston raised the prospect of introducing a new external investigator of complaints, ABC managing director Russell Balding pointed out that, of all complaints about ABC programs, only 2 per cent concerned bias — and that 'included bias for or against football teams, men, women, atheists, and Christians'.[15]

Businessman Bob Mansfield, who conducted the 1996 review, recommended in his report that the ABC create a way of monitoring 'balance and objectivity' in its news and current affairs, and the ABC introduced quarterly surveys of its accuracy, impartiality, and objectivity the following year. These showed 79 per cent of respondents thought the ABC 'balanced and even-handed in politics' and 95 per cent thought its news and current affairs 'reliable and accurate'.[16] After accusations that the ABC's coverage of the 1998 election was biased, the national broadcaster commissioned media-monitoring firm Rehame to assess coverage by commercial networks, SBS, and the ABC. Rehame concluded that the ABC was delivering the least-biased coverage.[17] Even so, as we noted, the Howard government continued to complain about bias in the ABC's journalism, with the result that the Election Coverage Review Committee was established to monitor each of the five most recent federal elections beginning with the one that saw Labor come to power in 2007. The primary conclusion of each report is that the ABC's election coverage has been comprehensive, fair, and professional.[18]

Despite what some like to say, measuring bias in journalism is a good deal more complicated than simply toting up the amount of airtime or column centimetres devoted to each political party. The ABC's review of its 2007 election reporting showed the proportion of time it spent on the coalition substantially outweighed time spent on Labor — 45.4 per cent to 38 per cent.[19] Coalition MPs did not loudly draw this to everyone's attention, perhaps (though we doubt it) because they know that 'share of voice' — as it is termed in the report — is a crude instrument. The media's attempt to represent politics in words, sounds, and images, however, is complicated and open to many shades of interpretation. As report author Paul Chadwick, then director of the ABC's editorial policies, noted, 'Time on-air tells you nothing about what was discussed'.[20] Nor does duration say anything about tone or context. Some voices are more effective through brevity, while others lack impact no matter how long they speak. Politicians may decline to be interviewed on the ABC. What does the ABC do then?

The complications of bias go well beyond the work of individual journalists. What about the organisations and companies they work for? Do journalists act autonomously, or do they follow directions from their managers and their proprietors? Or is it more complicated than that? These questions open up large topics, but what concerns us here is the notion among the ABC's critics that its journalists both lean to the left and are captured by groupthink. As mentioned in the last chapter, an academic study by Folker Hanusch about Australian journalists became a talking point because of the supposed finding that ABC journalists were far more likely to vote for Labor or the Greens than the coalition parties. There were several problems with this assertion — which, we will say again, fact-checkers concluded was 'flimsy'.[21] First, the figures cited were from a sub-sample of the survey, which meant the margin for error was too big to allow the results to be reported as representative of the ABC. Second, a hefty proportion of the total number of journalists surveyed — 38.5 per cent — said they either did not know who they would vote for at the next election or declined to say. Third, even if you chose to throw caution to the wind and quote the survey's figures on this point, why would you exclude the comparable figures for journalists working at Fairfax Media, which showed a slightly higher proportion saying they would vote for Labor or the Greens? And what of the journalists working at News Corp Australia? There, the figure for Labor and Greens voters was lower, but it was still a dominant 66.3 per cent, with coalition voters at 26.7 per cent.

Apart from wobbliness around statistics, there is a willingness among critics to use anything that can be found to paint ABC journalists as irretrievably left wing. Hanusch's study, published in 2013, was not the first to examine Australian journalists' worldviews and political beliefs. A 1998 study by John Henningham found what he described as a 'major ideological gulf between Australian journalists and the general public ... journalists are significantly more liberal than the public is'.[22] As media scholar Sally Young noted, however, the terms 'liberal' and 'left wing' are not interchangeable, and certainly not in Australia, which was the location of Henningham's study. Young wrote: 'Journalists do tend to be "liberal" — to support free speech, freedom of information and tolerance, for example — but they also tend to be anti-collective action and anti-bureaucracy'.[23] Scepticism and a willingness to ask difficult questions, especially of those in positions of power and authority, are baseline requirements of journalism. These are not intrinsically left- or right-wing qualities, though to the extent those on the right are conservative — that is, they prefer to conserve institutions and value traditions — these can feel at odds with journalists' questioning.

The waves of rhetoric about the ABC being full of lefties crash against a couple of other logical walls. If journalists in general and ABC journalists in particular are so left wing, how does that explain the overall centrist or centre-right position of the Australian news media? Historically, newspapers in Australia have overwhelmingly supported conservative political parties at election time, and even though commercial radio and television outlets don't have election-eve leader articles, their proprietors mostly support the coalition parties and occasionally make their views known publicly, as Kerry Packer, the long-time boss of Channel Nine, did via an interview on his own network in 1995, and as his father, Frank, did by ordering an editorial supporting the Liberal Party be screened during the 1972 election campaign.[24] This is not altogether surprising. The news media in Australia is produced primarily by big companies, who have a strong interest in a stable economy and all that goes with it — economic growth, lower rates of company tax, and industrial relations with employees who are quiet if not quiescent.[25] Yet if the world views and political beliefs of the managers and proprietors of media outlets are a strong — dominant in some outlets — force in shaping coverage, it is nevertheless important not to underestimate a core tenet of journalism, which is to report the news accurately and professionally regardless of your own personal beliefs. This is what is set down in the codes previously quoted, and it is what the majority of journalists — whether at the Nine newspapers or News Corp Australia or 2GB or Channel Seven or SBS or the ABC — strive to deliver. There is not only a logical hole in the argument that the ABC is systemically biased or left wing; there is little evidence supporting it.

Conversely, it is easy to find evidence of the ABC's journalism winning awards. The highest honours for journalism in Australia, the Walkleys, were established in 1956. Broadcast journalism was not included until 1978, a year which also saw the introduction of the Gold Walkley, for the year's most outstanding piece of journalism across all categories and all outlets. In the 43 years since, the Gold Walkley has been won 15 times by ABC journalists. The next most awarded media outlet has been *The Age*, with five winners, then *The Australian*, with four. If you roll together the Gold Walkleys won by Fairfax Media outlets from when the company fully acquired *The Age* in 1983 to when it merged with Nine in 2018, that number is 12 — three less than the ABC. If you compare the ABC to commercial radio and television, Channel Nine has won three Gold Walkleys, while Channel Seven has won one. With seven to its name, the ABC's premier investigative-journalism program, *Four Corners*, has won more Gold Walkleys than the rest of the broadcast media combined.

It is also easy to find evidence of how well the general public regards the ABC — not just in one poll and not just in one year. Since at least 2002 the ABC has commissioned an external company to ask people their views about its news and current affairs. It routinely garners an approval rating ranging between 74 and 83 per cent. In 2012, the Finkelstein inquiry into the media examined data from 21 separate opinion polls conducted between 1966 and 2011 and found the ABC consistently rated higher than its commercial counterparts on trust, accuracy, and fairness. The report concluded that the ABC is 'the most trusted news source in Australia'.[26] More recently, the University of Canberra News and Media Research Centre's annual digital news report asked respondents to rate the trustworthiness of a range of leading news-media outlets in Australia. In each year since 2018, the ABC has scored the highest.[27]

Complaining about the media: how's that working for you?

At the same time, it's also easy to find evidence of the ABC being more thoroughly scrutinised than any other media outlet in the country. Much of this attention flows from the ABC being governed by an act of parliament, but the ABC also scrutinises its own journalism through *Media Watch*, which began in 1989 and ever since has criticised the ABC as willingly as it has other media. The editorial culture at the ABC is robust enough for it to be common for ABC presenters to interview the ABC managing director and subject him or her to the same kind of questioning they would any other company's chief executive.[28]

Such self-scrutiny is less frequent in the rest of the news media, even at leading outlets like *The Age* and *The Sydney Morning Herald*. It is virtually ignored in commercial radio and television, and for that matter in the progressive titles published by Schwartz Media, which have rarely if ever discussed the controversies surrounding some of their editors' departures over the past two decades. Nor do newspapers in Australia have readers' editors, as *The Guardian* in the United Kingdom does, or ombudspersons, as *The Hindu* newspaper in India has.[29] After much of the US news media swallowed lines from the Bush administration that Saddam Hussein's weapons of mass destruction provided a pretext for going to war against Iraq, two leading newspapers, *The New York Times* and *The Washington Post*, analysed their own coverage, criticised its shortcomings, and published findings. No similar self-examination occurred at News Corp — or, if it did, it was not shared with readers.[30]

Instead, in News Corp Australia publications, self-scrutiny is confined to self-publicising. You'll be looking for a long time before reading a tough interview with Rupert Murdoch in one of his own outlets. You're far more likely to read articles praising him. Murdoch is undeniably a highly successful media businessman, but even he might have blushed at the description of him offered a few years ago by *The Australian*'s media editor as 'the most successful publisher the world has ever seen' and a 'visionary in a media industry largely populated by lesser executives who show more reservation than courage, more anxiety than insight, and more uncertainty than solutions'.[31] Conversely, that same newspaper is remarkably intolerant of those who criticise it, even someone like Ken Cowley, who devoted most of his working life to News. In an interview with *The Australian Financial Review* in 2014, Cowley made several critical remarks, but within days he was on the front page of *The Australian* saying that where he had been quoted calling *The Australian* 'pathetic', what he really meant was that it was 'the best newspaper in the country'.[32] Such obeisance was not enough for Cowley to be spared a bucket of criticism in the paper's Media section.[33]

What is evidently a rare habit of self-scrutiny in the ABC's own reporting is augmented by a range of internal and external means of scrutiny, beginning with the code of editorial policies, which — as has already been mentioned — is more extensive than other codes, and takes in regular commissioning of external reports by independent experts about aspects of news and current affairs. This is done both as a way of continually examining coverage and making recommendations for improvement, and to tease out how best to ensure the ABC's journalistic practice abides by the *ABC Act*.[34] The ABC also has an internal complaints-handling office that receives about 3,000 written editorial complaints each year, and it spends millions of dollars a year responding to them.[35] About half the complaints are dealt with by program-makers; the more serious are investigated by the complaints team. In 2020, about two-thirds of the complaints investigated were dismissed; a third were either upheld as breaches or resolved by the program team addressing the problems, obviating the need for the investigation team to reach a finding on the complaint. If a complainant remains unhappy, of course, they can take their complaint to ACMA.

Some do, but before describing what happens then — because therein lies an interesting tale — we need to finish listing the accountability mechanisms the ABC faces. It is, as mentioned, subject to federal election-coverage monitoring, it provides an annual report to parliament, which in 2021 ran to 252 pages, its managing director appears regularly before an estimates committee to be questioned by senators, it provides answers to questions on notice from the committee, it appears before a range of parliamentary committees, its activities are subject to the *Freedom of Information (FOI) Act*, and it responds to inquiries established by government. Some of the last named, like the Inquiry into the Competitive Neutrality of the National Broadcasters, were set up by the coalition government with political mischief in mind, even though it came to naught when the expert panel found the ABC and SBS were acting according to their charters and not causing distortions in the market that were beyond the public interest.[36] Naught, that is, except for the time and resources needed to answer the panel's queries.

Privately owned media outlets have some of the same obligations, but not many. They may well appear before a parliamentary committee, but they don't have to. For instance, Lachlan Murdoch, son of Rupert and co-chair of News Corp, declined an invitation in September 2021 to appear before a Senate-committee inquiry into media diversity in Australia, though News Corp's chief executive officer, Robert Thomson, did eventually appear.[37] They're also not subject to FOI laws, though they make good use of them, including requests to the ABC.

Scrutiny and double standards

All broadcast media (including what they produce online) are subject to ACMA's regulatory regime. As with the ABC, complaints about the commercial outlets' news and current affairs need to be directed to the outlets themselves first, in writing, and only come to ACMA if the complainant is not satisfied with the broadcaster's response after 60 days. (This makes a mockery of Senator Andrew Bragg's argument that the ABC's complaints-handling system was 'like Dracula and the blood bank' or akin to marking its own homework.)[38] Then ACMA investigates the complaint and makes a finding: upheld, rejected, or no finding. If a complaint is upheld, possible outcomes range from the very light (training for an errant broadcaster) to the very heavy (revoking a station's licence). The former outcome is common but ineffectual. How often have you heard broadcasters proclaiming training sessions were a 'road to Damascus' experience inspiring them to loftier journalistic standards? The latter outcome is rare — a commercial radio licence was suspended nearly two decades ago, in 2003, for failing to provide required audited returns — but unduly harsh and, so, ineffectual.[39] ACMA is seen by many in the media industry as legalistic, slow, and ineffectual. The general public does not know much about ACMA and what it does know it does not much like. In the past 20 years, there have been six reports — three to government, a Productivity Commission inquiry, a National Audit Office inquiry, and most recently a Senate inquiry into media diversity — all of them critical of ACMA's (and its predecessor's) processes and its effectiveness as a regulator.[40]

ACMA is a statutory body with an annual budget of $150 million, but it was set up primarily to be a self-regulatory or co-regulatory body. This was a marked shift from the Australian Broadcasting Tribunal (ABT), which operated between 1977 and 1992. When the Labor government passed the *Broadcasting Services Act* in 1992, its goals included regulation ensuring 'public interest considerations' that would not 'impose unnecessary financial and administrative burdens' on broadcasters. The act provided for an oversight body rather than 'an interventionist agency hampered by rigid, detailed statutory procedures, and formalities, and legalism'.[41] The ABT had had powers to conduct public hearings to determine whether an owner was a 'fit and proper person' to hold a broadcast licence; famously, the ABT tangled with Rupert Murdoch when he sought to expand his television holdings late in the 1970s and early in the 1980s.[42] The Labor government's legislation was suffused with the deregulatory fervour of the time, but it did not take long before the perils of light-touch regulation were exposed. Only six years later, the ABC's *Media Watch* — ironically — exposed the 'cash for comment' scandal, where high-profile commercial broadcasters like John Laws and Alan Jones were paid to present advertisers' messages as their own editorial comment.[43] (The program, presented by Richard Ackland, is one of the ABC's 15 Gold Walkley winners.)

Laws famously declared he was not a journalist but an entertainer — 'There's no hook for ethics here' — as if his only relationship to ethics was what might be imposed on him, but both he and Jones presented news and current affairs programs included in the codes that commercial networks had registered with ACMA, and so needed to abide by them. Jones again fell foul of ACMA in 2007, when it found he had encouraged violence and the vilification of Australians of Lebanese and Middle Eastern background on programs broadcast late in 2005 that preceded a riot at Cronulla beach in Sydney.[44] Despite the finding, nothing much happened and — as you may have noticed — Jones continued broadcasting for many years afterward. He stepped down from his high-rating breakfast program in 2020, citing doctor's advice, but soon resurfaced on Sky News 'after dark' and in the pages of *The Daily Telegraph*, where he was hired as a columnist. Late in 2021, he and Sky parted ways, leaving Jones, at least temporarily, without a gig on radio, television, or newspaper. Along the way, there have been 'incidents and accidents', 'hints and allegations', as Paul Simon once sang.

Jones is a shock jock and controversy is his stock-in-trade, but a comparison of the record of commercial broadcasters and the ABC in responding to complaints to ACMA is telling. We chose to look at complaints about news and current affairs on radio and television between 2010 and 2021. The results are in the following four tables.

Station	Upheld	Rejected	% upheld	% rejected
Radio National	3	41	7%	93%
Melbourne local radio (3LO, 774)	1	15	6%	94%
ABC Radio or News Radio	0	7	0%	100%
Sydney local radio (2BL, 702, Sydney)	0	6	0%	100%
Triple J	0	4	0%	100%
Adelaide local radio (5AN)	1	1	50%	50%
Brisbane local radio (612)	0	2	0%	100%
Perth local radio (720)	0	2	0%	100%
Canberra local radio (666)	0	2	0%	100%
Far North radio (Far North Qld)	0	2	0%	100%
Northern Tasmania	0	1	0%	100%
Darling Downs (4QS)	0	1	0%	100%
Total	**5**	**84**	**6%**	**94%**

Table 6.1: ABC news and current affairs programs on radio that attracted the most complaints to ACMA, January 2010 to July 2021

Programs	Upheld	Rejected	No finding	% upheld	% rejected	% no finding
Alan Jones	18	23	1	43%	55%	2%
Kyle & Jackie O	2	16	0	11%	89%	0%
Ray Hadley	8	8	0	50%	50%	0%
John Laws	4	6	1	36%	55%	9%
Michael Christian and Mel Greig	3	4	0	43%	57%	0%
Chrissie, Sam, and Browny	0	3	0	0%	100%	0%
Total	**35**	**60**	**2**	**36%**	**62%**	**2%**

Table 6.2: News and current affairs programs on commercial radio that attracted the most complaints to ACMA, January 2010 to July 2021

Program	Total	Upheld	Reject-ed	No finding	% upheld	% reject-ed	% no finding
Lateline	19	0	19	0	0%	100%	0%
News 24	33	0	33	0	0%	100%	0%
Foreign Correspondent	2	1	1	0	50%	50%	0%
7.30	67	4	63	0	6%	94%	0%
Media Watch	28	1	25	2	4%	89%	7%
Four Corners	38	2	36	0	5%	95%	0%
Q&A	23	0	23	0	0%	100%	0%
Newscasts	51	3	48	0	6%	94%	0%
The Drum	11	0	11	0	0%	100%	0%
Insiders	5	0	5	0	0%	100%	0%
Catalyst	21	1	20	0	5%	95%	0%
Total	**298**	**12**	**284**	**2**	**4%**	**95%**	**1%**

Table 6.3: ABC news and current affairs programs on television that attracted the most complaints to ACMA, January 2010 to July 2021

Program	Total	Upheld	Reject-ed	No find-ing	% up-held	% re-jected	% no finding
News	143*	49	94	0	34%	66%	0%
A Current Affair	72	22	50	0	31%	69%	0%
Today Tonight	70	5	65	0	7%	93%	0%
60 Minutes	27	8	19	0	30%	70%	0%
Sunrise	16	4	12	0	25%	75%	0%
Sunday Night	15	6	8	1	40%	53%	7%
Today	13	2	11	0	15%	85%	0%
The Project	8	0	8	0	0%	100%	0%
Total	**364**	**96**	**267**	**1**	**26.4%**	**73.3%**	**0.3%**

* From 142 code breaches alleged. For the sake of completeness, a no-breach finding in an investigation into coverage of the 2019 Christchurch massacre investigation has been added to the tally.

Table 6.4: News and current affairs programs on commercial television that attracted the most complaints to ACMA, January 2010 to July 2021.

What these show, first, is that the total number of complaints about ABC programs and commercial programs is similar in radio — 89 for the ABC, 97 for commercial outlets — and similar but less so for television — 298 for the ABC compared to 364 for commercial outlets. Second, the proportion of complaints upheld is not similar. The strike rate for complainants about ABC programs is low — 6 per cent for radio and 4 per cent for television — which suggests, as Alan Sunderland has argued, that the ABC's internal complaints-handling mechanism is effective. Third, the strike rate for complainants about commercial programs is still well below one in two — 36 per cent for radio and 26 per cent for television — but is much higher than for the ABC. Fourth, Alan Jones's program attracted more than twice as many complaints as any other program on commercial radio. It's worth noting Jones has also attracted two complaints over comments made on programs broadcast on Sky News in August 2020, in which he quoted selectively from peer-reviewed research about the effectiveness of masks and lockdowns to combat COVID-19. Parts of both complaints were found to have breached the code but were dismissed, mainly because the network posted clarifications on its website within the required 30 days.[45]

If you look at what prompted complaints to ACMA in the first place, and who made them, an interesting picture emerges. Many complaints about ABC programs stem from questions of accuracy or balance in programs about important issues in the public interest. Conversely, complaints about commercial programs tend to be about outrages against public taste. Think Kyle Sandilands and his comments about Magda Szubanski losing weight in a concentration camp, or his deeply misogynistic comments about a female journalist who reported negative Twitter comments about *The Kyle & Jackie O Show*.[46] We are not suggesting the complaints are illegitimate, just that they arise from the kind of material aired most commonly on public compared to commercial broadcasters. The exception on commercial radio is Jones, whose program routinely discusses political issues and who is politically engaged in a way that John Laws, for instance, has rarely been.

As to who lodges complaints, it can be anyone, and usually they remain anonymous. This means it is doubly striking that politicians are willing to complain to the ABC about its programs, as communications minister Mitch Fifield did at least six times during his four years in the role, and that, if not satisfied, they may well complain to ACMA, as former communications minister Richard Alston did in 2005 to ACMA's predecessor, the Australian Broadcasting Authority (ABA).[47] Remember that the ABC sits in these ministers' portfolios. How often do politicians, especially those in government, complain to ACMA about commercial programs? To the best of our knowledge, rarely if ever. This may have something to do with the ABC devoting more time to covering political issues, but it is also about the power of big commercial media companies, who are able and can be willing to make politicians' lives uncomfortable. As Jonathan Holmes has noted, 'The ABC has always copped it from the politicians: a lot of them reckon they own it, and all of them know it won't bite back the way some of the private empires do'.[48] Journalists Andrew Probyn and Laura Tingle both came to the ABC after long, successful careers in commercial media, though in newspapers rather than broadcast. Both were shocked to be on the receiving end of harassment and verbal bullying from coalition politicians far exceeding what they were accustomed to when working for commercial media. As Probyn told Holmes: 'The ABC is like that puny kid in the playground, easy to bash up because it's largely defenceless, because of all these ways in which we open ourselves up for scrutiny'.[49]

There is a whiff of this attitude even in some ACMA rulings. In 2011, Jones notoriously said at least twice on his program that then prime minister Julia Gillard was 'off her tree' and should be 'shoved into a chaff bag' and taken 'as far out to sea as they can' and be told 'to swim home'. ACMA found the comments 'very disrespectful and disparaging' but concluded they did not breach the code on inciting violence or inciting ridicule on the basis of gender.[50] Conversely, when Probyn in a 2017 report on the ABC's 7.00 pm news described Tony Abbott as 'the most destructive politician of his generation', ACMA said, 'If such a subjective statement in the nightly news by a news reporter does not place the ABC in breach of its duty to report the news with impartiality, it is difficult to understand what would'. It further said it 'beggars belief' the ABC could submit that Probyn's report was impartial. ACMA concluded Probyn should be reprimanded. Putting the rulings on Probyn and Jones side by side leaves a sour taste in the mouth. One is a personal, gendered attack, nearly a call to violence, that did not breach any code; the other is at worst debatable, at best accurate, but did breach a code. That said, as Jonathan Holmes showed, Probyn could have avoided trouble by rephrasing his description as though it was reportage, which is required in a news bulletin, rather than analysis — e.g. 'Tony Abbott, already regarded even by many in his party as a destructive force ...'[51]

Even when complaints are upheld, though, ACMA seems unwilling to take firm action. During a 2018 broadcast, Jones referred to finance minister Mathias Cormann as 'the nigger in the woodpile' in the context of the second leadership challenge in a week against then prime minister Malcolm Turnbull. ACMA found the racist phrase breached generally accepted standards of decency while also finding it did not breach the guideline on inciting hatred, serious contempt, or severe ridicule on the basis of race. No further action was taken by ACMA. In a 2019 broadcast, Jones said New Zealand prime minister Jacinda Ardern was 'a complete clown' who 'hasn't got a clue'. He urged Turnbull's successor, Scott Morrison, to give her 'a backhander' and 'shove a sock down her throat'. ACMA's investigation found his comments breached the code of practice on generally accepted standards of decency and were factually inaccurate: what Jones had asserted as fact about New Zealand's climate change mitigation targets was just speculation. Separate claims — that he had breached provisions about inciting violence, and of inciting ridicule on the basis of gender — were dismissed. No further action was taken by ACMA. Later in the year, ACMA upheld a complaint that Jones's station, 2GB, had failed to list on its website an advertising agreement whereby Jones was sponsored by Star, the Sydney casino operator, for his outside broadcasts of the Rugby World Cup in Japan. In this case, the licensee was ordered to 'conduct formal training with all relevant staff on the requirements of the Disclosure Standard within a period of six months'.

As a 2021 Senate inquiry would put it, ACMA's approach to managing misinformation and poor standards was 'woefully inadequate'. Further, the inquiry found, for a well-resourced agency in a rapidly changing media environment, ACMA was passive and lacked initiative. The agency's chair, Nerida O'Loughlin, told the inquiry that ACMA's 'responsibilities are enlivened when a complaint comes to us'. Translated from bureaucratese, this means ACMA does not see its role as identifying or monitoring issues in media standards.[52]

Hypocrisy and hot air

What this shows is the thoroughly distorted debate around the ABC. The public broadcaster is held to a higher standard than the rest of the news media, and actively attacked when it falls short by news organisations that, despite their own stated fidelity to high standards, themselves fall short, sometimes well short. The hypocrisy is breathtaking. Yet this trope about holding the ABC to higher standards has become a tactic used relentlessly by politicians and by commercial media outlets — loudly led by News Corp Australia — to erode public trust in the ABC. As Andrew Probyn told Jonathan Holmes, the mechanisms for scrutiny provided by the *ABC Act* greatly benefit audiences, but 'the same mechanisms can be used by government, and that's what they've been doing'.[53]

The ABC cannot be ignored because of its reach, and it is trusted far more by the public than other media outlets. Politicians attack the ABC on ideological grounds, but also to avoid scrutiny, and most of those complaining see the world in Manichean 'with us or against us' terms. Rival media outlets are driven by a combination of commercial self-interest and ideology. The ABC, like any media organisation, makes mistakes. In recent times, the broadcast of *Ms Represented* and *Juanita: A Family Mystery*, both produced independently and outside the purview of the ABC's news division, saw failures of editorial oversight that resulted in upheld complaints, lawsuits, and the withdrawal of *Juanita* from the ABC's iview. In response, the ABC has moved to rectify the underlying problem, by applying news-division standards of oversight to the entertainment and specialist programming division where appropriate. Despite these individual instances, there is no evidence that the ABC fails fundamentally in its mission and no evidence of systemic bias in its news and current affairs.[54] Its internal complaints-handling system works well, but the same cannot be said of the self-regulatory and co-regulatory systems for commercial broadcast media.

We haven't discussed the self-regulatory system for newspapers, magazines, and (some) online media run by the Australian Press Council, but — long story short — the picture is no happier than it is for ACMA.[55] The council is funded by publishers and 60 per cent of its funding comes from News Corp Australia, which is not only the news organisation most hostile to the ABC but the one about whom two former prime ministers, Kevin Rudd and Malcolm Turnbull, have been directing their campaign for a royal commission into the media.[56] News Corp Australia publications attracted two-thirds of all complaints to the Press Council in 2020–21, but as the overwhelming proportion of complaints do not come before an adjudication panel, whose findings members are obliged to publish, the results of hundreds of other complaints are known only to the complainant and the publisher. If you wanted to know, for example, how often someone had complained about Andrew Bolt's work, you would not be able to see that in the Press Council's annual report unless the matter had gone to adjudication.[57]

Media regulation, then, has been known to be weak and fragmented, but few in industry or government seem committed to improving it. Some are rightly sceptical about Rudd's campaign for a royal commission, but his petition to parliament gathered more signatures than any before it, and the Senate inquiry established in 2020 to examine media diversity attracted a lot of submissions — 5,068. Reporting in December 2021, the committee provided new information about the system's ineffectiveness by examining how YouTube had been able to achieve what others had not — requiring Sky News Australia to take down videos containing misinformation about COVID-19 on programs hosted by Jones, among others. It also heard from ABC Alumni how codes of practice for commercial media were being relaxed. The ABC requires program-makers to present a diversity of perspectives on an issue over time so that no significant strand of thought is excluded, but a similar standard no longer applies to commercial or pay TV: 'Anyone complaining to ACMA about the one-sided nature of Sky News's analysis and commentary ... would find that no clause of the relevant codes supports such a complaint'.

The inquiry was chaired by a Greens senator; whatever its findings, the coalition government was not obliged to do anything and has given no indication it will. Nothing new there, but, although the report was supported by Labor committee members, its recommendation for a royal commission into media diversity and regulation was swiftly rejected by Labor's shadow communications minister.[58] Labor may have been continuing its pre-election small-target strategy, but, more dispiritingly, despite abundant evidence, little action looks likely on media regulation. Again. Labor's response underscores how media policy is captured by governments and media companies that are acutely aware of their own interests and of the levers necessary to influence each other: legislation strengthening regulation can be staved off by threatened or actual negative coverage; media companies can be rewarded with government grants in return for positive coverage.

The ABC is not beholden to a private media proprietor, and its editorial culture is robust. Exactly how robust, at any given moment, is what governments are only too willing to test.

Chapter 7

REACHES, TOUCHES, FASHIONS
the ABC's influence on Australian culture

One of the most obvious features of the ABC is one of the most overlooked: its significance as a cultural organisation. Speaking in 2012, then chair James Spigelman argued that the ABC was the 'most important' such organisation in Australia. It had been so for many years, he said, and its capacity to contribute as such had only grown since the arrival of digital television, the internet, and the expansion of the ABC's radio services. With six television channels, 60 capital city, local, and digital radio stations, four national radio services, an array of online resources, and ventures in publishing, licensing, and live music, the ABC offers a diverse range of cultural content, both niche and generalist, in a wide variety of forms. Moreover, the ABC's longevity — especially as it approaches its tenth decade of operation — means it has built up an extraordinarily rich and diverse audio and audio-visual record and archive of cultural works. All of this, Spigelman pointed out wryly, could go unnoticed: 'I do not believe there are many, including many full-time employees of the ABC, who appreciate the depth and range of what we do.' But accounting for that, and understanding how it contributes to Australian life, would leave no one doubting the central argument Spigelman made and which we reiterate here: 'Without the ABC's contribution, Australian cultural life would be greatly impoverished.'[1]

Many points reinforce Spigelman's argument. First is the ABC's budget. With $1.13 billion in funding in 2020–21, its funding dwarfs that of any other cultural organisation in Australia. It receives more funding than SBS, the Australia Council for the Arts, Screen Australia, the state-based arts organisations (such as Create NSW), and the various national and state museums, libraries, archives, and galleries.[2]

Second, the ABC is a pervasive cultural organisation. Its national audience reach across television, radio, and online is 68.1 per cent. ABC television reaches just under eight million people each week, its radio stations reach more than five million per week, its news and current affairs offerings over six million, and its digital products see over 16 million unique weekly users. Furthermore, the ABC's reach extends beyond Australian shores, with users in the Americas, Europe, Asia, Africa, and Oceania accessing ABC websites, apps, and broadcasts in volume: the unique overseas audience for the ABC in 2020–21 was 15.2 million per month.[3]

Third, the ABC is perhaps the best-known and valued cultural organisation in Australia, even if not always recognised as a cultural organisation specifically. The ABC 'brand' is immediately recognisable and acknowledged to be of enduring quality. Surveys and polls repeatedly point to the trust and value accorded to its work. According to the ABC's national Corporate Tracking Program for 2020–21, 79 per cent of Australians believe the ABC performs a valuable role in the Australian community. A clear majority of respondents think its television and radio programming, and its online resources, are of good quality. The majority laud the ABC's fulfilment of its charter obligations and trust it to an extent almost without parallel in Australia. More than three-quarters of respondents believe the ABC to be 'distinctively Australian' and a contributor to an Australian national identity. They believe the ABC encourages and promotes the arts, provides educational programs, and balances wide appeal with specialised interests.[4]

Its fine reputation is the result of nearly nine decades of high-quality broadcasting, an achievement that should count as a fourth reason to regard the ABC as Australia's most significant cultural institution. Australians of a certain vintage, for example, will proudly recall admission to the Orders of the Dragon's Tooth or Golden Fleece, via *The Argonauts Club*, or tuning in to the Johnny O'Keefe-hosted *Six O'Clock Rock* (1959–62). Those who danced instead to *Countdown* (1974–87) will probably recall miniseries like *Power Without Glory* (1976), *Shark's Paradise* (1986), and *Brides of Christ* (1991), comedies such as *The Norman Gunston Show* (1975–79) and *The Gillies Report* (1984–85), and landmark current-affairs programs such as Chris Masters's Gold Walkley–winning exposé of the bombing of the Greenpeace vessel *Rainbow Warrior* (1985). Viewers in the 1990s and early 2000s might recall the children's show *Round the Twist* (1993–2001), adult fare like *SeaChange* (1998–2000) and *Changi* (2001), and comedies like *Frontline* (1994–97), *Kath and Kim* (2002–07), and the Chaser's various shows (2004, 2006–09, 2011–12, 2014–15). Viewers in the past decade, meanwhile, will have their own ABC memories, whether that's *Q&A* (2008–present), *Redfern Now* (2012–15), *Utopia* (2014–present), *Get Krack!n* (2017–present), and *The Code* (2014–16), or podcasts such as

Trace (2017–21) and *The Eleventh* (2020).

Such content reaches across nearly every facet of Australian life, and underscores how the ABC is a launchpad for locally produced film, television, and radio programming. Productions like the aforementioned should underscore this fifth reason to regard the ABC as Australia's most significant cultural institution. The amount invested in ABC film and television production has fluctuated, and been the subject of congratulations, controversy, and hand-wringing, but it is undeniable that the ABC is the enduring home for a large, broad range of Australian-produced content. Rural viewers have had *Bellbird* (1967–77) and *Back Roads* (2015–present); politics tragics have had a weekly dose for two decades with *Insiders* (2001–present), while those wanting in-depth analysis have enjoyed *Labor in Power* (1993), *The Howard Years* (2008), and *The Killing Season* (2015). There's been *The Search for Meaning* (1987–96) for people interested in spirituality and religious faith, and *Catalyst* (2001–present) for people curious about science. There have been documentary shows that have reached across the country and globe for individual and noteworthy stories: *Australian Story*, *Foreign Correspondent*. There have been innovative talk shows like *Enough Rope* (2003–08) and panel and game shows like *Good News Week* (1997–99) and *Question Everything* (2021). There have been fine-arts shows like *The Book Club* (2006–17) and sports shows like *Offsiders* (2005–present). There have been the loved series like *Miss Fisher's Murder Mysteries* (2012–15) and *Janet King* (2014–17), and there have been the juggernaut productions: *The Slap* (2011), *Paper Giants* (2011, 2013), *The Secret River* (2015), *Fires*, (2021) and — appropriately — *The Newsreader* (2021). The array of work broadcast on the ABC is enormous, and so too is the number of people who started their careers with the broadcaster. Whether they remained with the ABC or moved on — as Channel Nine executive Sam Chisholm once promised ABC executives, 'You train 'em and I'll pinch 'em' — the people who have been nurtured by the ABC constitute a richly talented list.[5]

The ABC's significant place in Australian culture stems from its charter obligation to broadcast programs 'that contribute to a sense of national identity and inform and entertain, and reflect the cultural diversity of, the Australian community', as well as 'encourage and promote the musical, dramatic, and other performing arts in Australia'. The purpose of this chapter is not to map the whole of the ABC's cultural footprint but to outline a few key areas where its work — in ways that are valuable and surprising — underscores our case that the ABC makes an extraordinary contribution to Australian life that is unsurpassed by commercial providers. It is also to point toward areas where the ABC's current predicament has compromised those contributions.

The ABC in music

It has been widely acknowledged that the ABC's greatest contribution to Australian cultural life is probably its involvement in the development and promotion of music.[6] Initially, the ABC's efforts were focused on classical music: with the assistance of federal and state governments in the mid-century, the ABC nurtured six full-strength symphony orchestras across the country, including the conservatorium and teaching resources required to support and maintain those orchestras. Renowned conductors from across the world, such as Eugene Goossens, worked with these orchestras, which went on tour in regional Australia to spread public experience and acquaintance with classical music. Performances were recorded and broadcast widely, and, though the ABC divested itself of these orchestras in the 1990s, it continues to record and broadcast concerts from major orchestral and operatic events in Australia and overseas.

Music remains core to much of the ABC's radio broadcasting. In varying proportions, ABC stations play classical, jazz, rock, and pop music, and present programs about music. Dedicated broadcasts on Radio National and ABC Classic, for example, explore the history, practice, and experience of music and musicians; meanwhile, Double J presents a mix of classic contemporary music, and Triple J presents an eclectic range of contemporary alternative music. Though now four decades old, that station remains vigorous and dedicated to appealing to new listeners. As Sydney radio station 2JJ, its inaugural broadcast in 1975 — of Skyhooks' 'You Just Like Me 'Cos I'm Good in Bed' — shocked moralists and competitors alike; today, its Hottest 100 countdown is an institution so venerated that its broadcast date is the subject of political debate.

One of the most successful of the ABC's contemporary initiatives in music is Unearthed. Sparked by the discovery of the band that became Silverchair, Unearthed began in 1995 as an attempt to find hidden musical talent in regional Australia. The results were immediate. Alternative rock band Grinspoon won the inaugural, Lismore-based competition. Their song 'Sickfest' became the number-one requested track on Triple J, and, after recording a partial EP, the band was signed to a commercial record deal the following year: it remains to this day a successful band that, until going on hiatus, was among the top tier of Australian rock artists.[7] Almost simultaneous with Grinspoon signing that deal, in 1996, was the success of alternative band Killing Heidi. They gained prominence through Unearthed, and in 1997 themselves signed a commercial record deal.

Unearthed has since seen a legion of artists tread a similar path, going from unknown to renowned: Missy Higgins, Flume, Boy & Bear, the Rubens, Rüfüs, Art vs Science, Courtney Barnett, Meg Mac, and Sticky Fingers, among others.

The focus of Unearthed shifted and the infrastructure evolved, particularly as online media came into its own. Today, Unearthed has a dedicated website where artists can upload music, and vote for and share that music, thereby creating a 'direct line' to audiences that is unlikely to otherwise have been available. A digital radio station, meanwhile, gets that music out to the world. 'The whole Unearthed project,' Triple J has argued, 'remains a valuable first step for Australian musicians trying to find an audience.'[8] It is, moreover, different to ostensibly similar commercial TV projects like *Australian Idol*, which are not only transparently, if unsurprisingly, commercial but also make music a device for competition rather than a way of finding and showing talent.[9]

While music-themed programming is less ubiquitous on television, the ABC still has form. *Countdown* was the most popular TV music program of its day, giving enormous exposure to Australian and international musicians, and remains a cultural touchstone. John Farnham, Olivia Newton-John, AC/DC, INXS, Kylie Minogue, Men at Work, and Marcia Hines, among many others, were given enormous publicity thanks to *Countdown* and its idiosyncratic host, Molly 'Do yourself a favour' Meldrum. Since 1987, music-video program *Rage* has become a fixture: its minimalist format, iconic scream, and Iggy Pop theme music have endured as long as its overnight broadcast time, while programs of a similar format on commercial television, such as *Nightmoves* and MTV, have not. Like Triple J, it has been friendly to less-mainstream musical acts; its respect for the artistic value of music videos has also proven to be unique.[10]

Education and children

If asked today to describe what suitable programming exists for children on the ABC, the average ABC television viewer — who, it should be said again, is in their late 60s — is likely to cast their mind back to their youth and reel off a few titles in the hope that they might still be on-air. *Play School* (1966–present) or *Bananas in Pyjamas* (1992–present) or the preternaturally youthful Wiggles (1991–present) are likely to feature. If they have grandchildren, and actually listen to them, those viewers might also mention *Bluey* (2018–present). But this, for most people, will be about it.

It should come as no surprise to know that the ABC does far more. The abundance of material the ABC produces for children is, in fact, staggering and unmatched by commercial providers. It has two television channels dedicated to children, in ABC Kids and ABC ME; an app and digital radio station, in ABC Kids Listen, which provides audio education and entertainment programs; and a treasure trove of online material including games, cooking tutorials and recipes, arts and craft, videos, and educational material for children ranging from age two — for whom content is badged with a cute 'Puggles symbol' — to school-age kids, for whom material is designed to 'reflect and celebrate the lives of young Aussies' and includes stories, news, cartoons, games, and podcasts that are educational and entertaining. The educational element in the ABC's offerings is informed by national frameworks for development and encompasses programs about Australian history (drawing on a rich archive of footage), Indigenous culture, and the contemporary world. The *Little Yarns* podcast (2019–present), for example, features First Nations people and music and art by First Nations composers and artists, and invites listeners to 'learn a word on Country from one of the hundreds of First Nations languages'.[11] Since 1968, meanwhile, *Behind the News* has presented news and current affairs in a way designed to appeal to and educate children, increasing their understanding of complex issues about politics, economics, the environment, and society. *BTN*, as it is commonly known, produces content based on key areas of the Australian Curriculum, hosts livestream question-and-answer sessions with its journalists, invites 'rookie reporters' to participate in the program, and makes a range of audio-only stories.

It is not always easy to discern the enormous value and study that go into the production of this material. On the surface, *Play School* may seem like a breezy musical lark. But it employs early childhood educators and everything from its sets to its songs to its routine elements is designed to 'stimulate learning, aid language, psychological and cognitive development, heighten social skills, and encourage youthful imaginations ... The makers of *Play School* hope that just as the program aims to represent, respond to, and reflect children's everyday world, so too will children take for their own the ideas, songs, and stories they see on *Play School* and make them part of their lives.'[12] The show has been praised for its representation of diversity in Australia and for its use of play to encourage engagement. It retains considerable popularity and bridges generations by retaining familiar elements and segments: young and old alike will recognise the rocket clock, Big Ted, and the 'look through the window' segment (used to present children with 'difference' as a concept).

The ABC has also been keen to be responsive to the public mood, as the material it produced for the public during the COVID-19 pandemic shows. When schools were first shut and communities locked down, in April 2020, the ABC provided key support for the educational and entertainment-based needs of children and young people.[13] As communications scholar Liz Giuffre noted, the ABC partnered with the Victorian state education department to provide learning materials to students via television, and linked its individual online materials to the NSW and South Australian education-department websites. Some of that material was directed toward public health education: there were *Play School*, Wiggles, and *Bluey* videos designed to persuade very young viewers to wash their hands. Other material was escapist and fun. The second season of the phenomenally successful children's show *Bluey* — so successful that Wil Anderson joked that the B in ABC stood for *Bluey* — was released on the same day Scott Morrison declared a lockdown. As Giuffre points out, the show provided a satisfying escape by featuring activities to which children could relate but not directly undertake while in lockdown.

For older children, meanwhile, the ABC produced the series *ME@Home*, a ten-minute show hosted by Grace Koh and taped in her home. Guests musical and famous featured, and the show blended fast editing, pop-culture references, do-it-yourself production values, and abundant references to the pandemic and coping strategies for the lockdown. Per Giuffre: '*ME@Home* provided a significant cultural and community connection for otherwise isolated Australian school-aged children ... [It] allowed young viewers to feel their experiences in isolation were being represented.'

For another, slightly older audience yet again, Triple J created Requestival, in which the station played music explicitly dictated by listeners between 6.00 am and 9.00

pm from 25 to 31 May 2020. The hope was to create an experience in which audiences actively participated with each other rather than the medium alone, by nominating songs and artists and providing an explanation for their choices. Thousands of these were shared on-air during the week-long program, which saw more than 70,000 requests and 1,225 songs played, creating a community of engaged listeners who not only developed jokes — such as a push to play 'Duel of the Fates', the orchestral music that accompanies a lightsabre duel in *Star Wars: The Phantom Menace* — but also paid tributes, most poignantly in the case of a push to play music by Geelong band Louie the Milk Man, whose lead singer had taken his own life shortly before Requestival began.[14]

Describing the ABC's efforts during COVID-19 as diverse and engaging, Giuffre argues the value of this work was significant: 'These outlets ensured that young Australians were able to feel connected despite being physically unable to gather together in their usual groups at school, day care, work or play.' These were efforts rarely if ever seen in other media outlets, and point to the crucial role the ABC has played and continues to play, in making and responding to Australian culture and its concerns.

This sporting life

The ABC has been an influential player in the broadcasting of Australian sport: indeed, memories of the ABC's sports broadcasting have, for many, often proven to be as potent as any other. 'For as long as I can remember, I was a regular listener to sport on ABC radio,' John Howard wrote in his autobiography. Elsewhere, Howard said ABC radio had meant more to him than any other medium when he was growing up; as prime minister, Howard would take considerable pleasure in joining the ABC's cricket commentators during a test match.[15]

Cricket dominated the ABC's efforts in sport for a substantial period: as media scholar Michael Ward noted in his survey of the ABC's televised sports broadcasting, coverage of the game in the 1950s to the 1970s constituted a quarter of its annual national and local sports output; during the summers, it was typical for this to constitute at least half of the ABC's sports coverage. Thanks to its national reach at a time when commercial television was limited by the 'two station' rule, the ABC was the only media organisation able to televise cricket across the country. It did so with aplomb, cementing a perception it was 'the long term and trusted media patron of cricket'.

In doing so, the ABC also laid the foundations for the game's commercial transformation by creating a national audience. Sensing the lucrative opportunities afforded by that audience, media proprietor Kerry Packer made a fruitless attempt to gain the television rights to test cricket, then created the short-lived World Series Cricket. The fallout from that affair saw exclusive cricket television rights go to Packer, but what is important — and rarely remembered or acknowledged — is that until 1991 the public broadcaster continued to carry test cricket broadcasts and paid through the nose for the privilege. Why did the ABC do so? To ensure regional viewers had access to the broadcasts.[16]

The ABC's cricket coverage on radio continues to be highly regarded, partly for its familiarity and, at a time when the ability to watch cricket on television is not necessarily free, for its accessibility. There remains, too, a certain purity to its coverage. As long-time commentator Jim Maxwell put it, the ABC's non-commerciality is a key strength. Those mainstays of the televised coverage Hawk-Eye and Hot Spot, he once observed, were fun gimmicks — but no more than that.[17] To this might be added the lack of ad breaks between overs and the calm, authoritative commentary: not for nothing has it long been said that many Australians watch the televised cricket with the volume down and the radio on.

The ABC's cricket coverage is not without fault. Decisions not to cover overseas test series in the West Indies, India, and New Zealand in the last decade, for example, have attracted criticism.[18] It is a tragic irony that at a time when the ABC has the chance to do so much, thanks to innovations in technology, it is more and more restricted by what Maxwell called 'budgets and bellyaches from our political leaders'.[19] But the ABC's coverage of cricket remains nonetheless constant — the 'sound of summer', as some have said.

The ambit of the ABC's sports coverage has long been wider. Historically speaking, the ABC has had extensive television and radio rights to cover everything from Australian Rules football and Rugby League to the Commonwealth and Olympic Games. This changed during the 1980s, when television rights for a sweep of major sports became too expensive for the ABC to compete with commercial providers, but the decade also saw the ABC increase its coverage of so-called 'minor' sports. Just as with cricket, the ABC's coverage of these sports helped to build audiences that aided their professionalisation and commercialisation. The professionalisation of women's netball is but one recent example.

But the ABC's ability to broadcast various sports is to a degree compromised by the galloping commercialisation of those and many other sports — a factor aggravated by funding pressures. It was sad but inevitable that in 2019 the ABC announced it would not pursue the radio broadcast rights for the coming Tokyo Olympic Games because of the immense cost involved. Speaking at the point when its funding had been cut, with no reprieve in sight, the ABC's head of radio commented that it was simply a 'money issue'.[20] Not only did this decision represent the end of a six-decade tradition of the ABC as the official, non-commercial radio broadcaster of the Olympics, it ensured coverage would go instead to a commercial station. The unwelcome development should underscore how important the ABC has been regarded for its contribution to sport in Australia. As Australian Olympic Committee chief Matt Carroll said, when the decision was announced: 'A great let-down to Australians who rely on their national broadcaster — from the smallest of communities to our suburbs.'[21]

ABC, everyday

But for *Q&A*, one might say the establishment of ABC Life in 2018 was one of the most controversial decisions made by the ABC in recent times. Pitched during Michelle Guthrie's era, ABC Life was launched, in part, to focus on younger Australians and to boost the ABC's digital storytelling capacity ahead of a time when the ABC's main efforts would be concentrated online. But it was embattled from the beginning. To the commercial networks, ABC Life was an encroachment on territory they thought they owned, and which they thought was beyond the bounds of the ABC's charter. 'The ABC should be asked to explain how its lifestyle initiative fits [with its charter],' said Free TV chief executive Bridget Fair.[22]

To which the ABC might merely have pointed Fair to the charter. For while the ABC's reach is wide, there were pockets of the community who did not necessarily regard the ABC as a part of everyday life. Younger audiences were only one missing piece. Others, as ABC Life deputy editor Osman Faruqi noted, included people living outside the inner cities and people from migrant backgrounds. Due to a lack of content that was appealing or relevant to them, they were far less likely to engage with the ABC than older, wealthier, and white audiences. It was a problem the ABC was obliged to confront, as Faruqi argued: 'Young Indian-Australian couples in Parramatta pay tax and deserve relevant ABC content as much as white retirees in Balmain.'[23]

Thus the establishment of ABC Life, and the production of content that might broadly be termed 'lifestyle journalism' — content that would reach and interest such young couples in Parramatta: articles, news segments, TV documentaries, and online packages about everything from sexual health to the nature of freelance work to quick dinner recipes to life with chronic pain. Critics ridiculed much of this. 'It's a vegan recipe, of course,' wrote Gerard Henderson, about an article on easy-to-make recipes in lockdown. 'Without ABC Life — who would have known how to cook chickpeas in rich tomato sauce?'[24] 'Only one in every four women is masturbating regularly, and our national broadcaster has hang-ups about that,' wrote Chris Kenny, after surveying the results of a survey of sexual health.[25]

Henderson and Kenny were doing exactly what they abhor in ABC presenters — sneering. But their sneers were given greater credence because of a long-running and gendered condescension about 'lifestyle journalism' that, in the case of ABC Life, was both misplaced and ignorant. For this kind of work was distinct and useful. As *Mumbrella*'s Brittney Rigby noted, part of ABC Life's appeal lay in the unique content it provided — advice on talking to children about racism, on giving up alcohol, on coping with unemployment, on personal finance planning — and, critically, the lack of a commercial edge: the ABC did all of this 'without trying to sell anything'.[26]

Another aspect of that distinctiveness was the ability of this material to augment 'hard' news coverage. During the first COVID-19 outbreak, for example, while ABC News kept audiences updated about government policies, daily infection rates, and the pandemic's toll on the economy, ABC Life offered information and insight about everyday concerns clearly shared among the public, such as whether an employer could ask you to reduce your hours under the government's JobKeeper program. There were interviews with people struggling with the enforced isolation of lockdowns, and suggestions on how to cope. There was coverage of eating disorders amid food shortages, and there was insight into the lives of people who, homeless during the pandemic, were grappling with the dilemmas of quarantine and self-isolation.

There was, furthermore, engagement with voices and communities otherwise marginalised and overlooked: not only was the ABC Life staff diverse in background, age, and demographics, it produced quality material that engaged with issues around identity, race, and class, and was integrated into the ABC's broader offerings, so a story produced for video series *Thanks*, about a boy caring for his dementia-afflicted father, was featured on *7.30*. The site also — a fact often overlooked — garnered an audience: Nielsen data showed it attracted 1.4 million views in March 2020.[27]

The enduring external criticism, however, was also echoed inside the ABC. There were some who thought the initiative a needlessly controversial distraction; others regarded it as a diversion of precious resources at a time when funding was being cut (particularly from the ABC's news division); yet others simply thought it 'soft' (an article on the need for sunscreen indoors was an oft-invoked example).[28] The combination of criticism internal and external, Faruqi wrote later, was 'draining'. The Tonagh and Bean efficiency review, completed in 2018, was glib and dismissive of the initiative, and its verdict — that ABC Life was 'further distant from the core' of the ABC charter — ultimately informed the decision to shut it down when the ABC launched a new five-year plan, in June 2020.[29] The idea was reconfigured, expanded to include regional and local content, and rebranded. At time of writing, it exists under the guise of ABC Everyday, providing information to 'navigate life's challenges and choices so you can stay on top of things that matter to you'.

The decision was unfortunate. Coming after supposed competitors such as *BuzzFeed News* and *10 Daily* were forced to close, the demise of ABC Life left a gap that was all the more gaping since the unit appeared to have achieved its goals. ABC Life had broadened the ABC's audience and engaged them in ways they rarely if ever had been before. Its lingering effect, in a cultural sense, is to remind us that a long-running thread in the ABC's work is to explain issues of everyday Australian life, and in doing so not only fashion that life but innumerable individual lives as well.[30]

Chapter 8

'REGIONAL AUSTRALIA WOULD BE SIBERIA'
the ABC in the bush

'A new era for Australia's media,' was the announcement. Changes drafted by the Liberal–National coalition government led by Malcolm Turnbull, debated in Senate hearings, and finally passed on a party-line vote in September 2017, suggested that the media industry in Australia would be strengthened, media diversity 'enhanced', and local journalism jobs — 'particularly in regional areas' — secured. 'These changes,' Turnbull trumpeted, 'bring Australia's outdated media laws into the 21st century.'[1]

Contemporaneous coverage, analysis, and feedback on the changes were much less celebratory. Generally, the consensus was that the government had squibbed a vital chance for media reform. There was general support for the abolition of rules that had prevented commercial television networks from exceeding 75 per cent of the national audience, but support for abolition of the 'two out of three' rule — whereby media proprietors were barred from owning significant shares in more than two of the three mediums of print, radio, and television in the same market — was tempered by a deep, continuing concern about the provision of news and current affairs coverage in rural and regional Australia. The government made some lacklustre moves to address this by mandating 'higher minimum local content requirements for regional television' should any television interest reach beyond a 75 per cent audience share, and it added a $60 million package for regional and small publishers, and scholarships and cadetships for journalists. This, Turnbull declared bullishly, would 'secure local jobs and make Australia's media industry more competitive'.[2]

This was a bold claim to advance. As discussed in earlier chapters, for the past four years Australia's two biggest print media companies, Fairfax Media and News Limited, had been shedding jobs at an enormous rate: around 1,500 journalists were made redundant in 2012 alone. The brunt of these job losses was initially felt in metropolitan areas; from 2015 on, however, the losses began to spread to rural and regional Australia. Losses at some larger regional dailies, such as the Albury-Wodonga *Border Mail*, the *Bendigo Advertiser*, the Warrnambool *Standard*, and the *Newcastle Herald*, were particularly deep — in the case of the *Newcastle Herald*, reducing overall staffing from more than 100 to just 24. Some smaller outlets, such as the *Cooma-Monaro Express*, which had endured for 135 years through the Depression, both World Wars, the turmoil of the 1980s, and the dotcom crash, were forced to close. The costs of this were acute. As journalism academic Brian McNair put it, readers could access all the national and global news they wanted through major media outlets — via, say, the ABC, CNN, or BBC World. 'But when it comes to how the local mayor is performing, or who is being born and who is dying in the community, or what multinational corporation is trying to get an LNG permit to dig up a neighbourhood beauty spot, we need local journalism to report, investigate, scrutinise, expose. To lose a title such as the *Cooma-Monaro Express* is to lose a central element of the infrastructure of local democracy.' What had been previously regarded as a near wholly metropolitan-based crisis in journalism was in fact nowhere more evident, McNair went on, than in the local and regional sectors.[3]

That crisis has only become more acute in the years since. Between 2008 and 2018, more than 100 local and regional newspaper titles across Australia were closed down; between 2011 and 2019, an estimated 3,000 journalism jobs — around a quarter of those existing in Australia — were cut.[4] In addition to auguring a dramatic shift from the crowded, well-resourced newsroom of old to ones that were much smaller and heavily reliant on outsourcing, these closures and job losses left gaps of coverage that were not filled by the new media outfits that had appeared in Australia — *The Conversation* and *The Saturday Paper*, the local editions of *The Guardian* and *The New York Times* — in the same period. The ACCC noted in 2019 that there were 21 local government areas without coverage from a single local newspaper, creating news deserts, where accountability would be next to non-existent.[5] Sixteen of those news deserts were in regional Australia. None of the new outlets was sufficiently large enough or well-resourced enough to offset job losses.

Then there was COVID-19. Even as people confined to their homes in 2020 discovered a new appetite for news, the lockdowns instituted by the state governments cut a swathe across the news and media industry. With advertising revenue dropping precipitously, commercial media outlets reacted with dramatic austerity: between April and September 2020, for example, News Corp Australia closed 36 of its titles and switched a further 76 from print to digital-only, with the brunt falling most on its local or regional titles; Australian Community Media, publisher of more than 170 titles, suspended publication of 'a number' of its non-daily papers.[6] The US-based *Atlantic* declared that the coronavirus was killing local news, but, given all that had been going on before, a more appropriate description might be that news in rural and regional areas had been killed already: the COVID-19 pandemic was merely burying it.[7]

The city and the country

It has long been a tenet of Australian governance that there has to be equity between the cities and the country. As political scientist Judith Brett has argued, this is an unacknowledged pillar in Australia's polity. There has been an enduring consensus that people who live in the country should be compensated for the costs of remoteness and sparse settlement.[8] As Brett put it: 'Since Federation, an important part of that Australian commitment to equality has been a commitment to regional equality, in keeping Australians' living standards relatively equal across the country, in order to prevent the development of very poor and very rich regions ... Built into the notion of what it was to be an Australian was an idea of certain social entitlements, shared access to basic services, a shared minimum standard of living.'

So enduring has this been that it has not only outlasted other pillars but also many of the instruments set up to deliver regional equality. Work done by the postmaster-general's department in the 1920s and 1930s, providing telegraph and wireless communications to remote areas in Australia, has survived to this day, even after that department was radically reconfigured and then privatised in three tranches: under its universal-service obligations, Telstra remains obliged to ensure that standard telephone services and payphones are reasonably accessible to all people in Australia, on an equitable basis, wherever they work or live.[9]

Broadcasting has been no different. When the forerunner of the ABC was established in 1929, via the two-class regulatory system of A- and B-category licences, the A-category-licence radio stations were obliged to 'extend the facility of broadcasting to places outside the capital cities, especially to distant country listeners'.[10] The replacement of that system in 1932, after passage of the *Australian Broadcasting Commission Act*, saw no change; as postmaster-general James Fenton said, 'Particularly in countries of wide expanses, the cities must contribute more or less to the privileges enjoyed by the rural folk.'[11] Twenty years later, when television broadcasting came onto the government agenda, the Menzies government agreed the ABC should be given responsibility to deliver a television service that would be national, out of a belief that, as media historian Mary Debrett has put it, Australia's 'geography and uneven spread of population' would render a national commercial venture unviable.[12] What would be viable, it was thought, were local or regional ventures. The 1954 royal commission into television declared that 'the commercial broadcasting service is intended to provide substantially a local or regional service on a commercial basis through separate broadcasting stations serving relatively restricted areas'.[13]

But the commercial media providers encountered significant obstacles in making their regional broadcasting efforts into commercially viable operations: for many years,

regional communities in Australia had access to only the
ABC and one local commercial television station, which was
usually sponsored by local radio, newspaper, or business
interests. And although this changed in the 1990s, to the
point that regional communities in Australia had access
to three commercial stations as well as the ABC and SBS,
the vast majority of the 54 regional commercial television
licences existing as of 2016 were controlled by one of three
regional television networks — Prime, WIN, and Southern
Cross. Alleviating cost pressures, those networks take
a substantial amount of their programs directly from a
metropolitan affiliate, with local news, advertising content,
and branding the only real point of differentiation. 'In many
respects, and despite being under independent ownership,'
wrote media scholars Michael Thurlow and Bridget Griffen-
Foley, 'Australia's regional commercial television networks
are little more than slave stations to their metropolitan
masters.'[14]

Those masters have been scathing about their
obligations. In 2016, while appearing before a Senate
committee inquiry into media ownership laws, then Nine
Entertainment Co. CEO Hugh Marks declared there was a
market failure in the provision of local news in rural and
regional Australia.[15] Noting that he was obliged to provide
news and current affairs services in rural and regional
areas, but that his first duty was to 'make sure we return the
best possible amount for our shareholders', Marks argued
it should not be incumbent on commercial broadcasters
to meet that obligation. 'I am not sure that imposing
additional costs on regional broadcasters, whose business
model is already threatened and challenged, will get the
outcome that people might think it would achieve.' He all
but disavowed a business interest in rural and regional
areas unless it was profitable: 'We are [a] content business.

What does adding an acquisition in regional Australia add to ourselves as a content business? I am not sure ... For us, the content business that we run is focused on expanding the number of platforms over which we provide content. The sorts of content we provide, and the business models around which we can monetise that content, are the focus for us as a business.'

Marks's comments might, on first reading, seem unremarkable. As a commercial media provider, Nine obviously has a duty to its shareholders and their demand for a commercial return. But the possibility of a return only exists because Nine has been given access to the scarce broadcasting spectrum that is owned by the public. That access comes with the obligation to provide certain amounts and types of material on that spectrum. This has been a long-understood part of the bargain of television broadcasting. As Menzies-government postmaster-general Charles Davidson said, during the introduction of the first television licences, 'Television stations are in a position to exercise a constant and cumulative effect on public taste and standards of conduct and, because of the influence they can bring to bear on the community, the business interests of licensees must at all times be subordinated to the overriding principle that the possession of a licence is, indeed, as the royal commission said, a public trust for the benefit of all members of our society.'[16]

For Nine, however, that public trust, and the demand for rural and regional material, be damned. Citing the creation of a one-hour news service for six sub-markets in northern NSW, Marks admitted that production of hyper-local content could draw an audience sufficient to earn a return. Nonetheless, Nine's preference was to abrogate entirely the obligations around local content, and to push the responsibility for the provision of this content onto the

ABC: 'Nine believes the ABC, as the public broadcaster, should be a mechanism for addressing what is a market failure.'[17]

The very reason the ABC could be mooted as such a solution is thanks to its construction of national, accessible radio and television broadcasting infrastructure. This has enabled the ABC to reach national audiences *as well as* local audiences, to the point that the ABC has become fundamental to servicing rural and regional Australia. The ABC has argued it is merely obeying its charter, which mandates its broadcast services work within 'national, commercial, and community sectors', and that its programs 'contribute to a sense of national identity and inform and entertain, and reflect the cultural diversity of, the Australian community'.[18] As we have seen, the duelling objectives implicit in these obligations have been both a cause for criticism and an opportunity for the ABC, which has also had to cross-reference these against what commercial competitors are doing, thereby requiring the ABC to take simultaneously a market-failure and market-competitive approach.[19]

But the ABC's activities in rural and remote areas have long been the object of praise. At the opening ceremony for the Australian Broadcasting Commission, in 1932, Country Party leader Earle Page said broadcasting might just be one more luxury for city-dwellers but for those in the bush it was a necessity, 'bringing news which affected the prices of their products'.[20] Contemporary leaders of that party, now known as the Nationals — who work in coalition with sceptical colleagues in the Liberal Party — have been effusive about the ABC and its value to regional and rural areas, particularly in the context of an unreliable commercial media sector. Tim Fischer (leader, 1990–99) was blunt when asked what might happen in the regions if the ABC were ever lost: 'No ABC? Where would we be?'[21] Fischer's successor, John Anderson (1999–2005), was of a similar view while in office: 'The National Party has sought to highlight the importance of the public broadcaster, in terms of its role as a provider of information to people in many parts of this country who do not, for example, have the luxury of being able to order a newspaper to be thrown over the back fence every morning ... We believe that the services offered by the ABC as part of its responsibilities [and] its charter, in rural and regional Australia, are very important.'[22] Warren Truss (2007–16) sang from the same song sheet: 'I think the ABC should have a presence in regional communities that is capable of delivering not just radio news services, but also television news services. That would certainly enrich the variety and the capacity of local communities to be well informed about what is happening in their areas.'[23] Michael McCormack (2018–21) was especially keen: 'I'm a big believer in the ABC, particularly in rural and regional Australia.'[24] Barnaby Joyce (2016–18, 2021–present) made the same point in 2014: 'Obviously, the ABC is an integral part of regional Australia.'[25] The following year, he made the point again: 'ABC regional radio is such an important part of life in the bush.'[26] (As Malcolm Turnbull joked, National and rural Liberal MPs generally have a high regard for everything hosted by people wearing Akubras.)[27]

Interviewed for this book, Darren Chester — the current MP for Gippsland, an independently minded Nationals member, and a former commercial newspaper and TV journalist — said the ABC was best placed to provide local voices and discuss local issues, the need for which had only become more acute since the withdrawal of commercial media from the regions.[28] Adding that the best of the ABC was seen during bushfires, floods, and cyclones, he argued the ABC 'is an important part of the fabric of regional life, and we need it to keep telling our stories in an unbiased and balanced way'. Even for him, at a personal level, the ABC's investment in the regions made his life and job easier. 'It used to be that for me to do a television interview, I would drive eight hours back and forth to Melbourne ... But the ABC has invested heavily in regional studios and has trained staff to provide multimedia content without the need to drive to Melbourne. Places like Sale have the capacity to do live crosses or pre-record interviews for the major city bulletins. As technology improves,' he added, 'I can also do a live cross from anywhere in my electorate, providing I've got a good mobile-phone signal.'

In 2019, the ABC acknowledged that due to the withdrawal of commercial media players it had become the only regional broadcaster in some areas of Australia. The ABC spelled out its efforts to provide news and information services to rural and regional areas. It employed more than 200 journalists (out of a total of 850 employed nationally) located in rural and regional areas, it maintained 47 non-metropolitan offices around the country, its local radio services were capable of reaching 99.58 per cent of the Australian population, and, in addition to establishing a regional division to meet the needs of rural and regional audiences, it had invested some $15.4 million to create content roles spread across the country. It had also increased the percentage of content produced by regional journalists and broadcast on national radio and television, focused on regional issues in news coverage, and, more than any other media outlet, was the biggest provider of local news and current affairs reporting in Australia. 'The ABC's role as a supplier of localised and distinct media content to all Australians, including those in rural and regional areas, has become increasingly important.'[29]

An increasingly important element of the ABC's work

in rural and regional Australia has been as an emergency broadcaster, disseminating official information, warnings, and advice to at-risk communities across the country during bushfires, floods, and other natural disasters. At one level, this has been one of the most praised parts of the ABC's work. In 2008, for example, Victorian state police and emergency services minister Bob Cameron presented ABC Local Radio Victoria with a Meritorious Service Award for its efforts to broadcast crucial information during emergencies — efforts that had become recurring: 'We've gone from a situation where the cricket was interrupted to give bushfire updates,' said Cameron, 'to one where the bushfire coverage is interrupted to give cricket scores!'[30] Similar praise was occasioned after Queensland's Lockyer Valley flooded in 2011: 'The ABC local radio was great at continually informing people about what was happening, where to go, and what not to do,' said Barnaby Joyce.[31] His successor (and, ultimately, predecessor) Michael McCormack would make the same point during the 2019–20 bushfires: 'Particularly in times of crisis, whether it's a flood or fire or drought, you see the ABC at its best. When [a] crisis happens, you can rely on the ABC to provide those updates, not just every hour but almost by the minute, and people rely on that service.'[32]

Apt examples of this pervade the pages of *Black Summer*, a collection of essays and reports by ABC journalists from the 2019–20 bushfires. In one, radio broadcaster Richard Glover writes movingly of taking calls from listeners from up and down NSW. 'They rang the radio station [to offer information], charting the progress of the southerly as it ran up the coast: first Nowra — extremely blustery — then Kiama — less strong — then Wollongong — a further weakening. By 2.45 am I was taking calls from listeners in Penrith, at the foot of the mountains ... A stomach-knotting night ended, a bit after 3 am, with a sigh of relief.' Later, a woman would explain how the information provided by Glover and those callers had given her the space to make decisions. By this time, however, Glover had obtained something of that experience himself: in the studio, he had heard that the fires were encroaching, then surrounding, then engulfing, the area where he and his family owned a mudbrick home.[33] This was not a unique experience: Adelaide ABC reporter Brittany Evins recalled watching from her work desk the fires move closer and closer to her home town, and then driving *toward* the fires to report on their progress.[34] Ipswich-based reporter Baz Ruddick flew to his old home town, Cobargo, which was devastated by the fires, and on the way counted the number of people he knew already whose homes had been razed and livelihoods devastated: 'Nine,' he noted.[35] ABC chief foreign correspondent Philip Williams, on the ground in the coastal town of Eden with cameraman Greg Nelson, saw firsthand the importance the ABC assumed to people fleeing the fires. 'For the next twelve hours,' Williams and Nelson wrote, 'we are the only media reporting from here. Everything we do is being broadcast across the ABC, on TV, radio, and the web. We feel a responsibility to be here, to tell the evacuees' stories, and to help keep them informed.' And while he noted he was not a local in these parts, Williams reiterated that this was not true of his colleagues: 'Our colleagues at ABC Local live here. This is their community. They know these people.'[36]

While the ABC's commitment to a role as an emergency broadcaster is clear, its capacity to be so is not. As academics Julie Freeman, Kristy Hess, and Lisa Waller noted in 2018, diversity and distance across rural and regional Australia and structure and resourcing changes present significant impediments to the ABC's ability to fulfil this role. Uneven radio coverage, a 'digital-first' focus, and the closures of local newsrooms — all, in part, forced by continuing funding cuts — point to a grimmer reality about the ABC's emergency-broadcasting capacities, and underscore a recognition that if we wish for the ABC to be an emergency broadcaster then it has to have the resources to be so.[37]

'Where is the local voice?'

The ABC may be a vital presence in regional and rural Australia, but it is not without critics, nor without its faults. One of the most striking faults, to those accustomed to hearing charges of the ABC's supposed bias toward a 'green left agenda', is a profound difference in its presentation of issues in rural and regional areas. As RMIT professor Lisa Waller said, during a keynote address at the Australian Media Traditions conference, in September 2021, 'Amid all the talk of left-wing bias at the ABC, there is little attention paid to right-wing bias in ABC Rural, which tends to speak to and on behalf of elite rural industries and interests.' An analysis by Waller and fellow academics Emma Mesikämmen and Brian Burkett showed this bias using *Country Hour*, the long-running ABC radio program for rural and regional Australia. Their study confirmed that the program tended to feature few stories about Indigenous peoples and that, when it did, it tended to present Indigenous people in conflict with farmers and drew only on narrow perspectives. *Country Hour* also typically reported favourably on land use that is geared toward commercial outcomes, such as 'improvement', production, and commercialisation, thereby valorising non-Indigenous uses of land and activity.[38]

Cuts to the ABC's funding have also seen the broadcaster make decisions that severely curtail its provision of news and information in rural and regional areas. In 2014, it shed 400 jobs, closed five regional radio stations, reduced the operations of its radio service in Newcastle, and halted production of a dedicated rural- and regional-focused news and current affairs program on Radio National, *Bush Telegraph*. Prompted by continuing, ever-tightening funding constraints in the past seven years, the removal of on-the-ground ABC journalists who work on local stories for broadcast to local audiences has caused considerable anguish, which has been compounded by the crisis within rural and regional commercial media providers: 'Where is the local voice talking to local people about local issues?' asked former ABC regional content director Ray Rigbye. The conclusion, for some, is that the ABC has been too ready or has been forced to cut at its regional and rural services, without due regard for the disproportionate effect that this has on rural and regional communities.

Complicating this withdrawal of resources has been the inequity of digital services. While the ABC has moved to expand online, and offers programming sometimes exclusively through platforms such as iview, the unevenness of access to digital technology in rural and regional Australia has given credence to arguments that the ABC has become over-reliant on digital technology as a substitute for a presence in rural and regional areas. The conclusion fostered by this is that the ABC's outlook is Sydney-centric — and, because of its decisions, ever more so — and misguidedly focused on the cultivation of a 'national identity', to the detriment of the diverse communities and myriad voices that make up Australia.[39]

And yet, if anything, these criticisms underscore the vital importance of a strong, well-funded ABC to the rural and regional areas of Australia. As Tim Fischer said in 2018, 'Regional Australia would be Siberia without the ABC.'[40]

Chapter 9

CLEARING THE BATTLEFIELD
governance, funding, and valuing the ABC

Among the many crises in the ABC's history, one of the most remarkable unfolded just before nine o'clock on the morning of Monday 24 September 2018. ABC chair Justin Milne came to the office of managing director Michelle Guthrie, at ABC headquarters in Ultimo, Sydney, with a letter terminating her employment immediately. The removal of a managing director was hardly unprecedented — as long-time observers are aware, Jonathan Shier left the position with similar abruptness in 2001 — but when Milne followed Guthrie out the door three days later, resigning amid allegations he had compromised the ABC's independence, even the most seasoned observers of the ABC were astonished. The ABC, Jonathan Holmes wrote, had never known a week like it.[1]

The ABC took nearly six months to move on from that turbulent week. It took until February 2019 for a new chair, in Ita Buttrose, to be announced; until March 2019 for Guthrie's unfair dismissal claim to be settled; and until May 2019 for managing director David Anderson to be confirmed in the post (Anderson had been passed over for the position when Guthrie was appointed in 2016 and was appointed managing director in an acting capacity after Guthrie's sacking). In the meantime, the ABC's dirty laundry was well and truly aired, with an array of current and former ABC staff, management, and board members going on the record about the problems that had riven the broadcaster in recent years. They revealed that at the core of the Guthrie and Milne crisis was a struggle over the ABC's future. Amid an imperative for cultural and directional change that would ensure the broadcaster remained relevant in an environment of rapidly changing audiences, technology, and media institutions, the two had set themselves on a collision course. Milne had regarded with apprehension journalistic and operational decisions that might endanger the ABC's relationship with the government and, by extension, the ABC's funding; Guthrie was apparently less willing to compromise on those decisions but was also contending with faltering support from her management team and an agenda being compromised each day by a government making successive cuts to the ABC's funding.

In hindsight, three key issues emerge from this mess that must be remedied if a repeat is to be avoided. The first concerns the governance of the ABC — in particular, the methods of appointment for the ABC board directors and chair, and the roles they must perform. This is an issue that has been raised in the past, but both the Guthrie and Milne imbroglio and the subsequent appointment of Ita Buttrose confirm that it remains a cancer that must be excised. In this chapter, we explore how this might be done.

The second key issue is in funding. As we have seen, funding for the ABC remains a continuing problem. Political scientist Henry Mayer argued in 1980 that this would always be the case, because the broad aims of the broadcaster, the lack of clarity around its priorities, and the inability to effectively judge waste and efficiency made it difficult to see how much money the ABC really needed. 'Endless disputes over funding and the use of funds,' he wrote, 'are built into the system.'[2] Some of these problems were addressed by the *Australian Broadcasting Corporation Act 1983*, which replaced the Australian Broadcasting Commission of which Mayer wrote, but disputes over the levels of funding for the ABC remain endemic. We do not share Mayer's pessimism, however, and thus see several areas where changes may see those disputes averted or settled. These include the length of the funding cycle, the nature of the commitment in that funding cycle, the use of tied funding, and the use of what are effectively efficiency dividends.

The third issue is around the government's interaction and relationship with the ABC. However misplaced it might have been, however inappropriate it was that he allegedly acted on it, Justin Milne's belief the government would be sensitive to decisions made by the ABC underscores just how important it is that government be alive to the impact, perceived and real, of what it says and does. In this chapter, we call on government to adjust its view and recognise that it is a custodian of an institution whose wellbeing should be nurtured, not neutered.

Dispelling the charades

That it is so normalised as to be unremarkable makes it no less egregious that the major political parties regard government-appointed positions as spoils of office. Whether it is the Administrative Appeals Tribunal or the board of the National Archives of Australia, governments of both persuasions have regularly appointed friendly or sympathetic people to these sinecures. The ABC board has been treated less often in this way, but over the past 20 years appointments that are overtly political have become more frequent, to the point that, as one observer put it, 'the ABC board became a political battlefield with obviously partisan appointments from both sides of politics'.[3]

As noted already, most board directors in the 1980s were inclined toward an ideal of stewardship and despite political ties were not partisan in that stewardship. The successive Howard-government appointments of Michael Kroger, Ron Brunton, Janet Albrechtsen, and Keith Windschuttle marked the end of that era, but the Rudd and Gillard governments moved to end this ideological stacking by establishing a formal arms-length, merit-based process for appointments to the ABC board. Under this process, a four-person panel, appointed by the Secretary of the Department of Prime Minister and Cabinet, worked with the Department of Communications to draft selection criteria for board positions, advertised the positions, and solicited interest and applications from candidates. The panel assessed applicants against the selection criteria, which required candidates possess substantial experience in a media or cultural industry, in business or financial management, or in corporate governance. The panel made a recommendation — generally via a shortlist — to the communications minister, who made the final decision by recommending appointments to the governor-general. The appointment of the chair followed a similar process, differing only in that the appointing panel made its report to the prime minister, who was required to consult with the leader of the opposition before making their recommendation to the governor-general.

Yet since the Liberal–National coalition came to power in 2013, this process has been hollowed out, subverted, and bypassed. For while members of the appointing panel have generally been non-partisan, there have been some who have brought an agenda much the same as those on the right wing. Former deputy Liberal Party leader Neil Brown, for example, appointed to the panel in 2014 alongside former ABC board member and trenchant ABC critic Janet Albrechtsen, announced he would search for board directors who would 'contribute' to maintaining balance on the ABC.[4]

Even so, the appointing panel has been regularly bypassed in favour of the old, unilateral system, with the communications minister appointing candidates *not* recommended by the panel. Late in 2015, for example, then communications minister Mitch Fifield appointed two new board directors who had not been recommended by the panel. Independent company director Kirstin Ferguson had applied for one of two vacancies and been assessed by the panel as 'very suitable'. Changing her mind, however, she withdrew her nomination, with the result that she was not subject to further scrutiny and her name did not appear on the list sent to the communications minister. She was persuaded to change her mind again by Albrechtsen, who then suggested her name to the minister's office, and Mitch Fifield duly appointed Ferguson to the board in November 2015 alongside Donny Walford, a leadership coaching executive and non-executive director. Wolford had not been assessed at all by the appointing panel: in what might have been a bumbling homage to Liam Neeson in *Taken*, Fifield declared Walford possessed undisclosed 'requisite skills'.[5] Just over a year later, Fifield made another two appointments: Georgie Somerset, a cattle farmer and 'rural leader' from Queensland, and Vanessa Guthrie (no relation to Michelle Guthrie), then chair of the Minerals Council of Australia. Both had been considered by the panel but with different results: Guthrie's appointment was not recommended, but Somerset's was (there is ambiguity in Somerset's appointment, however: Fifield would subsequently dub her 'one of the minister's recommendations').[6] Again, Fifield cited the possession by both women of 'requisite skills'.[7] Just over a year later, businessman Joseph Gersh was appointed to the ABC board after having been shortlisted, but not ultimately recommended, for appointment: no mention of requisite skills this time.[8] The effect was that, by the time Michelle Guthrie came to her end as ABC managing director, at least four of the seven non-executive directors of the ABC board — Ferguson, Walford, Guthrie, and Gersh — had gained their positions by the fiat of Mitch Fifield. None of the four, moreover, had any media experience.

Then there was the appointment of the chair. When Jim Spigelman's term as chair expired in 2017, the panel apparently recommended to prime minister Malcolm Turnbull that an old acquaintance and friend, in Justin Milne — then best known for his career with Telstra and OzEmail — be appointed. Milne was confident there was no potential of a collision between his relationship with Turnbull and his new job: there would be 'zero impact', he said.[9] All too soon, it turned out Milne was doing all he could to keep that declaration true. As he was to say later, no one had told him he was to be a wall against which the government might bash its fists: 'I think more likely what I am to be is a conduit.'

In the weeks following the exits of Guthrie and Milne, the role of the board was scrutinised. A Senate report into the matter was critical of the board's failure to inquire into the causes of tensions between Milne and Guthrie, and its decision to persist with Guthrie's sacking despite its knowledge of allegations of Milne's interference. But it was also damning of the government's repeated bypassing of the appointing panel.[10]

This is one area where a change is clearly warranted.

Janet Albrechtsen resigned from the panel in 2016 in frustration at the 'parameters that hindered the search for the smartest, most capable person', and in the following year Neil Brown stepped down as well.[11] Brown made public his disquiet at the appointments process, disputing (for example) that Milne's appointment as chair had been 'recommended' by the panel. He noted Milne had been only one of five people, and assessed as qualified only: 'That is not the same as a recommendation.' Further, Brown asserted Donny Walford's appointment 'came from nowhere', and that Walford's name was not on the list of nominated candidates. The decision to appoint Walford, then, was 'a clear breach of any recognition of the panel process being of any value whatsoever. In all of those cases,' Brown went on, 'the minister is holding up a figleaf in what is a government directive to appoint individuals, using the charade of going through the nominations panel process.'[12]

The repeated bypassing of a formal process — which, it should be stated, the government has denied — has two effects. The first is to discourage potential well-credentialled and worthy applicants from ever putting their names forward for consideration. Why waste the time and effort of undergoing the scrutiny of the process when it has been repeatedly shown to be of little to no value to the minister ultimately in charge of making the decisions?

Second, the repeated bypassing of the appointment process weakens the legitimacy of the board. All of those appointed by Fifield would probably cavil at suggestions that theirs was a partisan appointment or a stack. But the whiff of patronage is not easily dispelled. Transparency around the appointments process is the best way to do so. For appointees and public trust in the ABC, we believe it would be best if the option to override the panel were removed or, at very least, eschewed in all but the most exceptional of circumstances.

There has since been some evidence to suggest the government is mindful of the importance of the formal appointments process but, dishearteningly, also evidence that it remains too willing to override that process as expediency and opportunity arise. Ita Buttrose was chosen as the ABC's new chair by Scott Morrison, whose obligatory 'consultation' with opposition leader Bill Shorten was as cursory as Fifield's explanations and occurred only shortly before Buttrose's appointment was announced. At the time, Morrison trumpeted Buttrose's name recognition and considerable media experience. No one could deny the truth of either, but there was no getting around the plain fact that Buttrose had not applied for the job: 'I was busy doing other things,' she said later.[13] Though the prime minister's press release tried to imply otherwise — 'The Government has followed the legislative process for making this appointment, including considering the report of the independent nomination panel' — journalists quickly confirmed she had not been recommended by that panel, which after a search costing $160,000 had in fact recommended Greg Hywood (former chief executive of Fairfax Media), Kim Williams (former chief executive of News Limited), and Ian Robertson (national managing partner of law firm Holding Redlich).[14] Even if the result is a good one, the overriding of a legitimate process should be rejected.

Appointments to the board since have followed the formal process more closely, but simple, fruitful changes in approach — such as consultation with the ABC board itself about the skills and experience that might, in the interests of diversity, prove useful — have not been adopted. In September 2019, the government reappointed existing board member Peter Lewis to a second term; in 2021, after a period in which the board's ability to find a quorum was threatened by three resignations, communications minister Paul Fletcher appointed three new non-executive directors.[15] The first, Mario D'Orazio, was a veteran former journalist and executive of Channel Seven Perth who had been appointed to the board of Australia Post by then finance minister Mathias Cormann in 2019; the second, Peter Tonagh, was a former senior executive of News Corp Australia and had conducted an efficiency review into the ABC in 2018. Fiona Balfour, the third new director, was a former executive in information technology. No one could quibble with the qualifications and experience of each appointee, but there remained problems: Balfour was not recommended by the panel, and it was not known whether she even applied for the job. Who might have applied and, because of Balfour's appointment, missed out, remains unknown. Journalist Margaret Simons, a long-time critic of the process around board appointments, put the result forthrightly:

> The board is underweight in public and community sector experience more broadly. It remains light on journalistic experience, and overweight with conventional commercial corporate board experience. It lacks anyone with a practitioner's understanding of the arts, science, or academia. In other words, a lot is still wrong with the ABC board.[16]

Breaking the cycle

The ABC's negotiations for government funding have long involved rigorous preparation of budgets and strategic corporate plans; indeed, since 2013, the ABC has been required to prepare a corporate plan, budget estimates, and annual performance and financial statements, and has been subject to audits by the Commonwealth auditor-general.

Appropriations are made for a purpose best understood as a general summary of the ABC's chartered functions — in 2019–20, the federal government, through the Department of Communications and the Arts, made an appropriation to the ABC for a single outcome: 'Informed, educated, and entertained audiences — throughout Australia and overseas — through innovative and comprehensive media and related services'.[17]

The lack of detail about the appropriation is partly the result of there being no prescribed interpretation of the ABC's charter and a degree of independence that, in the long term, has obliged government to refrain from making directions to the ABC about its operations and spending. The responsible minister may direct the ABC to broadcast certain material, but this is a highly circumscribed and rarely used power. In general, the ABC has the independence to make decisions about how it spends appropriations, and it enjoys significant freedom when making programming decisions — albeit subject to legislative restrictions and regulations, particularly about programming requirements contained in its charter.

Yet the nature of ABC funding raises unavoidable tensions. Government has no part to play in the ABC's programming decisions, but via the budget allocations it shapes the context in which the ABC makes those and other decisions.[18] One facet of that involvement has been in the use of a three-year funding cycle. Triennial-based funding, instead of a year-by-year appropriation, was a goal of the ABC since the late 1940s and was eventually introduced in 1988 by the Hawke government amid the 'eight cents a day' funding campaign led by then ABC chair David Hill. The argument for triennial-based funding was that it improved the ABC's ability to make longer-term strategic decisions and deal with long lead times on television and radio productions. This key point has, time and again, been underscored by the ABC and external parties: triennial-based funding, argued Bob Mansfield in his 1997 review, offered the ABC certainty and direction, particularly as new technologies proliferated and investment in those technologies emerged as an imperative; ABC managing director Mark Scott extended the point in 2014 by noting that it allowed the ABC to enter into multi-year contracts and to make key planning decisions.[19] Plainly, there is a broad consensus that the three-year cycle of ABC funding has been for the better. But there is now increasing evidence that it may be appropriate to move from a three-year to a five-year cycle. The ABC has urged this change, a Senate inquiry has recommended it, and the Labor Party recently adopted it as policy.[20]

There are two good reasons for this. The first is to improve the ABC's ability to make long-term plans. As audience habits evolve and technological change continues to dramatically reshape the media landscape, the ABC would benefit from a longer planning term than a mere three years. The ABC espoused this view in its 2020–25 strategic plan, published in June 2020, which stressed the variables in play as it outlined how it would meet its charter obligations in the future. A three-year funding cycle was simply not long enough anymore, it argued: 'The Corporation can't forecast its long-term funding position because it operates within a three-year Budget appropriation.'[21] Aligning a five-year strategic plan — a timeframe widely used in business — with a five-year funding arrangement would better allow the ABC to invest in the infrastructure, resources, and programming that will enable it to remain a relevant and efficient organisation.

The second reason is to remove the ABC's triennial funding from the immediate heat of the three-year electoral cycle. During any and every election campaign, the main political parties jostle over whether they will increase, maintain, or cut ABC funding should they soon be sitting on the government benches. In the past, this has been open to gamesmanship, as has been discussed in earlier chapters concerning the 1996 and 2013 Liberal election campaigns.

Fights over election promises, and the various claims and counterclaims about cuts and funding, have made resourcing of the ABC a political football. It is not necessarily a problem that the ABC's reporting attracts heat — that's an inevitable result of good journalism — but the cut and thrust of threats around ABC resourcing is: it undermines the ABC's independence and risks making it a party-political plaything.[22] By extending the ABC's funding cycle from three years to five, it may be possible to distance the ABC from immediate political heat — a key point in safeguarding its independence.[23]

Another element ripe for change stems from the advent of that three-year funding cycle. When the Hawke government first agreed to move funding decisions to a triennial basis, one part of the agreement was that government would 'index and maintain the real value' of funding each year.[24] While there was no legal contract nor multi-year appropriation, there was a 'compact or understanding' (as a senior Department of Finance official put it, in 1997) about the level of funding.[25] Thus the cash figure of each yearly appropriation would be indexed according to an appropriate indicator, generally inflation, so as to preserve what Gareth Evans, as communications minister when that first triennial funding agreement was struck, called a 'real rate of return' on the sums agreed to at the start of the triennial.[26] On occasion, this has meant real funding for the ABC has decreased in the second or third year of the cycle: in 1989, for example, inflation turned out to be higher than forecast and the 1988–89 appropriation was slightly down on the previous year's in real terms. What is important to note is the good-faith element — in particular, the agreement that funding should retain its real value over the three-year cycle.

In May 2018, the Turnbull government announced it would freeze the indexation of the ABC's operational budget for the 2019–22 triennial period. Though presented as yet another reprieve for the ABC — on grounds it would be 'exempt from the government-wide efficiency dividend' — it was nothing of the sort. The money saved by the government, at $83.7 million, was a cut to the ABC, an efficiency dividend by another name, and it smelled just as sour. The government explicitly said the freeze in indexation was to 'ensure the ABC continues to find back-office efficiencies'; for good measure, it simultaneously announced yet another efficiency review. 'This will maintain the ABC's significant base operational funding at 2018–19 levels,' said communications minister Mitch Fifield, making clear it was a cut.[27] The government also admitted in its Portfolio Budget Statements that the indexation freeze — applied to the ABC's general operational revenue and not to its transmission appropriation — 'reduces funding to the ABC by $14.623m in 2019–20; $27.843m in 2020–21; and $41.284m in 2021–22'.[28]

The freeze and the totality of these cuts should belie any suggestion — as Fifield's successor, Paul Fletcher, gamely attempted — that the ABC is the recipient of 'stable' funding, with a budget that is 'secure'.[29] It is self-evidently not the case if a long-running principle of the triennial funding arrangements can be so breezily swept aside. In addition to extending the funding cycle from three to five years, governments of the future should honour their commitments and fund the ABC using the indicator that would maintain the real value of the agreed appropriation.

Next, government involvement in decisions around resourcing via the use of tied funding — that is, an appropriation, generally a one-off or short-term allocation, for specific projects and initiatives — should cease. Tied funding may sound benign, but its repeated use in the past two decades has normalised interference in what are at heart decisions that should be made by the ABC without involvement from government. In 2000, for example, after repeated rebuffs of requests for increased funding, the ABC board requested an additional $160 million that it said would be used for the conversion to digital television and for additional regional programming and Australian content. Responding, then communications minister Richard Alston requested new arrangements for accountability in the ABC, including annual meetings between the board and minister for performance reviews, ratings targets for programming, and the establishment of a 'monitoring unit' to apparently enhance editorial responsibility. When the prospect of this quid pro quo became public, it was immediately denounced and labelled for what it was. Then ABC managing director Brian Johns pointed out that Alston's proposals were an interference in the ABC's operations, and that funds must be spent as the ABC, not the government, saw fit.[30]

Failing to heed this point, Johns's successor, Jonathan Shier, submitted a request for $37 million in additional funding in 2001–02 and specifically tied it to 'programming and content initiatives of national significance', especially for better services for rural and regional Australia, involvement in new media, children's programs, and interactive material meant for schools. As ABC historian Ken Inglis would write, this was an unusual proposal: 'A statutory authority supposedly in control of its own budget was asking for a measure of tied aid.'[31] While the $17.8 million eventually provided to the 'National Interest Initiative', as it became known, eased some internal financial pressure for the ABC, it also set a precedent, whereby ABC projects and initiatives might only be funded if the government thought those projects and initiatives worthy. For even though Shier protested that the ABC was free to decide for itself how that money should be spent, government budget papers made clear where the money would go: 'the largest component of these funds will be applied to regional and rural programs' — i.e. to rural and regional areas where the government, ahead of the 2001 election, was vulnerable. Auditors, moreover, were there to make sure of it, just as they were when Shier's successor, Russell Balding, sought a renewal of the initiative in 2004 in the face of a continued refusal on the part of the Howard government to increase the ABC's triennial funding. Both the National Interest Initiative and the Rudd government's Children's Channel and Drama Funding Initiative, which provided $136.4 million over three years to develop a digital children's channel, may certainly be seen as valuable, worthwhile, and intrinsic to the ABC's work. But the provision of money for these projects based on approval for the projects by the government of the day is an encroachment on the ABC's independence.

The same point may be made about the Enhanced News Services initiative, included in the Gillard government's 2013–14 budget, which provided $20 million per year, over three years, to bolster the ABC's local and regional news gathering services, including the establishment of new bureaus, state-based digital news services, live-linking capacities in the regions, and the ABC's national reporting team and ABC Fact Check.[32] All were valuable uses of public money — core, it might be said, to what the ABC should be doing. But the use of this tied funding forced the ABC to make priorities of initiatives that were potentially not as pressing or as worthwhile as others; it made the ABC's work in this area captive to the caprice of government. Thus, when the Turnbull government settled the ABC's funding for the 2016–19 triennial period, in 2016, it rebuffed a request from the ABC for $30 million to expand its news operations in rural Australia. The government preferred to keep control, which it did by instead renewing the Enhanced News Services funding for another three years, on the grounds that in doing so it would 'support local news and current affairs services, particularly services located outside of capital cities'. A measure of that support, of course, might be gleaned from the drastically reduced funding for the initiative — it was cut by a third — while the craven decision-making and spin of the Morrison government are amply evident in the line it sold in 2019, when the next triennial of ABC funding was settled: the renewal of the Enhanced News Services initiative, at $43.7 million over three years, was presented as 'new' funding, a 'reprieve' for the ABC, and 'additional funding', when it was so only in the context of being *renewed*.[33]

Our conclusion is simple: the use of tied funding should stop.[34] The ABC should be given sufficient resources within the normal budget appropriations to attend to its core tasks and should have the freedom to decide the manner in which it does so. It should not have core tasks held hostage in the way that tied funding allows.[35]

Finally, a repeated claim of the present government has been that the ABC has not been subject to an efficiency dividend — a slight reduction, generally of 1–2 per cent, in yearly funding, supposedly to encourage government agencies to find savings. An increasingly common tool of the federal government, the efficiency dividend can be effective thanks to its predictability and near-universal applicability; it can also be a blunt instrument for agencies with significant non-discretionary costs.[36] The current government has instituted efficiency dividends of varying percentages for the past eight years, yet it has always denied subjecting the ABC to one. 'Commentators on this issue [of cuts to the ABC],' declared Paul Fletcher, airily, 'often fail to acknowledge that the ABC has been subject to the government-wide efficiency dividend since it was instituted, apart from one-off dividends in 1987–88 and 1996–97'.[37]

To this, one might point out that Fletcher fails in his own acknowledgement of what is plainly obvious. Having in 2013 promised there would be no cuts to the ABC, the Abbott government in its first budget, in May 2014, announced the ABC's funding would be cut by about 1 per cent — or $35.5 million over four years — as a 'down payment' on the results of an efficiency review it had commissioned four months before. In its Mid-Year Economic and Fiscal Outlook (MYEFO) update in November that same year, the government announced another cut of $254 million, spread over five years — or around 5 per cent of ABC funding — and again declared this would be achieved through efficiencies.[38] As we have discussed already, the $83.7 million cut delivered by the indexation freeze in 2018 was similarly framed around the ABC finding efficiencies.

The wilful denials by government ministers that the ABC has been exempt from efficiency dividends thus should be called out for what they are. The nature of the cuts made in the budget of 2014, in the MYEFO statement of November 2014, and in the indexation freeze of 2018, and the explanations of what each was supposed to achieve, is only too apparent. Rather than engage in obtuse denials of reality, government ministers today should have the courage to admit publicly what Tony Abbott and Mathias Cormann have each admitted: that these cuts were efficiency dividends.[39]

'Acid in the face'

'I feel disrespected,' Ita Buttrose said, late in 2020.[40] The cause for her feeling was the repeated leaking or publication of government correspondence with the ABC.[41] The first occasion had been in March: a letter sent by Paul Fletcher urging the ABC to consider selling its offices in Ultimo and Southbank made its way first to *The Sydney Morning Herald*.[42] Another Fletcher letter, meant for Buttrose and centring on the ABC's *Four Corners*, somehow made its way into a tweet that Fletcher posted before Buttrose had read it.[43] That same day, questions on the same topic that the government had supposedly sent the ABC were leaked to *The Australian*, which the next day included an article on the questions and the 'news' that the questions had been asked. The only issue, as the ABC pointed out, was that it had not yet received the questions: 'They appear to have been sent to *The Australian* first.'[44]

The lack of common courtesy here is glaring, and it speaks to the troubling disregard the government has for the ABC. It is one thing to believe the ABC can make do with less money, to think the processes for making board and chair appointments flawed, and to be angered by the ABC's journalism — whether for its criticism, its needling questions, or its mistakes.[45] It is another thing altogether to be as disrespectful and insulting as the government repeatedly has been about the ABC. It is a further step again to regard the ABC, as Darren Chester said many of his colleagues do, as 'the enemy'.[46] Whether or not it excites the Liberal and National Party 'base' to beat up on the ABC, as coalition insiders told Laura Tingle it did, should be immaterial, for this disregard feeds into behaviour more serious than the leaking of some correspondence.[47] Suddenly, it becomes legitimate to attempt to interfere in the

ABC's statutory independence, to question the patriotism of ABC employees, and to browbeat and harangue officials of an organisation with very limited means of responding.

As Buttrose has noted, criticism about the role of the public broadcaster has 'gone up a notch' in recent years, with accusations that the ABC pushes agendas, campaigns against private enterprise, and pursues partisan attacks.[48] It is in and of itself not wrong to be critical of the ABC, but the rhetoric around that criticism has become inflammatory, and spread far beyond the government. From Tony Abbott's question of whose side the ABC was on, to Liberal luminary Michael Kroger's claim that various ABC news programs are 'like political acid in the face of the Liberal Party', to *The Australian* editorialising (in the context of discussing ABC reporters Louise Milligan and Sally Neighbour) that 'the greatest enemy of truth is those who conspire to lie', the direction of the criticism and rhetoric is clear.[49]

Five years ago, *Quadrant* online editor Roger Franklin declared that it would have been better had a terrorist bombing in Manchester taken place instead in the ABC studio where an episode of *Q&A* was being recorded. Franklin was roundly criticised and his article — after a short-lived defence and hurried edit by the magazine — was eventually deleted.[50] It takes a special kind of licence to believe that it is acceptable to publicly imagine the death of a particular person (as Franklin did for one panellist, speculating about his state of mind as 'shrapnel of nuts, bolts, and nails' entered his body) and a particularly distasteful regard for the ABC and those working for it to declare, as Franklin did, that none of the likely casualties 'would have represented the slightest reduction in humanity's intelligence, decency, empathy, or honesty'.[51] It takes a similar kind of licence to not only retain such a person as the 'online editor' of your publication afterward, but also to allow them, in your pages, to continue for years thereafter to lecture the ABC on decency, civility, and morality in civic discourse.[52]

It's worth reflecting, too, if only briefly here, on the impact that the continual barrage of abuse and the relentless pressure from governments might have on those who work for the ABC. Ita Buttrose has worked for domineering media moguls like Kerry Packer in the past and yet even she seems to have been taken aback by how politicians interact with the ABC. A bemused Marie Mohr, less than a week into working as a supervising producer on *The 7.30 Report*, said to Kerry O'Brien, 'In twenty years at Ten, Nine, and Seven, I've never had a single accusation of bias. I'm here three days and suddenly I'm a biased Labor bitch. I want to know how you've managed to indoctrinate me in three days without me even knowing.'[53] Do ABC journalists simply absorb the heat and go on to the next story, or do they harbour resentment? If it is the latter, how does that show up in their work? Is there animus in their reports about their critics? As we said in chapter six, there is no evidence of serious or systemic bias in the ABC's journalism, but it is counterintuitive to conclude that the pressures and attacks have had no impact at all.

Take the 2021 program *Exposed: The Ghost Train Fire*, about which a good deal has been written, alleging inaccuracies and a campaign to undermine the reputation of former NSW Labor premier Neville Wran. The ABC commissioned an independent review, which was conducted by leading former ABC journalist Chris Masters and political scientist Professor Rodney Tiffen. They concluded that two-and-a-half parts of the three-part series were excellent journalism but that the final section of the third part made uncorroborated allegations about Wran. What was concerning was that instead of accepting the praise of two respected reviewers, acknowledging the need to improve editorial processes, and apologising for any inaccuracies and hurt caused, the ABC News, Analysis, and Investigation division responded with a rare, prickly defensiveness, which Tiffen described as more befitting a 'spin doctor than a news editor'.[54] The ABC also asked that the final report omit a finding that the program had failed to meet its editorial standards. In light of these reactions, Masters later said 'there was a formal endorsement' of what he termed 'lesser standards'.[55] It is only one example, of course, but the episode brought to mind the old adage: if you beat a dog all day, don't be surprised if it turns around and bites you.

That's not a response that will do anyone much good, but the ABC's wariness about replying to its critics does not appear to much help its journalists. It certainly does not help the public appreciate the level or impact of pressure and hostility directed at the ABC. What could help is a greater openness from the public broadcaster about the bullying and pressure that it has been subject to. Resigning as the ABC's news director in 2021, Gaven Morris talked of 'taking the arrows' from people trying to influence the ABC one way or the other, of putting on a 'shell' and protecting the people in the news division from even the knowledge of the phone calls that he received. It sounds noble — and it is. But it also has the effect of allowing the ABC's critics to continue regarding it as 'that puny kid in the playground, easy to bash up'.[56]

There is evidence now that the ABC understands this point, as do its journalists, and is increasingly willing to make clear to the public what is being done to it and why. Compare the statements made by Justin Milne during his time as ABC chair with those of current chair Ita Buttrose. During his time as chair, Milne preferred not to make criticisms of the government. In 2018, for example, he dismissed arguments about bias, errors, and budget cuts as unimportant compared with the ABC's digital future.[57] The only public statements that might be seen as critical came in 2017, when the government demanded the ABC disclose the names and salaries of employees earning above $200,000. Milne compromised on some points, stressed that privacy should be protected, but shrugged that, ultimately, pursuing it further was 'for the Parliament to decide'.[58] Buttrose's approach has been the opposite. She has highlighted attempts at editorial and governmental interference, cut through government folderol about the cuts it has delivered to the ABC's budget, and called out disingenuous reporting of the ABC. During an attempt by government senator Andrew Bragg late in 2021 to launch a Senate inquiry into the ABC's complaints-handling process, which would have run in parallel to an existing internal ABC inquiry, Buttrose was quick to call it out as a 'partisan political exercise'; the resultant outcry saw the inquiry dropped.[59] 'As ABC chair,' she said, in 2019, 'I will fight any attempts to muzzle the national broadcaster or interfere with its obligations to the Australian public. Independence is not exercised by degrees. It is absolute.'[60]

At its core, Buttrose's advocacy is a plea for the government to respect the ABC. It may feel quaint to call for this. But respect is fundamental to any working relationship, and if the members of the Liberal–National government who profess to venerate the contributions of Western civilisation should do anything, it should be to lift their gaze beyond their own short-term self-interest and recognise that they are custodians of office only, holding power for a passing time, and that they have a responsibility to pass on to their successors a country and government that are better off than they inherited. This includes this country's institutions, and it includes the ABC.

Chapter 10

WHO NEEDS THE ABC?

We began this book by asking you to imagine the world without the ABC. Now, let's ask: what does the coalition government want for it? In their ideal world, what would they like the ABC to do and not?

From various public remarks, news reports, and the raft of complaints traced in this book, we can venture a few ideas. One thing the government does not want from the ABC is for its comedians to be calling people 'cunts'.[1] We know the government doesn't want the ABC to use the phrase 'Invasion Day'.[2] We know the government didn't want the date of the Hottest 100 changed and indeed would probably prefer it go back to where it came from, so to speak — 26 January.[3] It wants the ABC to do more 'public-interest journalism', but not if it concerns allegations Australian troops killed unarmed men and children in Afghanistan, not if it concerns the affairs of government ministers, and definitely not if it concerns conspiracy-peddling friends who might have the ear of the prime minister. It does not want the ABC to ask about women in the Liberal–National Party ranks, nor utter the words 'climate change' and 'policy' in the same sentence; if anything, in fact, it would like the ABC to devote its investigative zeal to the problems of green energy.[4] It wants the ABC to have the highest editorial standards, but it does not necessarily mind lying to the ABC: 'Misleading the ABC,' said Tony Abbott in 2003, 'is not quite the same as misleading the Parliament as a political crime.'[5] As for *Q&A*, many government MPs would prefer to see it taken off air.

What does the government want for it? The government wants the ABC to be content with what they get. 'Everyone has to live within their means, including the ABC,' said Scott Morrison in 2018.[6] It does not want the ABC to respond to funding cuts by cutting programs: 'That would be cowardly,' declared Malcolm Turnbull. Nor by closing bureaus: 'A deliberate act of political vandalism,' Christopher Pyne said, of plans to close an office in his electorate.[7] It certainly does not want public campaigns about cuts, which senator James Paterson dubbed 'clumsy attempt[s] at political blackmail'.[8]

In 2018, Morrison scoffed at the idea of more ABC funding, and suggested with a hint of menace that those in the ABC pressing for more should be ashamed: 'They've been getting a free ride.'[9] According to the prime minister, the safest place for journalists to work is the ABC, precisely because it is government-funded.[10] Therefore, setting aside that ABC journalists are berated in a way that those at other news organisations are not, the government seems to have neither the time nor the inclination for questions about the manner in which it provides for the ABC. It would rather employees of the national broadcaster assumed a position of gratitude, said thank you, and went on their way.

We have seen that a good chunk of MPs in government, if given their own way, would like to see the ABC privatised. Others would prefer it downsized, made into a market-failure broadcaster only, with a charter that keeps it on a tight leash. A select few would prefer its ambit remain much as it is, though with a dramatically recalibrated understanding of 'objectivity'. To Tony Abbott, that would include 'some basic affection for the home team', an unwillingness to 'leap to be critical of your own country', and an openness to extending 'the benefit of the doubt' to government and the military.[11] To Malcolm Turnbull, this new objectivity — while not prompted by any problem of left-wing bias, he claimed — would include 'genuinely accurate and impartial' coverage, in which the ABC would rise above the fray.[12]

The more ABC-friendly in government think it should be more positive. Darren Chester told us that the ABC had a 'negative view of Australian culture and society', that it 'talks the country down a bit'. It should reconsider, he said. For a story on disadvantage in Indigenous communities, why not a 'more constructive' story about the solutions? Rural and regional communities were interested in lots of issues — sustainable jobs, natural-resource management, agriculture, transport. 'But we rarely hear positive stories or analysis of these topics.'[13] The ABC, in this thinking, should be much like its old nickname, Aunty: cheery, benign, inoffensive.

The more transactional think that the money government provides means the ABC should take direction from government. They have little time for niceties like editorial independence. 'We have to pay for you,' said Barnaby Joyce, when an ABC journalist pushed back on suggestions they should cover a particular story. 'And, you know, that's a substantive part of the budget.'[14]

Similarly, some in government think the ABC needs to be more responsive to complaints, and to reach out more: to find the mythical 'right-wing Philip Adams' and put them on air, preferably in prime time and on a prominent station. After all, one conservative commentator told Jonathan

Holmes, audiences on the right did not think anything on the ABC resonated with them. Which made them angry. 'They just don't see why they should go on paying for it,' remarked Holmes.[15]

From the energising effect of this anger, and the government's self-interest in fanning it in order to unite supporters in opposition to a common foe, it seems fair to surmise that the government, at the root of all its talk about bias and standards and funding security, would really like for Aunty to be Aunt Sally: a target for sticks and stones that never dodges or fights back, but stands, fixed in place, smiling and silent.

Leaders of the major media organisations in Australia doubtless have their own desires. Some would prefer the ABC continue to develop talent and content that they can poach. Others, aggrieved by a belief that they are shouldering unprofitable obligations, would prefer the ABC were given sole carriage of areas that they no longer have an interest in, like children's programming or rural and regional content. More, contending with a difficult and turbulent business environment, would prefer that the ABC were overhauled and constrained by legislation from doing anything that might duplicate what the commercial media does already.

The profit motive is conspicuous in all, but a particular ideological strand also infects these desires. When *The Australian*'s Paul Kelly argued that 'politics defines the market position of a media organisation', he was referring to the supposed hoax of an impartial public broadcaster in the modern era.[16] But Kelly could also have been writing about the organisation for which he has worked the better part of his journalistic career. To adopt his view of a politically defined media market is to see that News Corp Australia's newspapers and television broadcasts are positioned to cater to that right-wing audience to which Holmes referred, to attract subscription dollars and advertising revenue. There is a rampant ideological and commercial self-interest, then, in having the ABC to beat up — even on the most spurious of grounds.[17]

Where this leaves the ABC is at a buffeted intersection of criticism that is political, ideological, and commercial in nature: in effect, as one front in a broader culture war that ranges from the universities to the arts to the social welfare sector. It is an invidious place to be. The point of a culture war is never to vanquish the target of criticism. Culture wars, like those on terror or drugs or poverty, are never won, never declared over. They only exist to create and foster new lines of division.

We do not believe the ABC should be a player in that culture war, and in this book we have attempted to articulate its importance at a time when its role is much contested. We have tried to sketch the debate that surrounds the ABC and set out the context for much of the criticism that is made of the public broadcaster. We have explained the faults in much of that criticism, particularly in its lack of rigour and all too often its bad faith. We have pointed to several areas where we believe the case for the continuation of a thriving public broadcaster in Australia is clear, while acknowledging areas for improvement. And we have offered several solutions that might ameliorate the ABC's current circumstances.

These solutions are, at one level, technocratic. But to leave them to be implemented by technocrats and our elected representatives would be a mistake. The ABC's future is reliant less on the Liberal–National coalition and the Labor Party than it is on us. The ABC is a national institution that belongs to each of us, and its future should be of concern to all of us.

The impetus for enacting the solutions we have offered, and maintaining the future health of the ABC, must come from the public. It is not enough to talk about the ABC's future every few years when its triennial funding comes up for renewal. It is not enough to talk about it only when parliament is dissolved and political parties begin making election promises. What is required is our attention and our work to change the environment in which the ABC is discussed and treated: to set the climate for those triennial funding talks, to force the parties to listen to the broad public rather than to their party memberships. What is required is for the public to press and push and cajole and lobby and agitate for change in the way that the ABC is treated, so that the nature of its contribution to this country and its continuing value in contemporary life is understood — and continuously improved.

In 2007, when the ABC turned 75, *The Sydney Morning Herald* asked what Australia would look like without the ABC: 'You can imagine *an* Australia but not this Australia.' Let's reverse that question, too. Imagine the ABC if its funding had not been cut, if its governance had not been so politicised, if its journalism had not been so subject to self-interested attack, if it had not been sucked into the culture wars. Imagine if its role had been celebrated and championed instead of dismissed and damned. What would that look like?

It is possible to envision an ABC that is vibrant, relevant, and confident, producing and broadcasting programs of world-class quality, in a variety of forms, appealing to all comers; that is engaged with Australian life and culture; that explores with a liberal, adventurous spirit what might be possible. It is possible, too, to envision a world where both government and the ABC acknowledge the inherent tension in their relationship but act with respect for the institutions they each embody. It is possible, in short, to envision a national broadcaster of which we all are proud, and which continues to make an invaluable contribution to the life of this country.

Thus, as the ABC nears its 90th birthday and moves toward its centenary in 2032, we offer this answer to the titular question of this book: *Who needs the ABC?* We all do.

Appendix A

ABC CHARTER

The ABC in its modern iteration was established by the *Australian Broadcasting Corporation Act 1983*. Section six of that act (as amended to accommodate technological and institutional developments in the four decades since) describes the continuing functions and responsibilities of the ABC — that is, the ABC charter, which follows here:

Charter of the Corporation

(1) The functions of the Corporation are:
   (a) to provide within Australia innovative and comprehensive broadcasting services of a high standard as part of the Australian broadcasting system consisting of national, commercial and community sectors and, without limiting the generality of the foregoing, to provide:
      (i) broadcasting programs that contribute to a sense of national identity and inform and entertain, and reflect the cultural diversity of, the Australian community; and
      (ii) broadcasting programs of an educational nature;

(b) to transmit to countries outside Australia
broadcasting programs of news, current affairs,
entertainment and cultural enrichment that will:
>   (i) encourage awareness of Australia and an
>   international understanding of Australian attitudes
>   on world affairs; and
>   (ii) enable Australian citizens living or travelling
>   outside Australia to obtain information about
>   Australian affairs and Australian attitudes on world
>   affairs; and;

(ba) to provide digital media services; and

(c) to encourage and promote the musical, dramatic and
other performing arts in Australia.

(2) In the provision by the Corporation of its broadcasting
services within Australia:
>   (a) the Corporation shall take account of:
>   >   (i) the broadcasting services provided by the
>   >   commercial and community sectors of the
>   >   Australian broadcasting system;
>   >   (ii) the standards from time to time determined by
>   >   the ACMA in respect of broadcasting services;
>   >   (iii) the responsibility of the Corporation as the
>   >   provider of an independent national broadcasting
>   >   service to provide a balance between broadcasting
>   >   programs of wide appeal and specialized
>   >   broadcasting programs;
>   >   (iv) the multicultural character of the Australian
>   >   community; and
>   >   (v) in connection with the provision of broadcasting
>   >   programs of an educational nature — the
>   >   responsibilities of the States in relation to education;
>   >   and

(b) the Corporation shall take all such measures,
being measures consistent with the obligations of the
Corporation under paragraph (a), as, in the opinion of
the Board, will be conducive to the full development by
the Corporation of suitable broadcasting programs.

(3) The functions of the Corporation under subsection
(1) and the duties imposed on the Corporation under
subsection (2) constitute the Charter of the Corporation.

(4) Nothing in this section shall be taken to impose on the
Corporation a duty that is enforceable by proceedings in a
court.

Appendix B

ABC OPERATIONAL FUNDING DATA, 1983–2022
by Michael Ward[1]

When the ABC's budget is mentioned in public discussion, it is common to hear statements like this from the communications minister, Paul Fletcher: 'The ABC receives more than $1 billion of Government funding every year.'[2]

The implication is that the ABC is well funded, and that its budget is increasing. However, to understand the real story of ABC funding, we need to analyse it over time. Historical assessment of ABC funding is complicated by its different components (operational, one-off capital grants, capital user charges, short-term, and specific contracts) and by funding for distribution and transmission. At almost $200 million annually, the latter accounts for around 20 per cent of the ABC's budget, but this money does not go to the ABC but to companies supplying distribution and transmission services. More importantly, analysis of ABC funding needs to account for the impact of inflation on the real value of budget allocations over time.[3]

The stark fact is that operational funding for the ABC is at almost its lowest level in 40 years, having decreased in real terms from $274 million in financial year 1983–84 to $263 million in 2021–22.[4]

These findings are based on inflation-adjusted (1983–84 dollars), time-series data analysis of ABC funding from 1983–84 to 2021–22.[5]

Original research, examining annual Australian government budget papers and Australian Parliamentary Library reports, has analysed four periods of Australian government funding for the ABC: the Hawke/Keating, Howard, Rudd/Gillard/Rudd, and Abbott/Turnbull/Morrison governments.[6]

The data shows that there have been peaks and troughs since 1983 (see Figure B.1), but over time ABC funding has declined in real terms. Further, the shifts in funding reflect the political hue of the government of the day.

The following graphs show funding for ABC operational activities in real (inflation-adjusted) (Figure B.1) and nominal (Figure B.3) terms. Table B.1 compares average levels of funding by each of four governments in real and nominal terms. Figure B.4 contrasts nominal and real operational funding data. Figure B.2 contrasts the final year of each government's allocation to the ABC, with the Morrison government's 2021–22 funding being its last allocation as at time of writing.

Real cuts in funding[7]

Figure B.1 tracks the history of real operational funding for the ABC from financial year 1983–84 to the present, showing real funding ($ millions) at the beginning of each government.

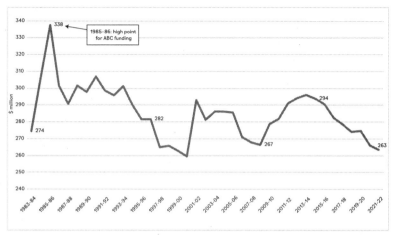

Figure B.1: ABC real operational funding, 1983-84 to 2021-22
($ millions, 1983-84 dollars)[8]

Figure B.1 shows real increases during the Hawke/Keating period, especially in 1984–85 and 1985–86, when funding increased by over 25 per cent compared to the last Fraser government budget, with smaller increases in three other budgets. However, there were other occasions when allocations decreased in real terms. While average funding of $299 million (1983–84 to 1995–96) was 13 per cent higher than the previous Fraser government's funding (see Table B.1), cuts in the late 1980s had a major impact on the ABC.[9] 1985–86, at $338 million in real terms, was the high point for ABC funding, not just for the Hawke/Keating governments, but for all subsequent years to date.

During the Howard government (1996–2007), average real funding for the ABC declined by 8 per cent from $299 million to $275 million per year. As in the previous government, there were years of cuts and increases. In 1996, communications minister Richard Alston announced a 12 per cent reduction in ABC funding to be implemented over two years.[10] After reaching the lowest point in ABC operational revenue in the past four administrations ($259 million in 2000–01), ABC funding increased in real terms for two years before declining again in 2002–03, stabilising and reducing again from 2005–06.

The Rudd/Gillard/Rudd governments (2007–13) provided a period of sustained real improvements in funding for the ABC with, as Figure B.1 shows, five consecutive budget increases, as average funding increased by 3 per cent to $285 million per year. The most significant increase was in 2009, with an extra $167 million over three years for a 'children's channel, increased Australian drama production, and regional broadband hubs'.[11] This funding was subsequently made a continuing part of the ABC operational budget.

Following the Rudd/Gillard/Rudd increases, average ABC operational funding has been cut by the Abbott/Turnbull/Morrison governments by a further 2 per cent in real terms, reducing to an average $278 million per year (Table B.1). While the Howard government's funding decrease of 8 per cent was greater overall, it also increased funding in some years. Eight consecutive real reductions have characterised the current government's allocation. Except for 2000–01, funding is now lower in real terms than at any time since 1980–81.

The following table shows the comparison of average funding levels of the past four governments. Overall, average Labor funding for the ABC was 6 per cent greater than coalition funding.

Government	Average ABC operating revenue (nominal)	Average ABC operating revenue (real)	% real change from previous government	% real cumulative change
Hawke/Keating	$434m	$299m	24%	
Howard	$586m	$275m	-8%	-8%
Rudd/Gillard/Rudd	$779m	$285m	3%	-5%
Abbott/Turnbull/Morrison	$871m	$278m	-2%	
				-7%
Labor compared to coalition (real)				
Average (Labor)	$543m	$294m	6%	
Average (coalition)	$700m	$276m	-6%	

Table B.1: Average government operational allocations for ABC, 1983–84 to 2021–22.[12] Note: totals and percentages have been rounded to the nearest whole number.

Coalition governments have cut real funding by 8 per cent (Howard) and 2 per cent (Abbott/Turnbull/Morrison) compared to the average level of the previous government. These contrast with real increases of 13 per cent during the Hawke/Keating governments and 3 per cent during the Rudd/Gillard/Rudd governments.

Comparing the changes in government allocations to the ABC

The following graph (Figure B.2) shows the level of ABC funding in real terms (1983–84 dollars) at the end of each of the last five Australian governments (the Morrison government figure is for the 2021–22 budget). The Hawke/Keating government's last budget allocation of $281 million (real) in 1995–96 was 7 per cent higher in real terms than the allocation of the Fraser government in 1982 ($264 million). The period of the Howard government (1996–2007) showed a decline of 5 per cent in real funding, from the $281 million to $268 million (real) in the budget for 2007–08. Funding increased during the Rudd/Gillard/Rudd government to reach $296 million (real) in 2013–14, an increase of 10 per cent over the term of the government. The current government shows the steepest decrease in ABC funding, dropping by 11 per cent from 2013–14's figure of $296 million to $263 million in 2021–22.[13]

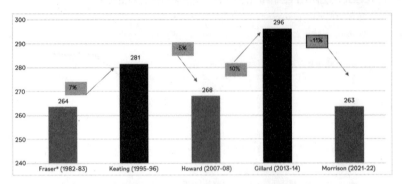

* Prime minister at the time of the last budget allocation.

Figure B.2: ABC funding at the end of each government's term and to 2021–22 for Morrison government ($ millions, 1983–84 dollars).[14] Note: totals and percentages have been rounded to the nearest whole number.

Nominal funding[15]

The following section shows the ABC funding levels in nominal terms. The nominal value in this data is the value of the original budget allocation as described in the relevant year's budget papers, without any adjustment for inflation. Figure B.3 shows the budget appropriation for ABC operational funding in nominal terms from 1983–84 to 2021–22. It is based on data shown in Table B.2.

Figure B.3 shows the importance of analysing the real

increase in funding levels, given that nominal levels mask the real value of funding allocations. Nominal values show an increase in ABC funding from $274 million in 1983–84 to $881 million in 2021–22, an apparent growth of 221 per cent. In nominal terms, the level of ABC funding increased during each period of government. Using nominal values, especially during periods of higher inflation, masks reductions in the value of budget appropriations.

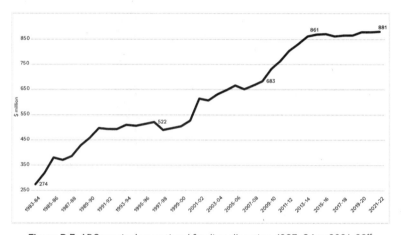

Figure B.3: ABC nominal operational funding allocation, 1983-84 to 2021-22[16]

The lower nominal increases during the current government reflect lower inflation and reduced real allocations, showing a flattening of funding compared to higher inflationary periods (e.g. the 1980s).

Figure B.4 compares nominal and real operational funding. The contrast in funding levels, noting the impact of inflation and static real funding levels, is clear. Once the effect of inflation is removed, an accurate picture of funding support is revealed.

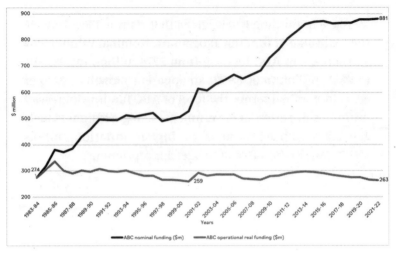

Figure B.4: Australian government ABC nominal and real operational funding, 1983-84 to 2021-22. Source: 1983-84 to 2005-06 (Jolly, 2014); 2006-07 to 2021-22, relevant PBS (DITRDC, 2021).

Operational and 'other' funding

As noted, analysis using the real value of money over time provides a more accurate comparison and test of arguments regarding the adequacy of operational funding levels for the ABC.

A second approach was undertaken to test the findings of changes in government financial support for the ABC. This approach again compares real and nominal levels of funding. However, the funding base is expanded to add 'other' — capital revenue and equity injections — to operational revenue while excluding transmission and capital user charges, which is consistent with an approach used by Jolly.[17] The rationale for excluding transmission and orchestra funding is described in the Notes at the end of this appendix.

Figure B.5 shows operational and 'other' revenue in real

terms from 1983–84 to 2021–22, which can be compared with Figure B.1. The funding level at the beginning and end of each government's term is shown on the graph. Even with 'other' funding added, the trend is the same as shown in Figure B.1 for operational revenue. That is, there was a real decline between 1983–84 and 2021–22. 1985–86, at $380 million (operational and other funding), remains the high point in ABC real funding.

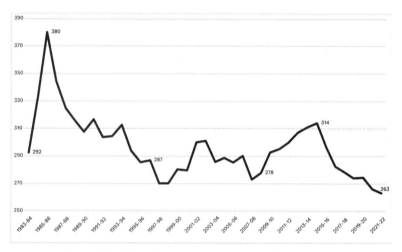

Figure B.5: ABC real operational and other funding combined, 1983-84 to 2021-22[18]

The next graph, Figure B.6, compares nominal and real (1983–84 dollars) levels of operational and 'other' funding. Again, the impact of inflation on funding levels is demonstrated in the graph. Figure B.6 shows a decline in both nominal and real funding since 2014–15.

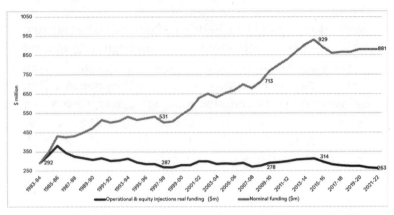

Figure B.6: ABC nominal and real operational and other funding,
1983-84 to 2021-22[19]

Figures B.5 and B.6, then, show similar trends for funding as those in Figures B.1 and B.4. Adjusted for inflation, real funding has decreased in overall terms since 1983–84. The periods of Labor government have shown moderate to significant increases in real funding. The inclusion of 'other' funds does show a slightly different trend when compared to operational revenue. Nominal funding has decreased significantly since 2014–15, from $929 million a year to $881 million. This reflects decisions such as the 2014 Abbott government's cancellation of a ten-year, $200 million international broadcasting contract with the ABC.[20]

Comparing real operational funds and operational plus 'other' funding

Figure B.7 confirms the trend by comparing real operational funding (grey line) and real operational revenue, capital, and 'other' funding (black line).

The beginning year of each government's term shows

the first year's budget allocation, with operational revenue plus capital and 'other' in plain text (e.g. \$292 million in 1983–84 and \$278 million in 2008–09), and operational revenue in boxed text (e.g. \$282 million in 1996–97, \$294 million in 2014–15, and \$263 million in 2021–22).

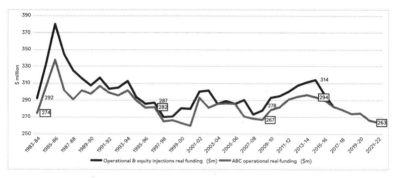

Figure B.7: ABC real operational and operational and other funding, 1983–84 to 2021–22[21]

While there is an increase in annual funding levels from 1983–84 to 2014–15 when 'other' funding is included, the real reduction in revenue is confirmed.

ABC staffing levels

A further comparison of the impact of funding can be made using ABC employment data. By 1985 the ABC was employing about 7,000 staff, having reached 5,000 in the 1960s and peaking at over 7,300 in 1975.[22] Figure B.8 shows the history of ABC staffing levels from 1986 to 2020.

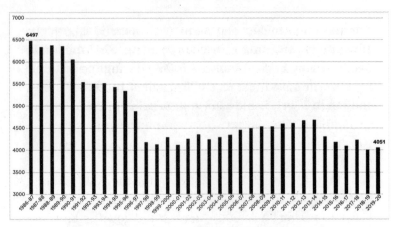

Figure B.8: ABC employment levels (FTEs), 1986–2020[23]

As Figure B.8 shows, in 1987, nearly 6,500 staff were employed at the ABC. While significantly higher than current levels, this was a drop from a decade earlier. Staffing levels continued to decline under both Labor and the coalition until 2001, when they reached 4,116 full-time-equivalent positions (FTEs).[24] The increase sustained between 2004–05 and 2013–14 has been followed since 2014–15 by a decline, though small and inconsistent increases occurred in 2019–20 and 2020–21.[25] Employment levels have been reduced at various times because of cuts across the ABC in radio, support, journalists and news-related positions, international services, and regional offices, and due to the outsourcing of television production.

Conclusion

Analysis of 40 years of budget data confirms other studies and commentary about the decline of public funding for the ABC.[26] Average ABC funding is now 7 per cent less in real terms than during the Hawke/Keating governments.

The most significant real reduction occurred during the Howard government (1996–2007), with an 8 per cent decline compared to average funding during the previous term.[27] The data reflects the impact of these decisions, showing a lower real level of ABC funding in 2020–21 than in 1983–84. This is notwithstanding the provision of a substantial range of new services in 2020–21 that were not delivered 40 years ago.

Analysing average real funding for the ABC across a government's term of office shows increases under the Hawke/Keating and Rudd/Gillard/Rudd governments and declines under the Howard and Abbott/Turnbull/Morrison governments. The comparison is starker when comparing real funding levels at the end of each government's term of office. The Hawke/Keating government's last budget allocation in real terms in 1995–96 was 7 per cent higher than the final budget of the Fraser government in 1982. The final budget for the Howard government showed a 5 per cent decline in real funding for the ABC. Conversely, by the time of the final budget of the Rudd/Gillard/Rudd government, real funding for the ABC had increased by 10 per cent. The current government shows the steepest decrease in real ABC funding, dropping by 11 per cent at the time of the 2021–22 budget.

Examining this near four-decade segment of the history of ABC funding, it is difficult not to reflect on the current government's determined, continuing cuts to ABC funding. In overseeing the most serious decline in funding (11 per cent down), compared to the previous government's last budget, six decisions have reduced ABC funding by almost $800 million.[28] ABC funding in real terms is now lower than it was in 1983.

Notes

The Australian Broadcasting Corporation receives an annual parliamentary funding allocation in the federal budget. Since 1989, its funding has been allocated notionally in three-year instalments, known as 'triennial funding', delivered each year. ABC funding consists of several components, including operational, capital, one-off funding from different agencies for specific activities, transmission, and, historically, funding for orchestras. Operational funding is for the ongoing activities of the organisation, such as audio-visual, audio, and other digital media content, and related business support such as information technology, legal, property, finance, human resources, payroll, and utilities (electricity, water, gas).[29]

The federal government's annual allocation of operational funding was identified as a basis for historical data analysis, enabling a 'like-for-like' comparison of ABC funding over time when adjusted for inflation to 'real' terms.

Calculations of the percentage change compares ABC funding over four periods of government using two approaches. First, as outlined in Table B.1, the average, real level of ABC operational funding is calculated by adding each year's allocation and dividing by the number of budgets delivered by that government. For example, the current government has allocated a total of $2.224 billion in operational funds to the ABC in eight budgets, or $278 million annually. The Hawke/Keating government allocated $3.9 billion in 13 budgets: $299 million annually.

The tables of time-series data of ABC operational funding have been built from two sets of data. For the financial years 2006–07 to 2020–21, the data is drawn from annual Portfolio Budget Statements (PBS) for the

ABC, released by the Australian government as part of the annual federal-budget appropriations. The figures used are 'estimated real' ABC operating revenues drawn from Tables 2.1 or 2.1.1 in each relevant PBS. These are considered the most accurate reflection of the real revenue allocated to the ABC in that year.

A second source of operational revenue data is used for ABC government appropriations from 1983–84 to 2005–06. This data is based on a 2015 Australian Parliamentary Library report, *The ABC: an overview*, specifically Table 1, 'ABC revenue: 1970–71 to 2017–18: actual dollars', and Table 3, 'Australian Government funding for the ABC: 1990–91 to 2012–13: actual dollars'. As the report notes, this data is derived from 'ABC Annual Reports, Financial Statements and Budget Statements'.[30]

The annual 'nominal' operational funding — the dollar figure in each annual budget paper — has then been adjusted for inflation/CPI to provide a 'real' figure for comparison over time. The 'nominal' value in this data is the value of the original budget allocation as described in the relevant year's budget papers, without any adjustment for subsequent inflation. The 'real' value is an adjustment to remove the impact of inflation on the value of money, using an index year. All annual values are then adjusted to the index year. In this model, the index year is 1983–84. All subsequent years are adjusted to 1983–84 values. Removing the distortion of inflation shows a comparable value across time.

Calculations of real data are based on the Australian Bureau of Statistics Consumer Price Index, Australia, 6401.0. Each year of ABC funding data has been presented in the attached tables with the relevant adjustment for inflation to build a time-series data comparison. Table B.2 shows annual nominal and real (inflation-adjusted) figures for ABC operational revenues from 1983–84 to 2021–22. The graphs (Figures B.1, B.3, and B.4) present that data as a comparison between 'real' and 'nominal' data.

To test the approach of using operational allocations, a second set of data was collected and built using operational funding, equity injections, and other allocations contained in the annual Portfolio Budget Statements or as noted in the Australian Parliamentary Library report — the data source for 1983–84 to 2005–06. For the reasons detailed below, and consistent with other approaches, other funding allocated such as transmission or orchestra funds was not included.

Operational revenue: excluding transmission and orchestra funding

Operational revenue has been selected as the main measure of ABC funding, excluding other funding for areas such as transmission, capital, one-off allocations, and orchestra funding for each year (see Figures B.1 to B.4 and Tables B.1 and B.2). By focusing on operational revenues, the table can exclude income sources that vary significantly from year to year and over time. This provides an objective basis for the historical comparison of 'like for like' government funding for the ABC.

As noted, for comparison purposes and to test the validity of findings, the second set of data includes operational funding, equity injections, and identified one-off funding (see Figures B.5 and B.6 and Table B.3). However, it excludes transmission and orchestra funding. Other forms of revenue have been excluded because they distort time-series comparison for several reasons. First, these sources of revenue were not allocated in the same way over time, ceased some years ago, or were ad hoc in their allocation, making consistent comparison impossible. For example, until 2007, the ABC received federal and some state funding for orchestras, which ceased when the orchestras became independent from the ABC in that year. That funding line is excluded. A second exclusion is ad hoc, separately identified funding for specific capital projects, such as property. Given this funding was separately allocated, it has been excluded from the analysis of real operational funding shown in Figures B.1 to B.4. The one-off capital injections relating to television digitisation in the early 2000s and other equity injections have been included in relevant graphs (Figures B.5 and B.6) and analysis, where indicated.

Transmission funding has been excluded. A further example of variables is the payments for transmission activities that are directed to commercial entities for contracts for transmission and distribution of ABC content. Prior to the early 1990s, transmission services were delivered by Telecom and the Department of Transport and Communications and were not separately recorded in ABC budget statements.[31] Following the privatisation and sale of the national transmission network, separate budget allocations have been made to the ABC for payments to commercial operators. The data set excludes funding appropriations for transmission services (television, radio, satellite, and digital).

ABC revenue from commercial activity

Finally, gross revenue from the sale of goods (licensing and products through ABC commercial activities, shops, etc.), which increased in the 1990s and early 2000s before effectively ceasing in the early 2010s, has been excluded. This is because this funding was not allocated by the Commonwealth government. The ABC's revenue raising had been formally sanctioned by parliament in 1985, extending longstanding activities such as concert sales.[32]

These expanded to include consumer sales through, for example, book and magazine publishing, CDs and DVD sales, as well as licensing of content for use by other broadcasters, distributors, airlines, and others.[33]

This figure expanded from $14 million in 1983–84[34] to a peak of $175 million in 2008–09,[35] or from $44 million to $304 million in 2019–20 dollars. The figures quoted are for gross revenue based on sales. They do not include the cost of goods sold and other expenses associated with commercial activity. Inglis notes that by 2004–05, the net contribution was $10.6 million, on estimated gross revenue of just under $150 million.[36] The most recent budget papers project ABC 'Sale of goods and services' to decline to $46 million (gross revenue) in 2021–22.[37]

Periods of government

The identification of the various periods of government (see graphs and data tables) is based on the budget year following the election of the new government. For example, the Rudd/Gillard/Rudd government was elected on 24 November 2007 and delivered its first budget in May 2008 for the 2008–09 year. It was defeated at the September 2013 election. The first Abbott-government budget was for the 2014–15 financial year. The following election dates (AEC, 2021) were used to calculate the periods of government:

- 5 March 1983 (Hawke/Keating government)
- 2 March 1996 (Howard government)
- 24 November 2007 (Rudd/Gillard/Rudd government)
- 7 September 2013 (Abbott/Turnbull/Morrison government)

Attached tables

Year	ABC nominal funding	Index (1983–84 =100)	CPI inflation — preceding FY to FY	ABC operational real funding ($m)	Real change — preceding FY vs current FY deflated
1983–84	$274m	100.0	0	$274m	0.00
1984–85	$320m	104.3	0.043	$306m	0.12
1985–86	$382m	113.1	0.084	$338m	0.10
1986–87	$373m	123.6	0.093	$301m	-0.11
1987–88	$386m	132.7	0.074	$291m	-0.04
1988–89	$429m	142.4	0.073	$301m	0.04
1989–90	$458m	153.9	0.081	$298m	-0.01
1990–91	$497m	162.1	0.053	$307m	0.03
1991–92	$494m	165.2	0.019	$299m	-0.03
1992–93	$494m	166.8	0.01	$296m	-0.01
1993–94	$512m	169.8	0.018	$301m	0.02
1994–95	$508m	175.3	0.032	$290m	-0.04
1995–96	$515m	182.8	0.043	$281m	-0.03
1996–97	$522m	185.2	0.013	$282m	0.00
1997–98	$491m	185.2	0	$265m	-0.06
1998–99	$499m	187.6	0.013	$266m	0.00
1999–00	$505m	192.1	0.024	$263m	-0.01
2000–01	$528m	203.6	0.06	$259m	-0.01
2001–02	$614m	209.5	0.029	$293m	0.13
2002–03	$607m	215.8	0.03	$281m	-0.04
2003–04	$632m	221.0	0.024	$286m	0.02
2004–05	$648m	226.3	0.024	$286m	0.00
2005–06	$667m	233.5	0.032	$286m	0.00
2006–07	$652m	240.5	0.03	$271m	-0.05
2007–08	$667m	248.7	0.034	$268m	-0.01
2008–09	$683m	256.4	0.031	$267m	-0.01
2009–10	$731m	262.3	0.023	$279m	0.05
2010–11	$763m	270.5	0.031	$282m	0.01
2011–12	$805m	276.7	0.023	$291m	0.03
2012–13	$832m	283.0	0.023	$294m	0.01
2013–14	$861m	290.7	0.027	$296m	0.01
2014–15	$868m	295.6	0.017	$294m	-0.01
2015–16	$871m	299.8	0.014	$290m	-0.01
2016–17	$861m	304.9	0.017	$283m	-0.03
2017–18	$866m	310.7	0.019	$279m	-0.01
2018–19	$865m	315.6	0.016	$274m	-0.02
2019–20	$879m	319.7	0.013	$275m	0.00
2020–21	$879m	330.1	0.0325	$266m	-0.03
2021–22	$881m	334.2	0.0125	$263m	-0.01

Table B.2: Australian government appropriation — ABC operating revenue, 1983-84 to 2021-22[38]

Year	Nominal funding	Index (1983–84 =100)	CPI inflation — preceding FY to FY	Operational & equity injections real funding	Real change — preceding FY vs current FY deflated
1982–83	$261m		7%	$279m	
1983–84	$292m	100.0	0%	$292m	0.00
1984–85	$347m	104.3	4%	$333m	0.14
1985–86	$430m	113.1	8%	$380m	0.14
1986–87	$426m	123.6	9%	$344m	-0.09
1987–88	$431m	132.7	7%	$325m	-0.06
1988–89	$450m	142.4	7%	$316m	-0.03
1989–90	$474m	153.9	8%	$308m	-0.03
1990–91	$514m	162.1	5%	$317m	0.03
1991–92	$502m	165.2	2%	$304m	-0.04
1992–93	$508m	166.8	1%	$305m	0.00
1993–94	$532m	169.8	2%	$313m	0.03
1994–95	$515m	175.3	3%	$294m	-0.06
1995–96	$522m	182.8	4%	$286m	-0.03
1996–97	$531m	185.2	1%	$287m	0.00
1997–98	$501m	185.2	0%	$270m	-0.06
1998–99	$507m	187.6	1%	$270m	0.00
1999–00	$539m	192.1	2%	$280m	0.04
2000–01	$570m	203.6	6%	$280m	0.00
2001–02	$629m	209.5	3%	$300m	0.07
2002–03	$650m	215.8	3%	$301m	0.00
2003–04	$632m	221.0	2%	$286m	-0.05
2004–05	$653m	226.3	2%	$289m	0.01
2005–06	$667m	233.5	3%	$286m	-0.01
2006–07	$698m	240.5	3%	$290m	0.02
2007–08	$679m	248.7	3%	$273m	-0.06
2008–09	$713m	256.4	3%	$278m	0.02
2009–10	$768m	262.3	2%	$293m	0.05
2010–11	$798m	270.5	3%	$295m	0.01
2011–12	$831m	276.7	2%	$300m	0.02
2012–13	$870m	283.0	2%	$307m	0.02
2013–14	$905m	290.7	3%	$311m	0.01
2014–15	$929m	295.6	2%	$314m	0.01
2015–16	$891m	299.8	1%	$297m	-0.05
2016–17	$861m	304.9	2%	$283m	-0.05
2017–18	$866m	310.7	2%	$279n	-0.01
2018–19	$865m	315.6	2%	$274m	-0.02
2019–20	$879m	319.7	1%	$275m	0.00
2020–21	$879m	330.1	3%	$266m	-0.03
2021–22	$881m	334.2	1%	$263m	-0.01

Table B.3: Government appropriation — ABC operating revenue and other (including equity injections), 1983-84 to 2021-22[39]

Appendix C

INTERNATIONAL COMPARISON OF PER CAPITA PUBLIC BROADCASTING FUNDING
by Michael Ward

The following table draws on publicly available information to compare per capita funding for public broadcasting across 23 selected countries.

On a per capita basis, Australia ranks 13th (equal with Japan), with total funding of A$66 per person. Per capita funding for public broadcasting is highest in Europe, where six public broadcasters receive equivalent to at least A$150 per person annually, with Switzerland the highest at A$274 per person.

Please note that the data is based on total funding, including licence fees, government appropriations, and revenue from other sources such as advertising sales. The Australian data uses total funding for public broadcasting (i.e. the ABC and SBS).

Country	Funding per capita (€)	Funding per capita (A$)
Switzerland	183	274
Denmark	158	237
Great Britain	125	188
Norway	120	181
Germany	117	175
Austria	114	171
Finland	86	129
Sweden	86	128
Ireland	80	120
Belgium	70	105
France	67	101
Netherlands	50	75
Japan	44	66
Australia	44	66
Croatia	43	64
Italy	41	62
Spain	33	50
Czech Republic	31	47
Canada	30	45
Hungary	29	44
Portugal	20	31
Poland	12	18
United States	9	13

Table C.1: Per capita funding for public broadcasting
(selected countries)[1]

The table compares 23 public broadcasters from a range of countries. The primary rationale for selection is to analyse countries with generally similar economic circumstances (e.g. OECD) to Australia. In addition to including Japan, there is a focus on European and North American broadcasters. This is due to the availability of funding data, especially from independent public agencies (e.g. the European Audiovisual Observatory and Ofcom). Selection is also based on previous research about public broadcasters and funding, including the work of the Public Media Alliance and academic research.[2]

Appendix D

ABC APPRECIATION AND ATTITUDE SURVEYS

by Michael Ward

ABC annual reports include information about community 'perceptions and beliefs about the value of the ABC's contribution to Australian society'.[1] The surveys provide a time-series snapshot of perspectives on accuracy and impartiality. Table D.1 presents data from 2002 to 2021 about the percentage of people who 'believe the ABC is accurate and impartial when reporting news and current affairs'. The data in the table shows a range of between 72 and 83 per cent of people holding a positive view, with a decline of 11 percentage points over 14 years from 2006 to 2020.

Year	Percentage
2002	79
2003	81
2004	80
2005	82
2006	83
2007	79
2008	81
2009	83
2010	82
2011	81
2012	80
2013	78
2014	77
2015	77
2016	77
2017	74
2018	75
2019	74
2020	72
2021	73

Table D.1: ABC news and current affairs: 'accurate & impartial', 2002–21[2]

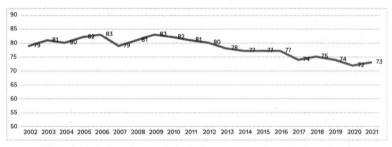

Figure D.1: ABC news and current affairs: 'accurate & impartial', 2002–21.[3]
Note: prior to 2008, the survey asked about ABC news and current affairs
being 'balanced and even handed'. Subsequently, the independent survey
asked about 'accuracy and impartiality'.

ACKNOWLEDGEMENTS

This is perhaps the longest short book ever written. It certainly took longer than any short book should. Someone — it might have been me, Matthew — had the bright idea in 2018 that someone should write a short book about the predicament facing the ABC, and a publisher said, 'Why don't you do it?' Good idea. And then I had that familiar 'have-I-just-overcommitted-myself?' feeling. How to get a book written quickly when I'm in the middle of co-editing another book project that required wrangling six authors to condense 4,885 pages of oral-history transcript into coherent chapters. Answer? Bring Patrick on board, which he was keen to do, despite working on his own other book projects. That is partly why this book has taken an unseemly length of time to produce; the other reason, of course, is COVID-19. The global pandemic did at least have the effect of keeping us indoors, but month after month of lockdown turns your brain to porridge. That said, the book is longer than the original planned 40,000 words because the more we delved into the topic, the more we felt needed to be said.

Who Needs the ABC? was conceived as a blend of

long-form journalism and contemporary history. Or, in the less than lyrical language of the modern university, as an NTRO (or to spell it out, a non-traditional research output). Translating this ghastly term for this project, we have taken a journalistic approach by identifying something about what is happening to the ABC that is particular to this moment in Australian political and cultural life. A decade ago, we would not have been able to write the book we've written, and, hopefully, in a decade's time, a book like this won't be needed. Right now, though, this is the book we believe has to be out there, prompting discussion and debate among the millions who consume ABC content. We chose to focus on the ABC since it became a corporation in 1983 because informative and interesting as the Australian Broadcasting Commission's history is, the more recent history is relevant and telling.

We would like to acknowledge those who agreed to be interviewed for this book: Mark Scott (on 5 March 2020), Karen Percy (18 March 2021), Emma Dawson (4 June 2021), and Darren Chester (13 August 2021). They are a former managing director of the ABC, a former senior ABC journalist, a former media policy adviser to a communications minister, and a current National Party MP. All four had useful things to tell us, and we are grateful for their time. By choice, we did not conduct a lot of interviews, because we were not planning to write an inside account of working life at the ABC. The story we wanted to tell was actually hiding in plain sight. You don't need a leak from inside federal cabinet to tell you the coalition government is hostile to the ABC. Most of the material in this book, then, is drawn from what is already on the public record, in reports to government, parliamentary inquiries, memoirs, ABC programs (especially *Four Corners* and *Media Watch*), academic studies, and so on.

That said, we know only too well that journalists have reported extensively on the ABC and made important disclosures. Among the many, we would particularly like to acknowledge the reporting and analysis of Andrew Dodd, Jonathan Holmes, Amanda Meade, Denis Muller, Kerry O'Brien, and Margaret Simons. We want to acknowledge scholars who have documented the ABC's history. First and foremost, Ken Inglis for his magisterial two volumes of history, the first of which was commissioned by the ABC, the second he researched and wrote as an independent scholar. Thank you to Bridget Griffen-Foley for her mammoth effort in editing *A Companion to the Australian Media*, which has been an authoritative source.

A number of colleagues and friends provided help on this project. Ken Haley read through a decade of *Media Watch Dog* for us and did a close read of the text. Emma Mesikämmen did a literature review about public broadcasting. Nicholas Payne did some research on News Corp Australia's reporting on the ABC. Thank you, all, especially Ken, who should be given five, if not ten, paws for his dedication to the task.

Thank you to Alex Wake for introducing us to Michael Ward, and a big thank you to Michael, who has produced invaluable material about the ABC's finances and standing that is in appendices B, C, and D. It has been a pleasure to work with you, Michael.

Thank you to those who read the manuscript and provided valuable comments: Andrew Dodd, Emma Dawson, Lisa Millar, and Denis Muller. Thanks also to colleagues and friends with whom we've discussed the ABC over the years: Peter Browne, Paul Chadwick, Phillip Chubb (sadly no longer with us), Cait McMahon, Katharine Murphy, Margaret Simons, Rod Tiffen, and Daniel Ziffer.

This is Patrick's third book with Scribe and Matthew's

first. Both of us have enjoyed the process and would like to thank Cora Roberts for her work publicising the title, David Golding for his careful, astute copyediting, Cressida McDermott for proofreading the manuscript, and publisher Henry Rosenbloom for believing in the project and at the outset offering us an idea that blossomed in how we framed the opening chapter.

Now for some individual thankyous:

For Matthew: first, I would like to thank colleagues at Deakin. The Communications course directors, Erin Hawley, Deirdre Quinn-Allan, and Chris Scanlon, shouldered more than they probably should have when their Head of Academic Group was deep in the manuscript. Katrina Clifford did the same for her co-editor of *Australian Journalism Review*. Kristy Hess stepped up on several occasions to act as Head of Academic Group while I focused on the book. And Lisa Waller, who moved from Deakin to RMIT in 2019, has always been a generous, supportive colleague. Thank you, all.

Second, I would like to thank Patrick for agreeing to co-author this book. We first met in Canberra when he asked me to be on his PhD supervision panel. I then asked him to tutor in various subjects I was running at the University of Canberra, and, apart from being an excellent teacher, Patrick was a great colleague to work with. He did research-assistant work for me after I arrived at Deakin, and that was how he began work on this book, but it soon became apparent that he could, and should, be a co-author. My early years in journalism taught me to be a lone wolf, but more recently, in academia, I have learned the value of collaborating, and done that on a good number of projects now. This collaboration has been a particularly happy experience. Patrick is not only highly intelligent but beneath his unruffled demeanour is a ferocious work ethic. He writes beautifully, is wonderfully generous, and has a deceptively subversive sense of humour. Who couldn't work with all that?

Finally, thank you to my family. My adult children, Gemma, Hayley, and Josh, have not only shown their customary interest in and support for this project but gradually, without it ever being planned, become ABC people. It began with exposure in childhood to the *0–9* music albums (on high rotation in the car) and *Round the Twist* (admittedly the first season was on Seven before moving to the ABC), discovering Triple J in their teens, and then as adults choosing ABC programs I've been following for years (*Four Corners*, *Media Watch*, and *RN Breakfast*), as well as tuning into newer offerings like Matt Bevan's *Russia, If You're Listening* podcasts. Hayley's own podcast six-part series, *Make Me*, has just been released on Spotify. For Gill, the end of 2021 saw not only a return to her workplace but the end of living in close proximity with someone working on two book projects that occupied the entire period Melbourne was in lockdown. If a vaccine for COVID-19 was found faster than anyone expected, one has yet to be developed for the book-writing virus. Thank you, darling, for your forbearance, support, and love. It means the world to me, as of course do you.

For Patrick: I owe a debt to colleagues at the University of Canberra's Centre for Creative and Cultural Research, who have provided generous support in the form of advice, references, stimulation, and the use of libraries and office facilities. I'm very grateful to Jen Webb, Katie Hayne, Tony Eaton, and Shane Strange, and thank them for their generosity and kindness over the time it took to write this book.

Writing is usually a solitary endeavour, exciting on occasions but more often characterised by the grim awareness that the words put on the page are inadequate to their purpose. Working in collaboration with Matthew on this book has seen very few instances of the latter and many more of the former. I am immensely grateful to him for asking me to join this project, and for the generosity, wisdom, and insight that he has shared with me throughout. It has been a delight and an honour to work with him: thank you.

This book would not have been possible without the vigilance and supervision provided by my dog, Grainger, the delightful chortles of my daughter, Claire, and the unstinting support, patience, and love of my wife, Kate. Thank you.

NOTES

Chapter 1. Who's Afraid of the ABC?

1 Adams is one of 37 national living treasures as chosen by a popular vote held by the National Trust (NSW), https://www.austlit.edu.au/austlit/page/v1293?mainTabTemplate=awardWorksAndAgents.

2 For full details of the ABC's funding and how it has changed over time, see Appendix B. For the 1984 staffing figure, see: Ken Inglis, *Whose ABC?*, Melbourne: Black Inc, 2006, p. 109.

3 *ABC Annual Report 2020–2021*, 21 October 2021, pp. 54–68, https://about.abc.net.au/reports-publications/abc-annual-report-2020-2021/.

4 Benjamin Wallace-Wells, 'The Sudden Rise of the Coronavirus Lab-Leak Theory', *The New Yorker*, 27 May 2021, https://www.newyorker.com/news/annals-of-inquiry/the-sudden-rise-of-the-coronavirus-lab-leak-theory.

5 Kerry O'Brien, *Kerry O'Brien: a memoir*, Crows Nest: Allen & Unwin, 2018.

6 *ABC Annual Report 2020*, 20 October 2020, p. 49, https://about.abc.net.au/press-releases/abc-annual-report-2020/.

7 Ken Inglis, *This Is the ABC*, Carlton: Melbourne University Press, 1983, p. 395.

8 Ken Inglis, *Whose ABC?*, Melbourne: Black Inc, 2006, pp. 30, 121.

9 Darren Chester to Matthew Ricketson, 13 August 2021.

Chapter 2. How the Internet ...

1 'John Laws', *The Australian Financial Review*, 6 April 1990, https://www.afr.com/companies/john-laws-19900406-kamcy.

2   Matthew Ricketson, 'Newspaper Feature Writing in Australia 1956–1996', in Ann Curthoys and Julianne Schultz, eds, *Journalism: print, politics, and popular culture*, Brisbane: University of Queensland Press, 1999, pp. 178–9.

3   Andrew Dodd and Matthew Ricketson, eds, *Upheaval: disrupted lives in journalism*, Sydney: NewSouth, 2021, p. 163.

4   Matthew Ricketson, *Writing Feature Stories*, Crows Nest: Allen & Unwin, 2004, p. 7.

5   France Bonner, 'Women's Magazines', in Bridget Griffen-Foley, ed., *A Companion to the Australian Media*, North Melbourne: Australian Scholarly Publishing, 2014, pp. 498–500.

6   'About the ABC: History of the ABC, the 90s', no date, https://archive.is/LNiE.

7   'About the ABC: History of the ABC, the 80s', no date, https://archive.is/20121208165604/http://abc.net.au/corp/history/hist6.htm.

8   Gavin Souter, *Company of Heralds: a century and a half of Australian publishing by John Fairfax Limited and its predecessors, 1831–1981*, Carlton: Melbourne University Press, 1981.

9   No byline, 'News Corp.'s Rupert Murdoch calls Myspace buy a "huge mistake"', *The Los Angeles Times*, 21 October 2011, https://latimesblogs.latimes.com/entertainmentnewsbuzz/2011/10/news-corps-murdoch-calls-myspace-a-huge-mistake.html.

10 Australian Competition and Consumer Commission, *Digital Platforms Inquiry Final Report*, 26 July 2019, pp. 40–56, https://www.accc.gov.au/publications/digital-platforms-inquiry-final-report.

11 'The 100 largest companies in the world by market capitalisation in 2020', Statista, no date, https://www.statista.com/statistics/263264/top-companies-in-the-world-by-market-capitalization/; 'Market capitalization of News Corp (NWS)', *Companies Market Cap*, https://companiesmarketcap.com/news-corp/marketcap/, accessed 11 January 2022.

12 Amanda Lotz, 'Putting a leash on Google and Facebook won't do much to save the traditional news model', *The Nieman Lab*, 29 July 2019, https://www.niemanlab.org/2019/07/putting-a-leash-on-google-and-facebook-wont-do-much-to-save-the-traditional-news-model/.

13 Australian Competition and Consumer Commission, *Digital Platforms Inquiry Final Report*, 26 July 2019, p. 58, https://www.accc.gov.au/publications/digital-platforms-inquiry-final-report.

14 Emily Bell, 'Facebook is eating the world', *Columbia Journalism Review*, 7 March 2016, https://www.cjr.org/analysis/facebook_and_media.php.

15 Australian Competition and Consumer Commission, *Digital Platforms Inquiry Final Report*, 26 July 2019, p. 302, https://www.

accc.gov.au/publications/digital-platforms-inquiry-final-report.

16 Lucy Clark, 'We've reached our goal of 150,000 *Guardian Australia* supporters. Thanks', *Guardian Australia*, 20 July 2020, https://www.theguardian.com/membership/2020/jul/20/guardian-australia-reached-goalof-150000-supporters.

17 MEAA, Submission 26, Senate Inquiry into Media Diversity in Australia, 11 December 2020, https://www.aph.gov.au/Parliamentary_Business/Committees/Senate/Environment_and_Communications/Mediadiversity/Submissions, p.3.

18 Australian Competition and Consumer Commission, *Digital Platforms Inquiry Final Report*, 26 July 2019, p. 561, https://www.accc.gov.au/publications/digital-platforms-inquiry-final-report.

19 Gary Dickson, 'The Australian Newsroom Mapping Project', Public Interest Journalism Initiative, https://anmp.piji.com.au/, accessed 22 September 2021.

20 Margaret Simons, Gary Dickson, and Rachel Alembakis, 'The Nature of the Editorial Deficit', Public Interest Journalism Initiative, 20 November 2019, p. 24, https://piji.com.au/wp-content/uploads/2019/11/piji-the-nature-of-the-editorial-deficit.pdf.

21 Katharine Murphy, *On Disruption*, Carlton: Melbourne University Press, 2018, pp. 51–2.

22 'The ABC's iview is now on Apple TV', *Business Insider*, 8 March 2016, https://www.businessinsider.com/the-abcs-iview-is-now-on-apple-tv-2016-3?IR=T.

23 Tim Burrowes, 'ABC Online launches investigations unit', *Mumbrella*, 11 February 2010, https://mumbrella.com.au/abc-online-to-launch-investigations-unit-17979.

24 ABC Investigations, https://www.abc.net.au/news/story-streams/investigations/.

25 Ken Inglis, *This Is the ABC*, Carlton: Melbourne University Press, 1983, p. 34.

26 Australian Senate, 'Media Diversity in Australia', report of the Environment and Communications References Committee, December 2021, p. xi.

27 'Bargaining with Big Tech', *Q&A*, ABC TV, 18 February 2021, https://www.abc.net.au/qanda/2021-18-02/13141040.

28 Andrea Carson, 'The Grand Bargain: Australia's news media bargaining code', in Gina Chua, *News in Asia*, Judith Neilson Institute, September 2021, https://newsinasia.jninstitute.org/chapter/the-grand-bargain-australias-news-media-bargaining-code/, accessed 20 October 2021.

29 Hal Crawford, 'Why Australia's dishonest News Media Code is a bad way to tax Google and Facebook', *Press Gazette*, 14 October 2021, https://pressgazette.co.uk/Australian-news-media-bargaining-

code/, accessed 20 October 2021. Other industry sources put the figure closer to $300 million.

30 Zoe Samios, 'Conversation, SBS snubbed by Facebook', *The Age*, 23 September 2021, p. 15.

Chapter 3. All Governments ...

1 '"There are no cuts": Morrison rejects criticism of ABC budget', *New Daily*, 25 June 2020, https://thenewdaily.com.au/news/national/2020/06/25/scott-morrison-cuts-abc/, accessed 28 August 2021.

2 The ABC charter, section 6 of the ABC Act, 1983, https://about.abc.net.au/how-the-abc-is-run/what-guides-us/legislative-framework/.

3 ABC Editorial Policies, updated, 15 January 2019, https://about.abc.net.au/wp-content/uploads/2017/11/A5print-15-01-2019.pdf.

4 Ken Inglis, *Whose ABC?*, Melbourne: Black Inc, 2006, p. 42.

5 Ken Inglis, *This Is the ABC*, Carlton: Melbourne University Press, 1983, p. 69.

6 Ibid., pp. 139, 188–9.

7 Ibid., p. 427.

8 Ibid., pp. 429–33.

9 Ken Inglis, *Whose ABC?*, Melbourne: Black Inc, 2006, pp. 8–9.

10 Ibid., p. 100.

11 Ibid., p. 33.

12 Ben Hills, 'It's his ABC', *The Sydney Morning Herald*, 16 March 1996, *Spectrum*, p. 1.

13 Alan Ramsey, 'Familiar ring to an ABC lament', *The Sydney Morning Herald*, 18 May 1996, p. 41.

14 Ken Inglis, *Whose ABC?*, Melbourne: Black Inc, 2006, p. 98.

15 Paul Chadwick, *Media Mates: carving up Australia's media*, South Melbourne: Macmillan, 1989.

16 Paul Barry, *The Rise and Rise of Kerry Packer*, Sydney: Bantam, 1993, pp. 309–31.

17 Gerard Henderson, 'For 8c a day, all the bias you can take', *The Sydney Morning Herald*, 22 January 1991, p. 11.

18 Ken Inglis, *Whose ABC?*, Melbourne: Black Inc, 2006, pp. 230–1.

19 Ibid., pp. 224–7.

20 Ibid., p. 237.

21 Rebecca Hawkings, 'Paul Keating's Creative Nation: A Policy Document that Changed Us', *The Conversation*, 30 October 2014, https://theconversation.com/paul-keatings-creative-nation-a-policy-document-that-changed-us-33537.

22 Ken Inglis, *Whose ABC?*, Melbourne: Black Inc, 2006, pp. 328–9.

23 Ibid., pp. 31–2, 307.

24 Ibid., p. 542.

25 Bernard Keane, 'John Howard can teach us a thing or two about respecting the ABC's independence', *Crikey*, 28 September 2018, https://www.crikey.com.au/2018/09/28/howard-and-the-abc/, accessed 28 August 2021.

26 Ken Inglis, *Whose ABC?*, Melbourne: Black Inc, 2006, pp. 408, 494.

27 In his 2019 memoir, *More to Life than Politics?* (Cleveland: Connor Court), Alston offers a lengthy and largely unpersuasive attempt to suggest that there was no broken promise (pp. 231–3). He claims that the coalition's election promise to 'maintain existing levels of funding to the ABC' was qualified by another promise to support triennial funding. Thus, in his view, the promise to maintain existing levels applied only to the last year of the triennial period; once the triennial funding expired, in June 1997, there was no promise to keep. This echoes Pamela Williams's account in *The Victory* (1997), but this hairsplitting interpretation is contrary to any plain reading of the coalition's Better Communications policy: according to it, the coalition undertook to 'maintain existing levels of Commonwealth funding and triennial funding for the ABC and SBS'. Alston also makes much of an election-night interview with ABC journalist Jim Middleton, who asked Alston whether the coalition's promise to maintain the ABC's funding in real terms over the term of the coming parliament would stand even if budget problems were worse than expected. Regarding this as a misrepresentation of the coalition's commitments (for which he blames Middleton), Alston sees no fault in his answer: 'Absolutely. John Howard has made it very plain that we want to honour all our commitments.' That is, in his own telling, Alston — who had developed the coalition's position on the ABC, who announced the coalition's promises for the ABC, and who was the incoming communications minister responsible for enacting those promises — failed to notice that Middleton had got the policy wrong, failed to correct Middleton's statement of coalition policy, and instead agreed that the coalition would maintain the ABC's funding, in real terms, over the term of the coming parliament, even if budget problems were worse than expected: 'Absolutely.' In a similar, connected vein, Alston also claims that the coalition's promise to maintain the ABC's funding was 'silent' on the indexation of funding: 'So "existing levels" on its face meant the same amount, not an increase in real terms,' he writes. Not only does this fly in the face of a convention established for nearly a decade wherein appropriations to the ABC were adjusted to preserve their real value, Alston's claim is also at odds with contemporary reportage, which had it that Alston promised the coalition would 'maintain funding in real terms' (see Anne Davies, 'Political ABC Rule at an

End: Coalition', *The Sydney Morning Herald*, 19 January 1996, p. 2). Even if one grants Alston every possible credit on these points, the question remaining is simple: why were he and the coalition so happy to be 'silent' about the specific meaning of their promise and, until the ballots were counted, perfectly content to allow misrepresentations about that policy to flourish, resulting in the apprehension that there would be no cuts to the ABC?

28   Ken Inglis, *Whose ABC?*, Melbourne: Black Inc, 2006, p. 387.

29   Ibid., p. 382.

30   Pamela Williams, *The Victory*, St Leonards: Allen & Unwin, 1997, p. 163.

31   Anne Davies, 'Political ABC rule at an end: Coalition', *The Sydney Morning Herald*, 19 January 1996, p. 2.

32   Ken Inglis, *Whose ABC?*, Melbourne: Black Inc, 2006, p. 426.

33   Ibid., pp. 425–6.

34   Ibid., pp. 526–7.

35   Chris Masters, *Jonestown: the power and the myth of Alan Jones*, Crows Nest: Allen & Unwin, 2006, pp. 302–3.

36   Ken Inglis, *Whose ABC?*, Melbourne: Black Inc, 2006, p. 544.

37   Ken Inglis, *Whose ABC?*, Melbourne: Black Inc, 2006, pp. 493–516; Kerry O'Brien, *Kerry O'Brien: a memoir*, Crows Nest: Allen & Unwin, 2018, pp. 496–508.

38   Richard Alston, *More to Life than Politics?*, Cleveland: Connor Court, 2019, p. 245.

39   Ibid.

40   Denis Muller, 'Media Accountability in a Liberal Democracy: An Examination of the Harlot's Prerogative', PhD thesis, University of Melbourne, 2005, pp. 213–23; Richard Alston, *More to Life than Politics?*, Cleveland: Connor Court, 2019, p. 246.

41   Ken Inglis, *Whose ABC?*, Melbourne: Black Inc, 2006, pp. 485–7.

42   Emma Dawson, 'Only the support of the people can save the ABC now', *Guardian Australia*, 17 May 2018, https://www.theguardian.com/media/commentisfree/2018/may/17/nly-the-support-of-the-people-can-save-the-abc-now.

43   Matthew Ricketson and Katharine Murphy, 'The Media', in Chris Aulich, ed., *From Abbott to Turnbull*, Echo Books, Canberra, 2016, p. 106.

44   *Commonwealth Parliamentary Debates House of Representatives*, 22 November 2010, pp. 3,253; *CPD Senate*, 20 June 2012, pp. 3,958–9.

45   Matthew Knott, 'ABC axes The Drum opinion website', *The Sydney Morning Herald*, 5 July 2016, https://www.smh.com.au/politics/federal/abc-axes-the-drum-opinion-website-20160705-gpyr18.html.

46   Ben Packham, 'Auditor-General slams government over tender process for Australia Network,' *The Australian*, 3 April, 2012,

https://www.theaustralian.com.au/news/auditor-general-slams-government-over-tender-process-for-australia-network/news-story/76c07466da5bb40542fbcfc983418e06.

47 'Triple j presenter told to delete Gillard "whore" tweet', *ABC News Online*, 2 December 2011, https://www.abc.net.au/news/2011-12-02/triple-j-presenter-told-to-remove-27whore27-gillard-tweet/3709644, accessed 22 August 2021; Annie Groer, 'Feminist icon Germaine Greer: Aussie PM Julia Gillard has "big arse" and bad jackets', *The Washington Post*, 16 May 2012, https://www.washingtonpost.com/blogs/she-the-people/post/feminist-icon-germaine-greer-aussie-pm-julia-gillard-has-big-arse-and-bad-jackets/2012/05/16/gIQAakiVTU_story.html, accessed 21 August 2021.

48 Interview with Emma Dawson, 4 June 2021.

49 David Knox, 'Stephen Conroy pressured ABC on Doctor Who', *TV Tonight*, 15 August 2013, https://tvtonight.com.au/2013/08/stephen-conroy-pressured-abc-on-doctor-who.html.

50 Julia Gillard, *My Story*, North Sydney: Knopf, 2014, p. 98; Elle Hunt, 'Julia Gillard attacks ABC's decision to finance sitcom At Home with Julia', *Guardian Australia*, 19 August 2016, https://www.theguardian.com/world/2016/aug/19/julia-gillard-attacks-abcs-decision-to-finance-sitcom-at-home-with-julia.

51 'No cuts to the ABC or SBS: Abbott', SBS, updated 30 January 2014, https://www.sbs.com.au/news/no-cuts-to-the-abc-or-sbs-abbott.

52 Sophie Elsworth, 'Sky News will launch its new channel on August 1 into regional Australia,' 25 July 2021, *The Australian,* https://www.theaustralian.com.au/business/media/sky-news-australia-will-launch-its-new-channel-on-august-1-into-regional-australia/news-story/62411ecf2179bc90614dcf7af0180404.

53 RMIT Fact Check unit, 'Paul Fletcher says ABC funding is rising each year. Is he correct?', *Crikey*, 20 July 2020, https://www.crikey.com.au/2020/07/20/paul-fletcher-says-abc-funding-is-rising-each-year-is-he-correct/; Jennifer Duke, '"Riddled with errors": Paul Fletcher slams ABC fact check', *The Sydney Morning Herald*, 17 August 2020, https://www.smh.com.au/politics/federal/riddled-with-errors-paul-fletcher-slams-abc-fact-check-20200814-p55ln8.html.

54 Zoe Samios and Rob Harris, 'ABC looks ahead after tough year', *The Age*, 18 December 2021, p. 18.

55 James Madden, 'Budget 2021: "Freeze" ends but ABC, SBS face cuts', *The Australian*, 11 May 2021, https://www.theaustralian.com.au/business/media/budget-2021-freeze-ends-but-abc-sbs-face-cuts/news-story/62ae07d6579559de9963571beddaee7e.

56 Tim Burrowes, *Media Unmade*, Melbourne: Hardie Grant, 2021, p. 94.

57 'Truth, trust, and treachery', *Media Watch*, 3 February 2014,

https://www.abc.net.au/mediawatch/episodes/truth-trust-and-treachery/9973608.

58 Matthew Ricketson, 'Six reasons Abbott's peace deal on *Q&A* isn't quite what it seems', *The Conversation*, 12 July 2015, https://theconversation.com/six-reasons-abbotts-peace-deal-on-qanda-isnt-quite-what-it-seems-44551.

59 Malcolm Turnbull, *A Bigger Picture*, Melbourne: Hardie Grant, 2020, p. 215.

60 Senate inquiry into allegations of political interference in the Australian Broadcasting Corporation, Environment and Communications References Committee, public hearing, Sydney, 6 March 2019, p. 13, https://parlinfo.aph.gov.au/parlInfo/download/committees/commsen/b40177a8-d496-4495-b1d0-401d47801b01/toc_pdf/Environment%20and%20Communications%20References%20Committee_2019_03_06_6991_Official.pdf;fileType=application%2Fpdf#search=%22committees/commsen/b40177a8-d496-4495-b1d0-401d47801b01/0000%22.

61 Jonathan Holmes, *On Aunty*, Carlton: Melbourne University Press, 2019, pp. 23–4.

62 Malcom Turnbull denied he had ever called Gaven Morris, the ABC's news director, to complain, and Morris, on leaving his job in late 2021, agreed but added: 'What I would notice is that other people would get phone calls that were very similar to the ones I was getting from other quarters ... So, the [Canberra] bureau would get a phone call from somebody. I would get a phone call from somebody else. Michelle [Guthrie, the then managing director] would get a phone call from somebody else ... We're all getting different phone calls, and the people involved would all be able to say that they never talked to so-and-so. But on a number of occasions, it was clear to me what was happening. It was quite a dangerous time in terms of the editorial independence of the ABC because of the different characters involved and the dynamic that was at hand'. See: Margaret Simons, 'Taking the Arrows', *Inside Story*, 12 November 2021, https://insidestory.org.au/taking-the-arrows/.

63 Jonathan Holmes, *On Aunty*, Carlton: Melbourne University Press, 2019, pp. 23–4.

64 Sarah Ferguson, 'Bitter End', *Four Corners*, ABC, 12 November 2018, https://www.abc.net.au/4corners/bitter-end/10490434.

65 Margaret Simons, 'Good news week', *Inside Story*, 21 May 2021, https://insidestory.org.au/good-news-week/.

66 'ABC statement editorial review: Impartiality of the Federal election 2019', 10 December 2020, https://about.abc.net.au/statements/abc-statement-on-editorial-review-impartiality-of-the-federal-

election-2019/, accessed 1 September 2021; Ita Buttrose to Scott Ryan, 10 December 2020, https://about.abc.net.au/wp-content/uploads/2020/12/Correspondence-from-Chair-to-Senate-President-FINAL-201210.pdf, accessed 2 September 2021.

Chapter 4. A Calm Voice in the Cacophony

1   Jonathan Holmes, *On Aunty*, Carlton: Melbourne University Press, 2019, pp. 1–2.

2   Georgina Born, *Uncertain Vision: Birt, Dyke, and the reinvention of the BBC*, London: Vintage, 2004, pp. 27–8.

3   Ibid., pp. 34–5.

4   Ibid., pp. 28–9.

5   'Statistics and Facts about the BBC', Statistica, 28 August 2020, https://www.statista.com/topics/3836/the-bbc/.

6   UNESCO, 2001, *Public Broadcasting: Why? How?*, https://unesdoc.unesco.org/ark:/48223/pf0000124058, accessed 14 September 2021.

7   'Total death toll: Over 606,000 people killed across Syria since the beginning of the "Syrian Revolution", including 495,000 documented by SOHR', Syrian Observatory for Human Rights, 1 June 2021, https://www.syriahr.com/en/217360/?__cf_chl_jschl_tk__=MCdb.OdOOkfDzirx13_TmXcx.C3vOf1aM8zpOjZhWaM-1636458623-0-gaNycGzNCNE.

8   Jenna Ross, 'The Ten Biggest Companies in the World', *Visual Capitalist*, 10 June 2021, https://www.visualcapitalist.com/the-biggest-companies-in-the-world-in-2021/.

9   Carole Cadwalladr and Emma Graham-Harrison, 'Revealed: 50 million Facebook profiles harvested for Cambridge Analytica in major data breach', *The Guardian*, 18 March 2018, https://www.theguardian.com/news/2018/mar/17/cambridge-analytica-facebook-influence-us-election.

10   Margaret Sullivan, 'Facebook is harming our society. Here's a radical solution for reining it in', *The Washington Post*, 5 October 2021, https://www.washingtonpost.com/lifestyle/media/media-sullivan-facebook-whistleblower-haugen/2021/10/04/3461c62e-2535-11ec-8831-a31e7b3de188_story.html

11   Yochai Benkler, Robert Faris, and Hal Roberts, *Network Propaganda: manipulation, disinformation, and radicalization in American politics*, New York: Oxford University Press, 2018.

12   Ibid., pp. 91–2.

13   Ibid., p. 221.

14   Elizabeth Dwoskin, 'Misinformation on Facebook got six times more clicks than factual news during the 2020 election', *The Washington Post*, 4 September 2021, https://www.washingtonpost.com/technology/2021/09/03/facebook-misinformation-nyu-study/.

15 Matt Bevan, 'YouTube bans all antivax content', ABC Radio National Breakfast, 'The Backstory', 30 September 2021, https://www.abc.net.au/radionational/programs/breakfast/the-backstory-with-matt-bevan/13564452.

16 Rasmus Kleis Nielsen, Richard Fletcher, Annika Sehl, & David Levy, 'Analysis of the Relation Between and Impact of Public Service Media and Private Media', The Reuters Institute for Study of Journalism, University of Oxford, 2016, p. 22.

17 Toril Aalberg and James Curran, eds, *How Media Inform Democracy: a comparative approach*, New York: Routledge, 2013.

18 David Cox, cited by Julian Petley, 'Impartiality in Television News: profitability versus public service,' in Stuart Allan, ed., *The Routledge Companion to News and Journalism*, London: Routledge, 2010, p. 612.

19 Victor Pickard, *Democracy Without Journalism?: confronting the misinformation society*, New York: Oxford University Press, 2020.

20 Reuters Institute Digital News Report 2021, Reuters Institute for the Study of Journalism, University of Oxford, 2021, p. 11, https://reutersinstitute.politics.ox.ac.uk/sites/default/files/2021-06/Digital_News_Report_2021_FINAL.pdf.

21 Jon Allsop, 'The BBC, Piers Morgan, and the real cost of the British-media culture war', *Columbia Journalism Review*, 17 September 2021, https://www.cjr.org/the_media_today/jess_brammar_bbc_piers_morgan.php.

Chapter 5. A Billion Reasons

1 Tom McIlroy, 'Labor targets Mayo candidate Georgina Downer in ABC scare campaign', *The Australian Financial Review*, 18 June 2018, https://www.afr.com/politics/coalition-cant-be-trusted-on-abc-privatisation-promises-michelle-rowland-20180618-h11i40, accessed 5 March 2021.

2 David Crowe, 'Liberal Party council votes to sell off the ABC and move Australian embassy to Jerusalem', *The Sydney Morning Herald*, 16 June 2018, https://www.smh.com.au/politics/federal/liberal-party-council-votes-to-sell-off-the-abc-20180616-p4zlut.html, accessed 24 February 2021.

3 Ibid.

4 Forum for Research and Policy in Communications, 'An analysis of CBC's financial history from 1937 to 2019: We tried to follow the money; Frodo had it easier', research paper, Ottawa, February 2020, https://frpc.net/wp-content/uploads/2020/02/Public-funding-of-CBC-operations-2020-4-February.pdf, accessed 1 October 2021.

5 Padraic McGuinness, *The Australian Financial Review*, 3 September 1984.

6   *The Australian Financial Review*, 13 March 1985.

7   John Nurick, *Mandate to Govern*, Perth: Australian Institute for Public Policy, 1987, pp. 176–81.

8   Glyn Davis, *Breaking Up the ABC*, Sydney: Allen & Unwin, 1988, p. 133.

9   Another call for privatisation, predicated entirely on economic grounds, is offered by Ross Jones. See: Ross Jones, 'Does Australia Really Need the ABC?', *Agenda*, vol. 4, no. 2, 1997, pp. 253–8.

10 Richard Alston, 'Left wing bias proves it is clearly their ABC', *The Australian Financial Review*, 12 January 2021. See too the similar affirmations of his memoir, *More to Life than Politics?*, Cleveland: Connor Court, p. 227.

11 Mitch Fifield, 'Speech to the Australian Adam Smith Club: Fiscal Contraception: Erecting barriers to impulsive spending', 7 October 2008, https://www.mitchfifield.com/2008/10/fiscal-contraception-erecting-barriers-to-impulsive-spending/, accessed 30 August 2021.

12 Lenore Taylor, 'ABC cuts not an "efficiency dividend", says Malcolm Turnbull, contradicting Abbott', *The Guardian*, 25 November 2014, https://www.theguardian.com/media/2014/nov/25/abc-cuts-not-an-efficiency-dividend-says-malcolm-turnbull-contradicting-abbott, accessed 26 August 2021.

13 James Paterson, 'Ignore the hysteria: it's time we privatised the tone-deaf, left-leaning ABC', *The Sydney Morning Herald*, 30 January 2014, https://www.smh.com.au/opinion/ignore-the-hysteria-its-time-we-privatised-the-tone-deaf-leftleaning-abc-20140130-31o39.html, accessed 14 August 2021.

14 David Crowe, 'Footage from Liberal Party meeting reveals who voted to sell the ABC', *The Sydney Morning Herald*, 18 June 2018, https://www.smh.com.au/politics/federal/footage-from-liberal-party-meeting-reveals-who-voted-to-sell-the-abc-20180618-p4zm5e.html, accessed 30 August 2021; 'Jim Molan calls for "defunding of the ABC" after Four Corners ran a "disgusting show"', *Sky News*, 10 November 2020, https://www.skynews.com.au/australia-news/jim-molan-calls-for-defunding-of-the-abc-after-four-corners-ran-a-disgusting-show/video/48ef8582a19ea59229b1a9ca25a8b962, accessed 29 August 2021; James McGrath, *CPD Senate*, 16 July 2014, p. 5178, and 21 June 2021, p. 68.

15 See, for example, 'Your ABC vs their IPA — ABC Alumni', Members ABC Alumni, 1 November 2021, https://www.youtube.com/watch?v=PT9UOdr-sqs.

16 Chris Berg and Sinclair Davidson, *Against Public Broadcasting*, Cleveland: Connor Court, 2018, p. 47.

17   Ibid., p. 52.

18   Ibid., p. 59.

19   Ibid., p 74.

20   Australian Competition and Consumer Commission, *Digital Platforms Inquiry*, June 2019, Canberra, p. 290.

21   Chris Berg and Sinclair Davidson, *Against Public Broadcasting*, Cleveland: Connor Court, 2018, p. 58.

22   Ibid., pp. 87–8.

23   Peter van Onselen, 'A billion good reasons to sell the broadcaster', *The Australian*, 25 May 2013.

24   William Hill, 'Privatise the ABC', *Spectator*, 16 January 2017, https://spectator.com.au/2017/01/privatise-the-abc/, accessed 14 April 2021.

25   Richard Alston, *More to Life than Politics?*, Cleveland: Connor Court, 2019, p. 225.

26   Peter van Onselen and Wayne Errington, *Who Dares Loses: pariah policies*, Melbourne: Monash University Publishing, 2021, pp. 34–7.

27   The cost of transmitting ABC services was treated either as free or went unrecorded, as transmission was provided by government entities. When the Howard government privatised the National Transmission Agency in 1999, the ABC needed an appropriation to purchase the transmission services.

28   Appendices A and B, 'Budget 2020–21', https://budget.gov.au/2020-21/content/overview.htm#two, accessed 15 April 2021.

29   The report remained secret, though a two-page summary that had been provided to the ABC board was leaked. See: 'ABC efficient but under-funded: KPMG report', 15 March 2006, https://www.abc.net.au/news/2006-03-15/abc-efficient-under-funded-kpmg-report/818370, accessed 21 March 2021.

30   *ABC and SBS Efficiency Study: Draft Report*, Department of Communications, Canberra, 2014.

31   Jennifer Duke and Fergus Hunter, 'Efficiency review questions the focus of ABC and SBS on lifestyle and food content', *The Sydney Morning Herald*, 5 March 2019, https://www.smh.com.au/business/companies/efficiency-review-questions-the-focus-of-abc-and-sbs-on-lifestyle-and-food-content-20190305-p511u7.html, accessed 5 March 2021; Australian Senate, 'Media Diversity in Australia', report of the Environment and Communications References Committee, December 2021, pp. 113–14.

32   Peter Tonagh and Richard Bean, *National Broadcasters Efficiency Review*, 2018, p. 11.

33   Chris Berg and Sinclair Davidson, *Against Public Broadcasting*, Cleveland: Connor Court, 2018, pp. 88–90.

34   Macquarie Bank, *Report to the Australian Broadcasting*

Corporation: an analysis of the ABC's funding relative to international public broadcasters and domestic peers, September 2002, https://apo.org.au/node/40274, accessed 20 March 2021.

35 Chris Berg and Sinclair Davidson, *Against Public Broadcasting*, Cleveland: Connor Court, 2018, p. 118.

36 Berg and Davidson also cite the salaries of various ABC journalists and presenters as an example of the ABC's 'crowding out' in the labour market. How exactly this is the case is unclear: if anything, Berg and Davidson simply seem stumped by how ABC presenters and journalists are remunerated.

37 It may also be worth noting that Berg and Davidson's source for this example is an *Australian* article reporting on a call for the ABC charter to be amended to include local content requirements in children's broadcasting.

38 Don Groves, 'Free-to-air broadcasters state their case to abolish children's TV quotas', *If*, 20 July 2017, https://www.if.com.au/free-to-air-broadcasters-state-their-case-to-abolish-childrens-tv-quotas/, accessed 4 October 2021.

39 Tim Burrowes, 'Crikey's Eric Beecher: ABC should not have launched The Drum', 11 October 2010, https://mumbrella.com.au/crickeys-eric-beecher-abc-should-not-have-launched-the-drum-34432, accessed 14 April 2021; Margaret Simons, *The Contentmakers*, Camberwell: Penguin, 2007, p. 147.

40 'ABC Open project may "shut rural papers"', *The Sydney Morning Herald*, 5 February 2010, https://www.smh.com.au/business/abc-open-project-may-shut-rural-papers-20100205-nido.html, accessed 14 April 2021.

41 Geoff Elliott, 'Eric Beecher is right to bag the ABC's Drum site', *The Australian*, 18 October 2010, https://www.theaustralian.com.au/business/media/eric-beecher-is-right-to-bag-the-abcs-drum-site/news-story/be8eb8b709bc0e6c3231838db7bc038b, accessed 14 April 2021.

42 Jason Wilson, 'ABC overlap: is it in the public interest?', *The Drum*, 12 November 2010, updated 6 February 2020, https://www.abc.net.au/news/2010-11-12/new_document/40928, accessed 17 April 2021.

43 Robert Kerr, Sandra Levy, and Julie Flynn, *Inquiry into the Competitive Neutrality of the National Broadcasters: report by the Expert Panel*, September 2018, Department of Communications and the Arts, 12 December 2018, https://apo.org.au/sites/default/files/resource-files/2018-12/apo-nid210591.pdf.

44 John Nurick, *Mandate to Govern*, Perth: Australian Institute for Public Policy, 1987, p. 177.

45 Chris Berg and Sinclair Davidson, *Against Public Broadcasting*, Cleveland: Connor Court, 2018, p. 103.

46   Ibid., p. 100.

47   Sinclair Davidson, 'Their ABC must be worried', 17 November 2020, https://ipa.org.au/publications-ipa/their-abc-must-be-worried, accessed 5 March 2021.

48   Folker Hanusch, 2013, 'Journalists in Times of Change: evidence from a new survey of Australia's journalistic workforce', *Australian Journalism Review*, vol. 35, no. 1, pp. 29–42.

49   'Fact check: Are ABC employees or journalists five times more likely to vote for the Greens than the general population?', 13 July 2018, https://www.abc.net.au/news/2018-07-13/fact-check3a-abc-greens-voters/9931782, accessed 5 March 2021.

50   Daniel Wild, 'Holding the ABC to account for staff-led, taxpayer-funded climate activism', 28 May 2020, https://ipa.org.au/research-areas/climate-change/holding-the-abc-to-account-for-staff-led-taxpayer-funded-climate-activism, accessed 5 March 2021; John Roskam and Daniel Wild, '20 policies to fix Australia', Institute of Public Affairs, 12 April 2019, https://ipa.org.au/wp-content/uploads/2019/04/IPA-Research-20-Policies-to-Fix-Australia.pdf, accessed 5 March 2021.

51   Chris Berg and Sinclair Davidson, *Against Public Broadcasting*, Cleveland: Connor Court, 2018, p. 111.

52   'Those at the ABC "aren't used to hearing frank, mainstream assessments"', *Sky News*, 6 April 2020, https://www.skynews.com.au/details/_6147363685001, accessed 5 March 2021; Gerard Henderson, 'Late-night tweets reveal truth about ABC's culture', *The Australian*, 24 October 2020. Henderson has long drawn this exclusion around such programs: *Counterpoint*, for example, was not 'prominent' on account of its broadcast time.

53   Tom Switzer and Amanda Vanstone, *Counterpoint*, 'Should the ABC be privatised?, 10 June 2013, https://www.abc.net.au/radionational/programs/counterpoint/should-the-abc-be-privatised3f/4740464, accessed 15 April 2021.

54   Gideon Rozner, 'Poll: Only 32% of Australians believe the ABC represents the views of ordinary Australians', https://ipa.org.au/publications-ipa/poll-only-32-of-australians-believe-the-abc-represents-the-views-of-ordinary-australians, accessed 5 March 2021.

55   *ABC Poll 2020*, Institute for Public Affairs, https://ipa.org.au/wp-content/uploads/2020/02/IPA-Research-ABC-Poll.pdf, accessed 5 March 2021.

56   Tom Switzer, 2013, 'Privatise the ABC', in Gary Johns, ed., *Really Dangerous Ideas*, Cleveland: Connor Court, 2013, pp. 125–31.

57   The ABC has long been attentive to reviewing its news and current affairs coverage. After the 2019 election, for example, the ABC

commissioned British journalist Kerry Blackburn to review its coverage. Blackburn 'did not find a pronounced bias in the framing of the narrative in favour or against either of the main parties'. Although Blackburn identified three individual programs out of 167 that gave more positive impressions of Labor than the coalition, the finding of her report was that the ABC's coverage 'consistently reflected a diversity of perspectives and covered a broad range of policy and campaign issues'. See: Kerry Blackburn, *ABC Editorial Review no. 19: impartiality of the Federal Election 2019*, https://about.abc.net.au/wp-content/uploads/2020/12/Correspondence-from-Chair-to-Senate-President-FINAL-201210.pdf, accessed 5 March 2021, pp. 12, 42.

58   Tom Switzer, 2013, 'Privatise the ABC', in Gary Johns, ed., *Really Dangerous Ideas*, Cleveland: Connor Court, 2013, pp. 125–31.

59   UNESCO, 2001, *Public Broadcasting: Why? How?*, https://unesdoc.unesco.org/ark:/48223/pf0000124058, accessed 13 April 2021.

60   Chris Berg and Sinclair Davidson, *Against Public Broadcasting*, Cleveland: Connor Court, p. 126.

Chapter 6. Identifying Bias Everywhere but Yourself

1   Judith Ireland, 'Tony Abbott blasts national broadcaster: ABC takes everyone's side but Australia's', *The Sydney Morning Herald*, 29 January 2014, https://www.smh.com.au/politics/federal/tony-abbott-blasts-national-broadcaster-abc-takes-everyones-side-but-australias-20140129-31lt8.html, accessed 28 August 2021.

2   Among the numerous academic studies and media investigations are: Robert Manne, *Bad News: Murdoch's Australian and the shaping of the nation, Quarterly Essay*, no. 43, Melbourne: Black Inc, 2011; Rodney Tiffen, *Rupert Murdoch: a reassessment*, Sydney: NewSouth, 2014; Andrew Dodd and Matthew Ricketson, 'The *Australian*'s Media Supplement: a lapdog, a watchdog, an attack dog, or all of the above?', *Media International Australia*, vol. 57, no. 1, November 2015, pp. 68–78; Eric Beecher, Emily Watkins, Christopher Warren, and Bernard Keane, 'Holy Wars: How *The Australian* attacks and targets its enemies', *Crikey*, 19 October 2017, https://www.crikey.com.au/feature/holy-wars-australian-targets-attacksenemies/#australian-journalisms-freak-show; Rodney Tiffen, 'Climategate', *Australian Journalism Review*, vol. 42, no. 1, 2020, pp. 23–36.

3   MEAA, *Ethics in Journalism*, Carlton: Melbourne University Press, 1997, p. 121.

4   Rhonda Jolly, *The ABC: an overview*, Commonwealth Parliamentary Library, 20 April 2011, https://www.aph.gov.au/About_Parliament/Parliamentary_Departments/Parliamentary_

Library/pubs/BN/101 1/ABC#_ftn23; ABC Editorial Policies,
15 January 2019, p. 3, https://about.abc.net.au/wp-content/
uploads/2017/11/A5print-15-01-2019.pdf.

5   Australian Press Council, Statement of General Principles, 1 August
    2014, https://www.presscouncil.org.au/statements-of-principles/.

6   Australian Senate, 'Media Diversity in Australia', report of the
    Environment and Communications References Committee,
    December 2021, p. 38.

7   Commercial Radio Australia, *Code of Practice*, 2017, http://
    www.commercialradio.com.au/CR/media/CommercialRadio/
    Commercial-Radio-Code-of-Practice.pdf.

8   Free TV, *Commercial Television Industry Code of Practice*, 2018,
    https://www.freetv.com.au/resources/code-of-practice/.

9   SBS, *Code of Practice*, 2021, https://www.sbs.com.au/aboutus/sites/
    sbs.com.au.aboutus/files/sbs_code_of_practice_july_2021.pdf.

10 Ray Finkelstein, assisted by Matthew Ricketson, *Report of the
    Independent Inquiry into the Media and Media Regulation*,
    Department of Broadband, Communications and the Digital
    Economy, 2012, p. 195.

11 The Herald and Weekly Times Limited Professional Practice Policy,
    reprinted in John Hurst and Sally White, *Ethics and the Australian
    News Media*, South Melbourne: Macmillan, 1994, pp. 287–97; *The
    Age* Code of Conduct, 1998, https://accountablejournalism.org/
    ethics-codes/Australia-Age-Code; *The Sydney Morning Herald*
    Code of Ethics, no date, https://www.abc.net.au/mediawatch/
    transcripts/0726_smh.pdf; News Corp Australia Editorial Code of
    Conduct, no date, https://www.theaustralian.com.au/editorial-
    code-of-conduct.

12 Ken Inglis, *Whose ABC?*, Melbourne: Black Inc, 2006, p. 294.

13 For an example, see Chris Mitchell, 'Lazy ABC groupthink at the
    heart of bias over Covid lockdowns', *The Australian*, 30 August
    2021, https://www.theaustralian.com.au/business/media/lazy-abc-
    groupthink-at-heart-of-bias-over-covid-lockdowns/news-story/6aa
    acfdcd024a438874e38f530e16169.

14 Ken Inglis, *Whose ABC?*, Melbourne: Black Inc, 2006, p. 398.

15 Ibid., p. 544.

16 Ibid., p. 427.

17 Ibid., p. 436.

18 Election Coverage Review Committee, ABC, https://about.abc.net.
    au/how-the-abc-is-run/what-guides-us/election-coverage-review-
    committee-ecrc/.

19 Paul Chadwick, *2007 Federal Election: Report of the Chairman,
    Election Coverage Review Committee*, ABC, February 2008, p. 7,
    https://about.abc.net.au/wp-content/uploads/2012/07/ABC-ECRC-

ChairmanReportFedElection2007.pdf.

20 Paul Chadwick, *2007 Federal Election: Report of the Chairman, Election Coverage Review Committee*, ABC, February 2008, p. 4.

21 Matt Martino, 'Fact check: Are ABC employees or journalists five times more likely to vote for the Greens than the general population?', ABC/RMIT Fact Check Unit, 13 July 2018, https://www.abc.net.au/news/2018-07-13/fact-check3a-abc-greens-voters/9931782.

22 Quoted in Sally Young, *How Australia Decides: election reporting and the media*, Port Melbourne: Cambridge University Press, 2011, pp. 233–4.

23 Ibid., p. 234.

24 Ibid., pp. 237–41; Patrick Mullins, *Tiberius with a Telephone*, Melbourne: Scribe, 2018, p. 583.

25 Sally Young, *How Australia Decides: election reporting and the media*, Port Melbourne: Cambridge University Press, 2011, pp. 239–40.

26 Ray Finkelstein, assisted by Matthew Ricketson, *Report of the Independent Inquiry into the Media and Media Regulation*, 2012, pp. 375–404. The quote is on p. 394.

27 Sora Park, Caroline Fisher, Glen Fuller, and Jee Young Lee, *Digital News Report: Australia 2018*, p. 28, https://apo.org.au/sites/default/files/resource-files/2018-06/apo-nid174861.pdf; Caroline Fisher, Sora Park, Jee Young Lee, Glen Fuller, and Yoonmo Sang, *Digital News Report: Australia 2019*, p. 78, https://apo.org.au/sites/default/files/resource-files/2019-06/apo-nid240786.pdf; Sora Park, Caroline Fisher, Jee Young Lee, Kieran McGuinness, Yoonmo Sang, Mathieu O'Neil, Michael Jensen, Kerry McCallum, and Glen Fuller, *Digital News Report: Australia 2020*, p. 76, https://apo.org.au/sites/default/files/resource-files/2020-06/apo-nid305057_0.pdf; Sora Park, Caroline Fisher, Kieran McGuinness, Jee Young Lee, and Kerry McCallum, *Digital News Report: Australia 2021*, p. 78, https://apo.org.au/sites/default/files/resource-files/2021-06/apo-nid312650_0.pdf.

28 For example: three weeks before David Hill resigned as managing director in 1994, the opening question he received from presenter Andrew Dodd on Radio National's *The Media Report* was, 'When are you going to resign?' See also: Kerry O'Brien, *Kerry O'Brien: a memoir*, Crows Nest: Allen & Unwin, 2018, pp. 492, 505–6, for forthright interviews with ABC chair Donald McDonald and managing director Jonathan Shier.

29 Ray Finkelstein, assisted by Matthew Ricketson, *Independent Inquiry into the Media and Media Regulation*, 2012, pp. 199–203. *The Sydney Morning Herald* did, for short periods in its history, have ombudspersons.

30 Rodney Tiffen, submission to the Senate inquiry into

media diversity, 2021, p. 6, https://www.aph.gov.au/
Parliamentary_Business/Committees/Senate/Environment_and_
Communications/Mediadiversity/Submissions.

31 Sharri Markson, 'Why newspapers have a shining future', *The Australian*, Media section, 26 May 2014.

32 Anne Hyland, 'Ken Cowley's judgment day', *The Australian Financial Review*, 1 June 2014, https://www.afr.com/companies/
media-and-marketing/ken-cowley-s-judgment-day-20140531-
ivd0c, accessed 29 August 2021; Sharri Markson, 'Cowley retreats on News criticism', *The Australian*, 2 June 2014, pp. 1–2.

33 Andrew Dodd and Matthew Ricketson, '*The Australian*'s Media Supplement: a lapdog, a watchdog, an attack dog, or all of the above?', *Media International Australia*, vol. 57, no. 1, November 2015, p. 72. There is an odd and peculiarly News Corp wrinkle to this point. In 2021, after many years of campaigning against the need to take action on human-induced climate change, News Corp Australia's tabloid newspapers did a backflip and began campaigning for it. The campaign did not extend to *The Australian*, nor to its high-profile columnist Andrew Bolt, who derided the new campaign as rubbish on his Sky News Australia program. Bolt's stance may have had something to do with the deep personal and reputational stake he has in his brand as a truth-teller on what he sees as the climate-change hoax. The differing editorial stances in a media company known for its ability to mount company-wide editorial campaigns may also have had something to do with Murdoch's sharp nose for protecting his commercial interests and for backing, or anticipating, changes in the political wind. See: 'News Corp's climate zeal', *Media Watch*, 18 October 2021, https://
www.abc.net.au/mediawatch/episodes/ep-37/13591482.

34 See, for instance: Denis Muller, *Quality Assurance Project 3: Impartiality (News Content)*, ABC, July 2008, https://about.abc.net.au/wp-content/uploads/2012/06/
QAProject3ImpartialityNewsContentJul2008.pdf.

35 Alan Sunderland, 'Don't blame umpire on ABC complaints', *The Age*, 14 July 2021, p. 19.

36 Robert Kerr, Julie Flynn, and Sandra Levy, *Inquiry into the Competitive Neutrality of the National Broadcasters: Report by the Expert Panel*, September 2018, p. 11, https://www.communications.
gov.au/documents/inquiry-competitive-neutrality-national-
broadcasters-report-expert-panel.

37 Amanda Meade, 'Executive decision: Lachlan Murdoch turns back on media inquiry to re-open Fox News,' *Guardian Australia*, 3 September 2021, https://www.theguardian.com/media/2021/
sep/03/executive-decision-lachlan-murdoch-turns-back-on-media-

inquiry-to-reopen-fox-news.

38 Craig McMurtrie, 'The essential role of the ABC's Audience and Consumer Affairs unit in investigating complaints', *ABC Backstory*, 15 November 2021, https://www.abc.net.au/news/backstory/2021-11-15/abc-craig-mcmurtrie-on-abc-complaints-handling-inquiry/100620738.

39 Ray Finkelstein, assisted by Matthew Ricketson, *Report of the Independent Inquiry into the Media and Media Regulation*, 2012, p. 170.

40 Ibid., p. 177–80; Australian Senate, 'Media Diversity in Australia', report of the Environment and Communications References Committee, December 2021, p. xii.

41 Ray Finkelstein, assisted by Matthew Ricketson, *Report of the Independent Inquiry into the Media and Media Regulation*, 2012, p. 160.

42 George Munster, *Rupert Murdoch: a paper prince*, Ringwood: Viking, 1985, pp. 186–203; Rhonda Jolly, *Media Ownership and Regulation: a chronology, part 2: 1972 to 1995: moguls, miscreants, and new regulatory brooms*, Parliamentary Library, 18 February 2018, pp. 23–32, https://apo.org.au/sites/default/files/resource-files/2018-02/apo-nid132646.pdf.

43 Rob Johnson, *Cash for Comment: the seduction of journo culture*, Sydney: Pluto Press, 2000.

44 Matthew Ricketson and Russell Skelton, 'Shock and awe', *The Age*, 13 April 2007, p. 11.

45 Australian Communications and Media Authority, *Investigation Report BI-568*, 17 December 2020.

46 Tim Burrowes, *Media Unmade*, Melbourne: Hardie Grant, 2021, pp. 117–21.

47 Jonathan Holmes, *On Aunty*, Carlton: Melbourne University Press, 2019, p. 62.

48 Ibid., p. 52.

49 Ibid., pp. 64–5.

50 Jonathan Holmes, *Media Watch*, ABC, 18 July 2011, updated June 2012, https://www.abc.net.au/mediawatch/episodes/personal-or-policy-you-be-the-judge/9974236.

51 Australian Senate, 'Media Diversity in Australia', report of the Environment and Communications References Committee, December 2021, pp. 65, 55.

52 Zoe Samios and Rob Harris, 'ABC looks ahead after tough year', *The Age*, 18 December 2021, p. 18.

53 Jonathan Holmes, *On Aunty*, Carlton: Melbourne University Press, 2019, p. 60.

54 For a summary, see: Margaret Simons, 'The watchdog that sometimes barked', *Inside Story*, 2 July 2021, https://insidestory.org.au/the-watchdog-that-sometimes-barked/. For more detail,

see: Matthew Ricketson, 'Why the MEAA left the Press Council and why that matters', *Australian Journalism Review*, vol. 43 no. 1, July 2021, pp. 11–21. Disclosure: one of the authors of this book, Matthew Ricketson, has been the MEAA's representative on the Press Council since 2016.

55 Jonathan Holmes, *On Aunty*, Carlton: Melbourne University Press, 2019, p. 65.

56 Amy Remeikis, 'Kevin Rudd and Malcolm Turnbull challenge News Corp over reports of "foreign interference" in petition', *Guardian Australia*, 18 November 2020, https://www.theguardian.com/media/2020/nov/18/kevin-rudd-and-malcolm-turnbull-challenge-news-corp-over-reports-of-foreign-interference-in-petition.

57 Neville Stevens, evidence to the Senate inquiry into media diversity, public hearing, 22 October 2021, pp. 13–14, https://parlino.aph.gov.au/parlInfo/download/committees/commsen/25071/toc_pdf/Environment%20and%20Communications%20References%20Committee_2021_10_22.pdf;fileType=application%2Fpdf#search=%22committees/commsen/25071/0000%22.

58 Australian Senate, 'Media Diversity in Australia', report of the Environment and Communications References Committee, December 2021, https://parlinfo.aph.gov.au/parlInfo/download/committees/reportsen/024602/toc_pdf/MediadiversityinAustralia.pdf;fileType=application%2Fpdf; James Madden, 'Labor rejects push for judicial inquiry into media regulation', *The Australian*, 9 December 2021, https://www.theaustralian.com.au/nation/politics/push-for-media-inquiry-doomed/news-story/7326815c77fc7e572cc30fe2336a7a68. Labor's response to the Senate report brought to mind how in 2012 British prime minister David Cameron stood up in parliament to bemoan how politicians, including him, had been cowed in the face of media power, and promised to implement the findings of any inquiry into phone hacking — and then rejected Lord Leveson's central recommendation within hours of his 2,000-page report being released. See: Patrick Wintour and Nicholas Watt, 'Leveson report: David Cameron rejects call for statutory press regulation', *The Guardian*, 30 November 2012, https://www.theguardian.com/media/2012/nov/29/leveson-report-david-cameron-rejects.

Chapter 7. Reaches, Touches, Fashions

1 Jim Spigelman, 'The role of the ABC in Australian culture', 22 November 2012, address for the 30th anniversary of Conversazione, Melbourne, http://about.abc.net.au/speeches/the-role-of-the-abc-in-australian-culture/, accessed 1 July 2021.

2 While the Commonwealth's 2020–21 appropriation was $1.065

billion, the ABC was forecast to earn a further $64 million from other sources while retaining a $6.7 million cash reserve. See: 'Australian Broadcasting Corporation: Entity resources and planned performance', Portfolio Budget Statements, 2020–21, p. 125.

3   *ABC Annual Report 2020–2021*, 21 October 2021, p. 68, https://about. abc.net.au/reports-publications/abc-annual-report-2020-2021/.

4   Ibid., pp. 56–7.

5   Annie Lawson, 'Out of the hot seat', *The Age*, 8 September 2005, https://www.theage.com.au/entertainment/out-of-the-hot-seat-20050908-ge0ult.html, accessed 1 September 2021.

6   Quentin Dempster, 'The ABC', in Bridget Griffen-Foley, ed., *A Companion to the Australian Media*, Australian Scholarly Publishing, 2014, pp. 42–6.

7   'Grinspoon', *Howlspace: Music from Australia & NZ*, 27 July 2012, https://webarchive.nla.gov.au/awa/20120726200945/http:// pandora.nla.gov.au/pan/14231/20120727-0512/www.howlspace. com.au/en4/grinspoon/grinspoon.htm, accessed 14 August 2021.

8   'About Unearthed: Discover', *Triple J Unearthed*, no date, https:// www.triplejunearthed.com/comps-and-resources/about, accessed 16 August 2021.

9   Liz Giuffre, 2009, 'Maintaining *Rage*: counting down without a host for over 20 years', *Perfect Beat*, vol. 10, no. 1, pp. 39–47.

10 Ibid.

11 *ABC Annual Report 2020*, 20 October 2020, p. 30, https://about.abc. net.au/press-releases/abc-annual-report-2020/

12 Elizabeth Mackinlay and Katelyn Barney, 2008, '"Move over and make room for Meeka": the representation of race, otherness, and indigeneity on the Australian children's television program *Play School*', *Discourse*, vol. 29, no. 2, pp. 273–88.

13 This paragraph draws on Liz Giuffre, 2021, 'Blue, Requestival, Play School, and ME@Home: the ABC (Kids) of communication cultures during lockdown', *Media International Australia*, vol. 178, no. 1, pp. 63–76; and *ABC Annual Report 2020*, 20 October 2020, p. 22, https:// about.abc.net.au/press-releases/abc-annual-report-2020/.

14 In addition to playing the band's music, Triple J presented a news story on the band and the campaign, and offered links to help listeners with mental health issues.

15 John Howard, *Lazarus Rising: a personal and political autobiography*, Pymble: HarperCollins, 2010, p. 12; Ken Inglis, *Whose ABC?*, Melbourne: Black Inc, 2006, pp. 372–3.

16 Michael Ward, 'ABC television and the development of televised cricket', *Sporting Traditions*, vol. 35, no. 1, May 2018, pp. 79–96.

17 'In the box seat: Jim Maxwell profile', *RadioInfo*, 4 January 2007,

https://www.radioinfo.com.au/news/box-seat-jim-maxwell-profile, accessed 28 August 2021.

18   See John Faulkner's remarks: *CPD Senate*, 19 March 2013, https://www.aph.gov.au/Parliamentary_Business/Hansard/Hansard_Display?bid=chamber/hansards/c06d5112-f3de-47b9-88ce-ad5ee5a1a980/&sid=0196, accessed 28 August 2021.

19   Jim Maxwell, *The Sound of Summer: a memoir*, Crows Nest: Allen & Unwin, 2016, p. 71.

20   Joshua Hodson, 'Australian Olympic Committee calls for ABC to pursue Tokyo 2020 radio rights', *Ministry of Sport*, November 2019, https://ministryofsport.com.au/australian-olympic-committee-calls-for-abc-to-pursue-tokyo-2020-radio-rights/, accessed 28 August 2021.

21   Amanda Meade, 'ABC drops Tokyo Olympics live radio coverage, blaming budget cuts', *The Guardian*, 11 November 2019, https://www.theguardian.com/media/2019/nov/11/abc-drops-tokyo-olympics-live-radio-coverage-blaming-budget-cuts, accessed 1 September 2021.

22   Jennifer Duke, '"Hard to justify": Free-to-air TV slams ABC lifestyle project', *The Sydney Morning Herald*, 3 August 2018, https://www.smh.com.au/business/companies/hard-to-justify-free-to-air-tv-slams-abc-lifestyle-project-20180802-p4zv54.html, accessed 1 September 2021.

23   Osman Faruqi, 'Closing ABC Life is more about politics and appeasement than good outcomes', *The Guardian*, 25 June 2020, https://www.theguardian.com/commentisfree/2020/jun/25/closing-abc-life-is-more-about-politics-and-appeasement-than-good-outcomes, accessed 1 September 2021.

24   Gerard Henderson, 'Media Watch Dog', no. 497, 22 May 2020, https://thesydneyinstitute.com.au/blog/issue-497/, accessed 1 September 2021.

25   Chris Kenny, 'ABC Life hits a new high on the wokeness scale', *The Australian*, 11 September 2019.

26   Brittney Rigby, 'ABC Life's "rebrand" is a loss; it published pieces that would never find homes with its commercial critics', *Mumbrella*, 26 June 2020, https://mumbrella.com.au/abc-lifes-rebrand-is-a-loss-it-published-pieces-that-would-never-find-homes-with-its-commercial-critics-632395, accessed 1 September 2021.

27   Broede Carmody, 'Controversial lifestyle website ABC Life to be renamed', *The Sydney Morning Herald*, 14 December 2020, https://www.smh.com.au/culture/tv-and-radio/controversial-lifestyle-website-abc-life-to-be-renamed-20201211-p56mt4.html.

28   Zoe Samios, 'ABC stands by "Life" website amid internal staff tensions', *The Sydney Morning Herald*, 1 June 2020, https://www.

smh.com.au/business/companies/abc-stands-by-life-website-as-commercial-rivals-crumble-20200531-p54y4v.html, accessed 1 September 2021.

29   Tonagh and Bean's report gives two examples of ABC Life content that are not representative (but much in the vein of those noted by Henderson and Kenny), is doubtful of information that ABC Life was of low cost and leveraged existing content, and, in calling it 'distant from the core', place ABC Life as a secondary priority to the ABC's journalism. Given that the same review was also doubtful that SBS's sports coverage — in particular, the Tour de France and FIFA World Cup — were central to its charter, there are grounds to consider that Tonagh and Bean were overly narrow in their regard for these programs and misread the charters. See Peter Tonagh and Richard Bean, 'National broadcasters efficiency review', December 2018, p. 58.

30   Broede Carmody, 'Controversial lifestyle website ABC Live renamed', *The Sydney Morning Herald*, 14 December 2020, https://www.smh.com.au/culture/tv-and-radio/controversial-lifestyle-website-abc-life-to-be-renamed-20201211-p56mt4.html, accessed 1 September 2021.

Chapter 8. 'Regional Australia Would Be Siberia'

1   Malcolm Turnbull, 'A new era for Australia's media', 14 September 2017, https://www.malcolmturnbull.com.au/media/a-new-era-for-australias-media, accessed 19 July 2021.

2   Ibid.

3   Brian McNair, 'Memo to Michelle Guthrie: as local newspapers die, might the ABC help out?', 10 May 2016, *The Conversation*, https://theconversation.com/memo-to-michelle-guthrie-as-local-newspapers-die-might-the-abc-help-out-58983, accessed 19 July 2021.

4   Simon Crerar, 'Coronavirus and the crisis in regional news', 9 April 2020, https://www.uts.edu.au/research-and-teaching/our-research/centre-media-transition/news/coronavirus-and-crisis-regional-news, accessed 19 July 2021; Matthew Ricketson, Andrew Dodd, Lawrie Zion, and Monika Winarnita, '"Like Being Shot in the Face" or "I'm Glad I'm Out": journalists' experiences of job loss in the Australian media industry, 2012–2014', *Journalism Studies*, vol. 21, no. 1, 2020, pp. 54–71.

5   Australian Competition and Consumer Commission, *Digital Platforms Inquiry Final Report*, Canberra, June 2019, p. 18.

6   Amanda Meade, 'News Corp Australia warns of coronavirus crisis job cuts as smaller regional papers close', *Guardian*, 25 March 2020; Amanda Meade, 'Dozens of Australian newspapers stop printing

as coronavirus crisis hits advertising', *Guardian*, 14 April 2020; Amanda Meade, 'News Corp announces end of more than 100 Australian print newspapers in huge shift to digital', *The Guardian*, 28 May 2020.

7   Steven Waldman and Charles Sennott, 'The Coronavirus is killing local news', *The Atlantic*, 25 March 2020, https://www.theatlantic.com/ideas/archive/2020/03/coronavirus-killing-local-news/608695/, accessed 19 July 2021.

8   Judith Brett, 2007, 'The Country, the City, and the State in the Australian Settlement', *Australian Journal of Political Science*, vol. 42, no. 1, March, pp. 1–17. See, too, Judith Brett, 'Fair Share: country and city in Australia', *Quarterly Essay*, no. 42, Melbourne: Black Inc, 2011, which draws on the above paper.

9   Telstra, 'Universal Service Obligation (USO)', https://www.telstra.com.au/consumer-advice/customer-service/universal-service-obligation, accessed 17 July 2021.

10   Committee of Review of the Australian Broadcasting Commission, *The ABC in Review: national broadcasting in the 1980s*, Australian Government Publishing Service, Canberra, 1981, p. 56.

11   James Fenton, *CPD*, 9 March 1932, pp. 840–7.

12   Mary Debrett, *Reinventing Public Service Television for the Digital Future*, Bristol: Intellect, 2010, p. 81.

13   'Report of the Royal Commission on Television', Commonwealth Government Printer, Canberra, 1954, pp. 28–9.

14   Michael Thurlow and Bridget Griffen-Foley, 'Station Break: a history of Australian regional commercial television ownership and control', *Australian Journalism Review*, vol. 38, no. 1, 2016, pp. 117–30.

15   This comment and more from Marks are drawn from: *Official Committee Hansard, Senate, Environment and Communications Legislation Committee*, 'Broadcasting Legislation Amendment (Media Reform) Bill 2016', transcript, Friday 29 April 2016, Melbourne, pp. 25–33.

16   Charles Davidson, 'Broadcasting and Television Bill, 1956', *HoR CPD*, 19 April 1956, pp. 1,531–42. This echoed comments from Labor leader H.V. Evatt to the effect that 'the guiding principle [of television broadcasting] must be services to the community and not merely profit'.

17   What might also be added is Marks's simultaneous declaration that Nine's television production costs were 30 per cent more efficient than the ABC's: thus his solution is to make the ABC produce local and regional content despite the much-increased cost to the taxpayer.

18   Mary Debrett, *Reinventing Public Service Television for the Digital*

Future, Bristol: Intellect, 2010, p. 82. The ABC has regarded the charter as sufficient prescription for its work in rural and regional Australia, and opposed attempts in 2016 by Nationals senator Bridget McKenzie to make explicit provisions for ABC services and journalism in rural and regional Australia on grounds that her draft bill was reliant on 'a narrow conception of localism'.

19   Ibid.

20   Ken Inglis, *This Is the ABC*, Carlton: Melbourne University Press, 1983, p. 5.

21   Ken Inglis, *Whose ABC?*, Melbourne: Black Inc, 2006, p. 576.

22   John Anderson, *HoR CPD*, 31 October 2000, p. 21,693–4.

23   Jared Owens, 'Warren Truss: ABC must provide local TV news', *The Australian*, 20 January 2016, https://www.theaustralian.com. au/business/media/warren-truss-abc-must-provide-local-tv-news/ news-story/009b3ada2083774891bddb34489bc877, accessed 19 July 2021.

24   'Transcript: Interview with Craig Zonca and Loretta Ryan', ABC Radio Brisbane, 13 November 2018', https://www. michaelmccormack.com.au/media-releases/2018/11/13/transcript- interview-with-craig-zonca-and-loretta-ryan-abc-radio-brisbane- 13-november-2018, accessed 19 July 2021.

25   Barnaby Joyce, *CPD HoR*, 25 November 2014, p. 13,100.

26   Barnaby Joyce, 'ABC's Heywire a huge opportunity for New England electorate youth', 26 July 2015, https://barnabyjoyce.com. au/news/releases/abcs-heywire-a-huge-opportunity-for-new- england-electorate-youth, accessed 19 July 2021.

27   Malcolm Turnbull, *A Bigger Picture*, Melbourne: Hardie Grant, 2020, p. 215.

28   Darren Chester to Matthew Ricketson, 13 August 2021.

29   *ABC Submission to the ACCC Digital Platforms Inquiry*, 20 April 2018, p. 5, https://www.accc.gov.au/system/files/Australian%20 Broadcasting%20Corporation%20%28April%202018%29.pdf, accessed 19 July 2021.

30   Hilary Harper, 'ABC awarded for emergency coverage', *ABC Local*, 1 April 2008, https://www.abc.net.au/local/ stories/2008/03/28/2202193.htm, accessed 19 July 2021.

31   Barnaby Joyce, *CPD Senate*, 8 February 2011, p. 27.

32   'Transcript: Interview with Craig Zonca and Loretta Ryan, ABC Radio Brisbane, 13 November 2018', https://www. michaelmccormack.com.au/media-releases/2018/11/13/transcript- interview-with-craig-zonca-and-loretta-ryan-abc-radio-brisbane- 13-november-2018, accessed 19 July 2021.

33   Richard Glover, 'The Fire Near Me', in Michael Rowland, ed., *Black Summer: stories of loss, courage, and community by ABC journalists*

on the ground during the 2019–20 bushfires, Sydney: HarperCollins, 2021, pp. 40–60.

34 Brittany Evins, 'The Faces of Fire', in Michael Rowland, ed., *Black Summer: stories of loss, courage, and community by ABC journalists on the ground during the 2019–20 bushfires*, Sydney: HarperCollins, 2021, pp. 62–75.

35 Baz Ruddick, 'Building Community in a Scorched Summer', in Michael Rowland, ed., *Black Summer: stories of loss, courage, and community by ABC journalists on the ground during the 2019–20 bushfires*, Sydney: HarperCollins, 2021, pp. 251–62.

36 Philip Williams and Greg Nelson, 'Dark Days', in Michael Rowland, ed., *Black Summer: stories of loss, courage, and community by ABC journalists on the ground during the 2019–20 bushfires*, Sydney: HarperCollins, 2021, pp. 110–24.

37 Julie Freeman, Kristy Hess, and Lisa Waller, 'Communication Life Line?: ABC emergency broadcasting in rural/regional Australia', *Communication Research and Practice*, vol. 4, iss. 4, 2018, pp. 342–60.

38 Lisa Waller, Emma Mesikämmen, and Brian Burkett, 'Rural Radio and the Everyday Politics of Settlement on Indigenous Land', *Media, Culture & Society*, vol. 42, no. 6, 2020, pp. 805–22.

39 Julie Freeman, Kristy Hess, and Lisa Waller, 'Making Inroads: a critical examination of the ABC's commitment to local news', *Media International Australia*, vol. 165, no. 1, 2017, pp. 117–30.

40 Tim Fischer, *ABC News Breakfast*, 11 November 2018.

Chapter 9. Clearing the Battlefield

1 Jonathan Holmes, 2019, *On Aunty*, Carlton: Melbourne University Press, p. 7.

2 Henry Mayer, 'Media', in Henry Mayer and H. Nelson, eds, *Australian Politics: a fifth reader*, Melbourne: Longman Cheshire, 1980, p. 551.

3 Bill Browne and Fergus Pitt, *Depoliticising the ABC Board and Appointment Process*, Australia Institute, September 2018, http://australiainstitute.org.au/wp-content/uploads/2020/12/Depoliticising-the-ABC-Board-WEB.pdf, accessed 15 August 2021.

4 Sharri Markson, 'Brown: I'd scrap ABC and start over', *The Australian*, 4 July 2014, p. 1, http://at.theaustralian.com.au/link/aea57c639520de8077d4b84f8233c405?domain=theaustralian.com.au, accessed 16 August 2021. Albrechtsen confirmed later that she was invited to join the panel by Tony Abbott. See: Janet Albrechtsen, 'Fan-girl Ferguson would be a poor fit to chair ABC', *The Australian*, 2 October 2018, p. 12.

5 Mitch Fifield, 'Media release — appointment of two new directors

to the ABC board', 18 November 2015, https://www.mitchfifield.
com/2015/11/media-release-appointment-of-two-new-directors-to-
the-abc-board/, accessed 15 August 2021.

6   Anne Davies, 'ABC board members appointed by Fifield despite
    being rejected by merit-based panel', *The Guardian*, 28 September
    2018, https://www.theguardian.com/media/2018/sep/27/abc-board-
    members-appointed-by-fifield-despite-being-rejected-by-merit-
    based-panel, accessed 16 August 2021.

7   Mitch Fifield, 'Media release — appointment of two new directors
    to the ABC board', 27 February 2017, https://www.mitchfifield.
    com/2017/02/appointment-of-two-new-directors-to-the-abc-
    board/, accessed 15 August 2021.

8   Mitch Fifield, 'Appointment of new directors to the ABC and
    SBS boards', 11 May 2018, https://www.mitchfifield.com/2018/05/
    appointment-of-new-directors-to-the-abc-and-sbs-boards/,
    accessed 16 August 2021.

9   Matthew Knott, 'New ABC chair Justin Milne says "high-minded"
    Malcolm Turnbull will not interfere', *The Sydney Morning Herald*,
    27 March 2017, https://www.smh.com.au/politics/federal/new-abc-
    chair-justin-milne-says-highminded-malcolm-turnbull-will-not-
    interfere-20170327-gv756t.html, accessed 16 August 2021.

10 'Allegations of political interference in the Australian Broadcasting
    Corporation', Environment and Communications References
    Committee, Australian Senate, April 2019, https://www.aph.gov.au/
    Parliamentary_Business/Committees/Senate/Environment_and_
    Communications/ABCInterferenceAllegations/Report, accessed 18
    August 2021.

11 Janet Albrechtsen, 'Fan-girl Ferguson would be a poor fit to chair
    ABC', *The Australian*, 2 October 2018, p. 12.

12 Stephen Brook and Rachel Baxendale, 'Coalition "ignored" best
    ABC choices', *The Australian*, 2 October 2018, p. 3.

13 Narelle Hooper, 'ABC chair Ita Buttrose on governing the
    national broadcaster', *Australian Institute of Company Directors*,
    1 December 2019, https://aicd.companydirectors.com.au/
    membership/company-director-magazine/2019-back-editions/
    december/abc-chair-ita-buttrose-on-governing-the-national-
    broadcaster, accessed 17 August 2021.

14 Scott Morrison and Mitch Fifield, 'Media release: Chair of the
    ABC', 28 February 2019, https://www.pm.gov.au/media/chair-abc,
    accessed 16 August 2021; Yasmin Jeffery and staff, 'Who is new
    ABC chair Ita Buttrose and how did she get the top job?', *ABC News
    Online*, 28 February 2019, https://www.abc.net.au/news/2019-
    02-28/ita-buttrose-abc-chair-announcement-who-is-media-
    veteran/10855214, accessed 16 August 2021; Margaret Simons, 'Good

news week', *Inside Story*, 21 May 2021, https://insidestory.org.au/good-news-week/, accessed 16 August 2021.

15   Paul Fletcher, 'Media release: reappointment of ABC and SBS board directors', 20 September 2019, https://www.paulfletcher.com.au/media-releases/media-release-reappointment-of-abc-and-sbs-board-directors, accessed 16 August 2021; Paul Fletcher, 'Media release: ABC board appointments', 17 May 2021, https://minister.infrastructure.gov.au/fletcher/media-release/abc-board-appointments, accessed 16 August 2021.

16   Margaret Simons, 'Good news week', *Inside Story*, 21 May 2021, https://insidestory.org.au/good-news-week/, accessed 18 August 2021.

17   *Appropriation Bill (No. 1) 2019–20*, Schedule 1, p. 43, https://parlinfo.aph.gov.au/parlInfo/download/legislation/bills/r6374_aspassed/toc_pdf/19132b01.pdf;fileType=application%2Fpdf, accessed 16 August 2021.

18   Tyson Wils, 'Funding the Australian Broadcasting Corporation', 4 November 2019, Parliamentary Library research paper, https://parlinfo.aph.gov.au/parlInfo/download/library/prspub/7006636/upload_binary/7006636.pdf, accessed 15 August 2021.

19   Bob Mansfield, *The Challenge of a Better ABC, vol. 1: a review of the role and functions of the ABC*, Canberra: Australian Government Publishing Service, 1997, p. 7; Mark Scott, 'Present Challenges, Future Audiences', speech to the University of Melbourne, 13 October 2014, http://about.abc.net.au/speeches/present-challenges-future-audiences/, accessed 16 August 2021.

20   See, too, Emma Dawson, *It's Our ABC: a research report for GetUp! by Per Capita*, May 2020, https://percapita.org.au/wp-content/uploads/2020/05/2749-ABC_Report.pdf, accessed 17 August 2021; Australian Senate, 'Media Diversity in Australia', report of the Environment and Communications References Committee, December 2021, p. 130.

21   ABC, *Five-Year Plan: 2020–2025*, June 2020, p. 12, https://about.abc.net.au/wp-content/uploads/2020/07/ABC-Five-Year-Plan-FINAL-Updated.pdf, accessed 16 August 2021.

22   Richard Alston claims that it was Menzies who first dubbed the ABC a publicity department for the ALP. See: Richard Alston, *More to Life than Politics?*, Cleveland: Connor Court, 2019, p. 223. No reference is offered for this apparent remark. Tony Abbott suggested that the ABC should show 'some basic affection for the home team' and criticised it for 'taking everyone's side but Australia's' for its reporting on asylum seekers. See: 'Australia's Tony Abbott calls broadcaster ABC unpatriotic', *BBC News*, 29 January 2014, https://www.bbc.com/news/world-asia-25925312, accessed 16 August 2021.

23 See, too, ABC managing director David Anderson's remarks on this:
    Amanda Meade, 'ABC managing director rejects Scott Morrison's
    claim broadcaster's funding "increasing every year"', *The
    Guardian*, 8 July 2020, https://www.theguardian.com/media/2020/
    jul/08/abc-managing-director-rejects-scott-morrisons-claim-
    broadcasters-funding-increasing-every-year, accessed 16 August
    2021. It may also be worth noting that the 2018 efficiency review
    into the ABC and SBS recommended that both adopt ten-year
    business plans and that government move to a ten-year funding
    cycle. See Peter Tonagh and Richard Bean, *National Broadcasters
    Efficiency Review*, December 2018, p. 47.

24 Gareth Evans, 'Australian Broadcasting Corporation: budget
    allocation', *CPD Senate*, 18 August 1989.

25 Fisher, House of Representatives Standing Committee on Com-
    munications, Transport, and Microeconomic Reform, 'Inquiry
    into federal road funding', 26 June 1997, https://parlinfo.aph.gov.
    au/parlInfo/search/display/display.w3p;db=COMMITTEES;id=
    committees%2Fcommrep%2Frcomw970626a_rtc.out%2F0003;
    query=Id%3A%22committees%2Fcommrep%2Frcomw970626a_rtc.
    out%2F0003%22, accessed 16 August 2021.

26 Gareth Evans, 'Australian Broadcasting Corporation: budget
    allocation', *CPD Senate*, 18 August 1989.

27 Mitch Fifield, 'Strengthening Australia's connectivity, creativity
    and cultural heritage', press release, 8 May 2018, https://www.
    mitchfifield.com/2018/05/strengthening-australias-connectivity-
    creativity-and-cultural-heritage/, accessed 16 August 2021.

28 Mitch Fifield and Bridget McKenzie, *Portfolio Budget Statements:
    Budget related paper 1.3: Communications and the Arts portfolio,
    2018–19*, Australian Government, p. 72, https://www.transparency.
    gov.au/sites/default/files/2018-19_pbs_-_final_accessible_
    version_09.05.2018a04d.pdf, accessed 16 August 2021.

29 Katie Burgess, 'Communications minister Paul Fletcher blames
    ABC management for job cuts', *The Canberra Times*, 1 July 2020,
    https://www.canberratimes.com.au/story/6814425/fletcher-blames-
    abc-management-for-job-cuts/, accessed 16 August 2021; Paul
    Fletcher, 'ABC funding explainer', https://www.paulfletcher.com.
    au/sites/default/files/attachments/ABC%20funding%20-%20
    explained.pdf, accessed 16 August 2021. Given the government's
    own admission in its Portfolio Budget Statements, it should also be
    pointed out that Fletcher's claim that there had been 'no cut in the
    ABC's budget' is risible.

30 Ken Inglis, *Whose ABC?*, Melbourne: Black Inc, 2006, p. 460.

31 Ibid., p. 491.

32 Nick Leys, 'ABC 2016–2019 funding', 3 May 2016, https://about.abc.net.

au/press-releases/abc-2016-2019-funding/, accessed 16 August 2021.

33 Fergus Hunter, 'ABC gets budget relief as Morrison government extends "enhanced" news-gathering funding', *The Sydney Morning Herald*, 2 April 2019, https://www.smh.com.au/politics/federal/abc-gets-budget-relief-as-morrison-government-extends-enhanced-news-gathering-funding-20190402-p519ve.html, accessed 16 August 2021.

34 Or the government should give the ABC money on the same terms it gave Foxtel $40 million to screen women's soccer matches on its subscribers-only service — a deal now subject to review by the auditor-general.

35 Alexandra Wake and Michael Ward, 'The ABC didn't receive a reprieve in the budget. It's still facing staggering cuts', *The Conversation*, 9 April 2019, https://theconversation.com/the-abc-didnt-receive-a-reprieve-in-the-budget-its-still-facing-staggering-cuts-114922, accessed 16 August 2021.

36 Nicholas Horne, *The Commonwealth efficiency dividend: an overview*, Parliamentary Library, 13 December 2012, https://www.aph.gov.au/About_Parliament/Parliamentary_Departments/Parliamentary_Library/pubs/BN/2012-2013/EfficiencyDividend#_Toc343007823, accessed 15 August 2021.

37 Paul Fletcher, 'ABC funding explainer', https://www.paulfletcher.com.au/sites/default/files/attachments/ABC%20funding%20-%20explained.pdf, accessed 16 August 2021.

38 See, for example, Malcolm Turnbull, 'Speech: The future of our public broadcasters', 19 November 2014, https://www.malcolmturnbull.com.au/media/the-future-of-our-public-broadcasters, accessed 17 August 2021.

39 Lenore Taylor, 'ABC cuts not an "efficiency dividend", says Malcolm Turnbull, contradicting Abbott', *The Guardian*, 25 November 2014, https://www.theguardian.com/media/2014/nov/25/abc-cuts-not-an-efficiency-dividend-says-malcolm-turnbull-contradicting-abbott, accessed 16 August 2021; Primrose Riordan, 'ABC funding reduction is an efficiency dividend, not a cut: Mathias Cormann', *The Sydney Morning Herald*, 20 November 2014, https://www.smh.com.au/public-service/abc-funding-reduction-is-an-efficiency-dividend-not-a-cut-mathias-cormann-20141120-11q8th.html, accessed 16 August 2021.

40 Nick Tabakoff, '"I feel disrespected": Ita strikes back', *The Australian*, 14 December 2020, p. 20.

41 Amanda Meade, 'ABC chair Ita Buttrose accuses government of "political interference" in draft letter to Paul Fletcher', *The Guardian*, 14 December 2020, https://www.theguardian.com/media/2020/dec/14/abc-chair-ita-buttrose-accuses-government-of-

political-interference-in-draft-letter-to-paul-fletcher, accessed 28 August 2020.

42 Jennifer Duke, 'ABC urged to consider selling inner-city offices', *The Sydney Morning Herald*, 2 March 2020, p. 1.

43 Fletcher's letter is dated 30 November but in the tweet that made the letter public, at 10.29 am on 1 December, Fletcher states that he wrote the letter that day (i.e. 1 December). See Fletcher to Buttrose, 30 November 2020, in Paul Fletcher (@PaulFletcherMP), 'Today I have written …', 1 December 2020, https://twitter.com/PaulFletcherMP/status/1333553873219248130, accessed 28 August 2021.

44 Amanda Meade, 'ABC accuses Morrison government of using News Corp to attack its journalism', *The Guardian*, 2 December 2020, https://www.theguardian.com/media/2020/dec/02/abc-accuses-morrison-government-of-using-news-corp-to-attack-its-journalism, accessed 28 August 2021.

45 There are some grounds on which to suggest that it was mistakes in the ABC's journalism that most exercised Malcolm Turnbull, not necessarily that its coverage was adverse. See, for example, his comments on *Q&A* in November 2018, waving aside complaints about bias in the press ('I'd given up on that years ago') and his comments reiterating the importance of news that was 'accurate and objective'. The extent to which this attitude was shared by his staff, however, is debatable.

46 Darren Chester to Matthew Ricketson, 13 August 2021.

47 Laura Tingle, '"You've got to play to the base": why the ABC is a political football', *ABC News*, 9 June 2018, https://www.abc.net.au/news/2018-06-09/laura-tingle-why-the-abc-is-a-political-football/9850360, accessed 28 August 2021.

48 Examples are legion but, to offer one, Richard Alston claims in his memoirs that *7.30* runs 'pre-packaged' stories about workers who have been maltreated, underpaid, and/or undervalued. These stories, he claims, 'are clearly carefully wrapped up and hand delivered to the ABC, presumably on the understanding that no serious alternative viewpoint, let alone rebuttal, is presented'. Alston does not explain how 'an alternative viewpoint' might mitigate a story about workers being underpaid, nor does he offer any justification for why such a story should not be run. Nor, having put into the public arena his claim about the compromised integrity of ABC journalists, does he see fit to offer any evidence to support it. See: Richard Alston, *More to Life than Politics?*, Cleveland: Connor Court, 2019, p. 251.

49 Amanda Meade, 'ABC board defends Ita Buttrose against "disrespectful" spray by Liberal powerbroker', *The Guardian*, 3 June 2021; 'Greatest enemy of truth is those who conspire to lie',

The Australian, 8 June 2021, p. 10.

50 Franklin called his article 'an attack on terrorism', and, asked to comment, *Quadrant* editor Keith Windschuttle said, 'You're talking bullshit, don't call back.' See: Nick O'Malley, 'Quadrant article laments blast wasn't against ABC', *The Age*, 25 May 2017, p. 6.

51 Amanda Meade, 'Manchester bomb should've been exploded on ABC's Q&A, Quadrant's Roger Franklin says', *The Guardian*, 24 May 2017, https://www.theguardian.com/australia-news/2017/may/24/manchester-bomb-shouldve-been-exploded-on-abcs-qa-quadrant-writer-says, accessed 28 August 2021.

52 Roger Franklin, 'The ABC and its Feral Audience', *Quadrant*, 17 March 2021, https://quadrant.org.au/opinion/media/2021/03/the-abc-and-its-feral-audience/, accessed 28 August 2021.

53 Kerry O'Brien, *Kerry O'Brien: a memoir*, Crows News: Allen & Unwin, 2018, p. 484.

54 Amanda Meade, 'ABC rejects criticism of treatment of Neville Wran in Luna Park ghost train fire series', *Guardian Australia*, 31 August 2021, https://www.theguardian.com/media/2021/aug/31/abc-rejects-criticism-of-neville-wran-treatment-in-luna-park-ghost-train-fire-series.

55 Zoe Samios and Rob Harris, 'ABC looks ahead after tough year', *The Age*, 18 December 2021, p. 18.

56 Andrew Probyn in Jonathan Holmes, *On Aunty*, 2019, Melbourne: Melbourne University Press, pp. 64–5.

57 Justin Milne, 'An ABC Fit for the Future', 11 July 2018, https://about.abc.net.au/speeches/an-abc-fit-for-the-future/.

58 Justin Milne, 'Letter from ABC chairman Justin Milne to Communications Minister the Hon Mitch Fifield', 10 November 2017, https://about.abc.net.au/statements/letter-to-senator-the-hon-mitch-fifield/.

59 Matthew Ricketson and Patrick Mullins, 'Is the latest ABC inquiry really just "business as usual"', *The Conversation*, 16 November 2021, https://theconversation.com/is-the-latest-abc-inquiry-really-just-business-as-usual-171824.

60 Ita Buttrose, 'Statement by Ita Buttrose, ABC Chair, on the public's right to know', ABC, 7 June 2019, https://about.abc.net.au/statements/statement-by-ita-buttrose-abc-chair-on-the-publics-right-to-know/.

Chapter 10. Who Needs the ABC?

1 Amanda Meade, 'Minister rebukes ABC over Tonightly's "vitriolic" Australian Conservatives skit', *The Guardian*, 21 March 2018, https://www.theguardian.com/media/2018/mar/21/minister-rebukes-abc-over-tonightlys-vitriolic-australian-conservatives-

skit, accessed 30 August 2021.

2   Tom Stayner, 'Paul Fletcher takes aim at the ABC as the broadcaster
     defends "Invasion Day" article', *SBS*, 25 January 2021, https://
     www.sbs.com.au/news/paul-fletcher-takes-aim-at-the-abc-as-the-
     national-broadcaster-defends-invasion-day-article/54f9ab22-1127-
     49cc-9c1e-9140c0fadedd, accessed 30 August 2021.

3   Fergus Hunter, 'Communications minister Mitch Fifield savages
     "dumb" Triple J decision on Hottest 100', *The Sydney Morning
     Herald*, 28 November 2017, https://www.smh.com.au/politics/
     federal/communications-minister-mitch-fifield-savages-dumb-
     triple-j-decision-on-hottest-100-20171128-gztzn8.html, accessed 28
     August 2021.

4   See Barnaby Joyce's comments to Hamish McDonald on UK
     climate policy: *ABC Breakfast*, 24 September 2021, https://www.abc.
     net.au/radionational/programs/breakfast/barnaby-joyce-net-zero-
     regional-economy/13556308, accessed 24 September 2021.

5   Mark Kenny, 'A government of lies, damned lies and gymnastics',
     The Canberra Times, 6 March 2020, https://www.canberratimes.
     com.au/story/6663742/a-government-of-lies-damned-lies-and-
     gymnastics/, accessed 4 October 2021.

6   'Budget cuts millions from ABC to pay for Captain Cook statue at
     Botany Bay', SBS, 9 May 2018, https://www.sbs.com.au/nitv/nitv-
     news/article/2018/05/09/budget-cuts-millions-abc-pay-captain-
     cook-statue-botany-bay, accessed 28 August 2021.

7   Malcolm Turnbull, 'ABC funding to be cut by $254 million over
     five years, Communications Minister Malcolm Turnbull says', *ABC
     News*, 20 November 2014, https://www.abc.net.au/news/2014-11-
     19/abc-funding-cuts-announced-by-malcolm-turnbull/5902774,
     accessed 29 August 2021; Sara Garcia, 'Federal MP Christopher
     Pyne launches online petition to save ABC jobs in Adelaide', *ABC
     News*, 19 November 2014, https://www.abc.net.au/news/2014-
     11-19/christopher-pyne-launches-petition-to-save-abc-jobs-in-
     adelaide/5902010, accessed 29 August 2021.

8   James Paterson, 'ABC keeps pushing beyond charter', *The
     Australian Financial Review*, 28 May 2018.

9   Josh Taylor and Alice Workman, 'The treasurer wants Shaun
     Micallef's "Mad as Hell" spared from $83 million in ABC budget
     cuts', *Buzzfeed*, 9 May 2018, https://www.buzzfeed.com/joshtaylor/
     scott-morrison-wants-mad-as-hell-spared-from-abc-cuts, accessed
     28 August 2021.

10   '"There are no cuts": Morrison rejects criticism of ABC budget',
     The New Daily, 25 June 2020, https://thenewdaily.com.au/news/
     national/2020/06/25/scott-morrison-cuts-abc/, accessed 28 August
     2021.

11 Judith Ireland, 'Tony Abbott blasts national broadcaster: ABC takes "everyone's side but Australia's"', *The Sydney Morning Herald*, 29 January 2014, https://www.smh.com.au/politics/federal/tony-abbott-blasts-national-broadcaster-abc-takes-everyones-side-but-australias-20140129-31lt8.html, accessed 30 August 2021.

12 Malcolm Turnbull, *A Bigger Picture*, Melbourne: Hardie Grant, 2020, p. 215.

13 Darren Chester to Matthew Ricketson, 13 August 2021.

14 Barnaby Joyce to Hamish McDonald, *ABC Breakfast*, 24 September 2021, https://www.abc.net.au/radionational/programs/breakfast/barnaby-joyce-net-zero-regional-economy/13556308, accessed 24 September 2021.

15 Jonathan Holmes, *On Aunty*, Carlton: Melbourne University Press, 2019, pp. 85–6.

16 Paul Kelly, 'We need the ABC — it's time it realised that it needs us', *The Australian*, 3 October 2018, p. 14.

17 A very good example was provided in September 2021, when *Australian* media writer Sophie Elsworth drew on unpublished IPA research to argue that the ABC was obsessed with News Corp and the Murdoch family. The problem was that the research, which included 1,700 occasions where 'Murdoch' and 'News Corp' were mentioned in ABC programs, also included guests who were affiliated with Murdoch University, a chef named Lauren Murdoch, stockmarket reports that mentioned News Corp's performance, breakfast shows where the day's papers were read out, and streets and towns named Murdoch, as well as individually counting material that had been syndicated (i.e. repeated) across multiple stations. The obsession, then, was rather muted, and if anything appeared to run the other way. Elsworth failed to notice any of this and uncritically ran quotes from the IPA's Evan Mulholland to the effect that the ABC was prosecuting a campaign against a media rival. See: Sophie Elsworth, 'Growing evidence of ABC's obsession with News Corp', *The Australian*, 6 September 2021, p. 19; 'IPA ABC News Corp research', https://docs.google.com/spreadsheets/d/1zJMZZ9PDmWqz50gK5oDIc3mUOX4o83OGNx9FPbNrNXs/edit#gid=2055104688, accessed 7 September 2021.

Appendix B. ABC Operational Funding Data ...

1 Michael Ward is researching public service media, national identity, and women's sport as part of a PhD in the Media and Communications Department of the University of Sydney. Prior to this work, he was a senior executive with the Australian Broadcasting Corporation from 1999 to 2017.

2 Paul Fletcher, 'ABC Funding Explainer', 2020, https://www.

paulfletcher.com.au/pauls-blog/abc-funding-explainer.

3   See notes below for details of the components of ABC funding.

4   The only year lower than 2021–22 ($263 million in 1983–84 dollars) since 1981–82 ($225 million) is 2000–01 ($259 million).

5   Calculations are based on analysis of relevant Portfolio Budget Statements. See: Department of Infrastructure, Transport, Regional Development, and Communications, 'Budgets', https://www.infrastructure.gov.au/department/statements/index.aspx, accessed 22 July 2021 [DITRDC, 2021]; Rhonda Jolly, 'The ABC: an overview', Australian Parliamentary Library Research Paper series 2014–15, https://www.aph.gov.au/About_Parliament/Parliamentary_Departments/Parliamentary_Library/pubs/rp/rp1415/ABCoverview, accessed 16 July 2021 [Jolly, 2014]. For detailed references and explanation of data calculations, see attached notes and tables.

6   DITRDC, 2021; Jolly, 2014; Tyson Wils, Funding the Australian Broadcasting Corporation, Australian Parliamentary Library Research Paper Series 2019–20, 4 November 2019, https://www.aph.gov.au/About_Parliament/Parliamentary_Departments/Parliamentary_Library/pubs/rp/rp1920/FundingABC, accessed 27 July 2021.

7   Adjusted or real values are in baseline 1983–84 financial-year dollars.

8   DITRDC, 2021; Jolly, 2014.

9   Ken Inglis, *Whose ABC?*, Melbourne: Black Inc, 2006.

10   Allan Brown, 'Australian Public Broadcasting Under Review: the Mansfield report on the ABC', *Canadian Journal of Communication*, vol. 26, no. 1, 2001.

11   Mary Debrett, 'Riding the Wave: public service television in the multi-platform era', *Media, Culture & Society*, 31(5), 2009, p. 823.

12   DITRDC, 2021; Jolly, 2014.

13   2021–22 budget papers show ABC funding declining further to $257 million in real terms in 2022–23. See: *2021–22 Portfolio Budget Statement*, https://www.infrastructure.gov.au/department/statements/index.aspx, accessed 22 July 2021.

14   DITRDC, 2021; Jolly, 2014.

15   Nominal: not adjusted for inflation; the dollar figures appearing in annual budget papers.

16   DITRDC, 2021; Jolly, 2014.

17   'The ABC's financial statements classified all Commonwealth appropriations as revenues from government until 1999–2000, when a payment of $33.2 million was classified as an injection of equity and not included in total operating revenues. This payment and subsequent equity injections have been included in capital revenues to maintain consistency with previous years'. See: Jolly, 2014, p. 60.

18 DITRDC, 2021; Jolly, 2014.

19 Ibid.

20 Annmaree O'Keefe and Chris Greene, 'International Public
    Broadcasting: a missed opportunity for projecting Australia's soft
    power', Lowy Institute, 2019, https://www.lowyinstitute.org/sites/
    default/files/Okeefe%2C%20Green_International%20Public%20
    Broadcasting_WEB.pdf.

21 DITRDC, 2021; Jolly, 2014.

22 Ken Inglis, *Whose ABC?*, Melbourne: Black Inc, 2006, p. 109; Ken Inglis,
    This Is the ABC, Carlton: Melbourne University Press, 1983, p. 408.

23 ABC annual reports, 1997–2020; Allan Brown and Catherine
    Althaus, 'Public Service Broadcasting in Australia', *Journal of
    Media Economics*, vol. 9, no. 1, 1996, pp. 31–46.

24 ABC annual reports, 1997–2001.

25 ABC annual reports, 1997–2020.

26 See, for example, Ben Goldsmith, 'Cut Here: reshaping the ABC',
    The Conversation, 16 July 2014, https://theconversation.com/cut-
    here-reshaping-the-abc-29166, accessed 27 July 2021; Alexandra
    Wake and Michael Ward, 'The ABC Didn't Receive a Reprieve in
    the Budget. It's Still Facing Staggering Cuts', *The Conversation*, 9
    April 2019, https://theconversation.com/the-abc-didnt-receive-
    a-reprieve-in-the-budget-its-still-facing-staggering-cuts-114922,
    accessed 2 August 2021.

27 DITRDC, 2021; Jolly, 2014.

28 Alexandra Wake and Michael Ward, 'The ABC Didn't Receive
    a Reprieve in the Budget. It's Still Facing Staggering Cuts', *The
    Conversation*, 9 April 2019, https://theconversation.com/the-abc-
    didnt-receive-a-reprieve-in-the-budget-its-still-facing-staggering-
    cuts-114922, accessed 2 August 2021.

29 *ABC Corporate Plan 2019–20*, https://about.abc.net.au/wp-content/
    uploads/2019/08/ABC-Corporate-Plan-201920.pdf, accessed 27 July
    2021.

30 Jolly, 2014, p. 63.

31 Jolly, 2014.

32 Ken Inglis, *Whose ABC?*, Melbourne: Black Inc, 2006, p. 211.

33 *ABC Annual Report 2004/05*, https://about.abc.net.au/reports-
    publications/page/17/, accessed 2 August 2021.

34 Jolly, 2014, p. 60. A note of caution: in Jolly's data, 'revenue
    from independent sources' includes sales of goods, rendering
    of services, interest, and disposal of assets. However, it can be
    assumed that the great majority of the figure, especially from the
    1990s, is for ABC commercial activity.

35 This is for sale of goods and services.

36 Ken Inglis, *Whose ABC?*, Melbourne: Black Inc, 2006, p. 576.

37 *2021–22 Portfolio Budget Statement*, p. 127, https://www.
    infrastructure.gov.au/department/statements/index.aspx, accessed
    22 July 2021.

38 DITRDC, 2021; Jolly, 2014. Note: operating revenue from 2006–07
    to 2021–22 is estimated actuals as reported in the following year's
    PBS (e.g. 2020–21 figure is as reported in 2021–22 PBS), inflation-
    adjusted figures are calculated using the RBA Inflation Calculator
    Tool, inflation rates for FY21 and FY22 are forecast CPI sourced
    from the RBA May 2021 Statement on Monetary Policy Economic
    Outlook, and equity injections, transmission, capital user charges,
    and orchestral subsidies are excluded.

39 Ibid.

Appendix C. International Comparison ...

1   *2015–16 Portfolio Budget Statement*, https://webarchive.nla.
    gov.au/awa/20200828201756/http://pandora.nla.gov.au/
    pan/181345/20200829-0006/www.communications.gov.au/who-
    we-are/department/budget/2015-16-budget-communications-
    portfolio.html, accessed 22 July 2021; 'Revenue and Other Sources
    of Funds. Annual Report 2016/17', https://site-cbc.radio-canada.ca/
    site/annual-reports/2016-2017/financial-sustainability/revenue-
    and-other-sources-of-funds-en.html, accessed 13 September 2021;
    NHK Overview, 2021, https://www.nhk.or.jp/corporateinfo/english/
    corporate/; *Yearbook 2016 Key Trends*. Strasbourg: European
    Audiovisual Observatory, Corporation for Public Broadcasting;
    'Table 2, Public Broadcasting Revenue by Public Television and
    Radio System and Source of Revenue, Fiscal Year 2016–2017', *Public
    Broadcasting Revenue, Fiscal year 2017*, https://www.cpb.org/files/
    reports/revenue/2017PublicBroadcastingRevenue.pdf, accessed 27
    August 2021.

2   For example: Benson, Powers & Neff, 'Public Media Autonomy
    and Accountability: best and worst policy practices in 12 leading
    democracies', *International Journal of Communication*, vol. 11,
    2017, pp. 1–22; Edelvold Berg, & Brink Lund, 'Financing Public
    Service Broadcasting: a comparative perspective', *Journal of
    Media Business Studies*, vol. 9, no. 1, 2012, pp. 7–21; Lowe & Berg,
    'The Funding of Public Service Media: a matter of value and
    values', *International Journal on Media Management*, vol. 15, no.
    2, 2013, pp. 77–97; Saurwein, Eberwein & Karmasin, 'Public Service
    Media in Europe: exploring the relationship between funding
    and audience performance', *Javnost — The Public Journal of the
    European Institute for Communication and Culture*, vol. 26, no. 3,
    2019, pp. 291–308.

Appendix D. ABC Appreciation ...

1 ABC Corporate Tracking Program, *Measures of Community Satisfaction*, ABC, 2019.
2 ABC Annual Reports, 2002–20, accessed 28 August 2021. ABC Annual Report 2021, accessed 15 November 2021.
3 Ibid.